Illustrated Series™

Microsoft® Office 365® PowerPoint® 2021

Comprehensive

Cengage

Australia • Brazil • Canada • Mexico • Singapore • United Kingdom • United States

Illustrated Series® Collection Microsoft® Office 365® & PowerPoint® 2021 Comprehensive
David Beskeen

SVP, Product: Erin Joyner

VP, Product: Thais Alencar

Product Director: Mark Santee

Senior Product Manager: Amy Savino

Product Assistant: Ciara Horne

Learning Designer: Zenya Molnar

Content Manager: Grant Davis

Digital Delivery Quality Partner: Jim Vaughey

Developmental Editor: Julie Boyles

VP, Product Marketing: Jason Sakos

Director, Product Marketing: Danaë April

Executive Product Marketing Manager: Jill Staut

IP Analyst: Ann Hoffman

IP Project Manager: Ilakkiya Jayagopi

Production Service: Lumina Datamatics, Inc.

Designer: Erin Griffin

Cover Image Source: 4khz/Getty Images 472634414

For product information and technology assistance, contact us at **Cengage Customer & Sales Support, 1-800-354-9706 or support.cengage.com.**

For permission to use material from this text or product, submit all requests online at **www.copyright.com.**

Library of Congress Control Number: 2022904923

Student Edition ISBN: 978-0-357-67513-7
Looseleaf ISBN: 978-0-357-67514-4*
*Looseleaf available as part of a digital bundle

Cengage
200 Pier 4 Boulevard
Boston, MA 02210
USA

Cengage is a leading provider of customized learning solutions with employees residing in nearly 40 different countries and sales in more than 125 countries around the world. Find your local representative at **www.cengage.com.**

To learn more about Cengage platforms and services, register or access your online learning solution, or purchase materials for your course, visit **www.cengage.com.**

Brief Contents

Contents

Illustrated Series™

Microsoft® Office 365®
PowerPoint® 2021

Comprehensive

Getting to Know Microsoft Office Versions

Cengage is proud to bring you the next edition of Microsoft Office. This edition was designed to provide a robust learning experience that is not dependent upon a specific version of Office.

Microsoft supports several versions of Office:

- **Office 365:** A cloud-based subscription service that delivers Microsoft's most up-to-date, feature-rich, modern productivity tools direct to your device. There are variations of Office 365 for business, educational, and personal use. Office 365 offers extra online storage and cloud-connected features, as well as updates with the latest features, fixes, and security updates.

- **Office 2021:** Microsoft's "on-premises" version of the Office apps, available for both PCs and Macs, offered as a static, one-time purchase and outside of the subscription model.

- **Office Online:** A free, simplified version of Office web applications (Word, Excel, PowerPoint, and OneNote) that facilitates creating and editing files collaboratively.

Office 365 (the subscription model) and Office 2021 (the one-time purchase model) had only slight differences between them at the time this content was developed. Over time, Office 365's cloud interface will continuously update, offering new application features and functions, while Office 2021 will remain static. Therefore, your onscreen experience may differ from what you see in this product. For example, the more advanced features and functionalities covered in this product may not be available in Office Online or may have updated from what you see in Office 2021.

For more information on the differences between Office 365, Office 2021, and Office Online, please visit the Microsoft Support site.

Cengage is committed to providing high-quality learning solutions for you to gain the knowledge and skills that will empower you throughout your educational and professional careers.

Thank you for using our product, and we look forward to exploring the future of Microsoft Office with you!

Using SAM Projects and Textbook Projects

SAM Projects allow you to actively apply the skills you learned live in Microsoft Word, Excel, PowerPoint, or Access. Become a more productive student and use these skills throughout your career.

To complete SAM Textbook Projects, please follow these steps:

SAM Textbook Projects allow you to complete a project as you follow along with the steps in the textbook. As you read the module, look for icons that indicate when you should download **sam'** ⬇ your SAM Start file(s) and when to upload **sam'** ⬆ the final project file to SAM for grading.

Everything you need to complete this project is provided within SAM. You can launch the eBook directly from SAM, which will allow you to take notes, highlight, and create a custom study guide, or you can use a print textbook or your mobile app. Download IOS or Download Android.

To get started, launch your SAM Project assignment from SAM, MindTap, or a link within your LMS.

Step 1: Download Files

- Click the "Download All" button or the individual links to download your **Start File** and **Support File(s)** (when available). You <u>must</u> use the SAM Start file.

- Click the Instructions link to launch the eBook (or use the print textbook or mobile app).

- Disregard any steps in the textbook that ask you to create a new file or to use a file from a location outside of SAM.

- Look for the SAM Download icon **sam'** ⬇ to begin working with your start file.

- Follow the module's step-by-step instructions until you reach the SAM Upload icon **sam'** ⬆.

- Save and close the file.

Step 2: Save Work to SAM

- Ensure you rename your project file to match the Expected File Name.

- Upload your in-progress or completed file to SAM. You can download the file to continue working or submit it for grading in the next step.

Step 3: Submit for Grading

- Upload the completed file to SAM for immediate feedback and to view the available Reports.

  - The **Graded Summary Report** provides a detailed list of project steps, your score, and feedback to aid you in revising and re-submitting the project.

  - The **Study Guide Report** provides your score for each project step and links to the associated training and textbook pages.

- If additional attempts are allowed, use your reports to assist with revising and resubmitting your project.

- To re-submit the project, download the file saved in step 2.

- Edit, save, and close the file, then re-upload and submit it again.

For all other SAM Projects, please follow these steps:

To get started, launch your SAM Project assignment from SAM, MindTap, or a link within your LMS.

Step 1: Download Files

- Click the "Download All" button or the individual links to download your **Instruction File**, **Start File**, and **Support File(s)** (when available). You <u>must</u> use the SAM Start file.

- Open the Instruction file and follow the step-by-step instructions. Ensure you rename your project file to match the Expected File Name (change _1 to _2 at the end of the file name).

Step 2: Save Work to SAM

- Upload your in-progress or completed file to SAM. You can download the file to continue working or submit it for grading in the next step.

Step 3: Submit for Grading

- Upload the completed file to SAM for immediate feedback and to view available Reports.

  - The **Graded Summary Report** provides a detailed list of project steps, your score, and feedback to aid you in revising and resubmitting the project.

  - The **Study Guide Report** provides your score for each project step and links to the associated training and textbook pages.

- If additional attempts are allowed, use your reports to assist with revising and resubmitting your project.

- To re-submit the project, download the file saved in step 2.

- Edit, save, and close the file, then re-upload and submit it again.

For additional tips to successfully complete your SAM Projects, please view our Common Student Errors Infographic.

Creating a Presentation in PowerPoint

CASE ▸ JCL Talent, based in Atlanta, Georgia, is a company that provides comprehensive recruitment and employment services for employers and job seekers worldwide. You work for Dawn Lapointe in the Technical Careers division. You have been asked to help her create a presentation on global workforce trends that she will give at an upcoming recruiters convention. Use PowerPoint to create the presentation.

Module Objectives

After completing this module, you will be able to:

- Define presentation software
- Plan an effective presentation
- Examine the PowerPoint window
- Enter slide text
- Add a new slide
- Format text
- Apply a design theme
- Compare presentation views
- Insert and resize a picture
- Check spelling
- Print a PowerPoint presentation

Files You Will Need

Support_PPT_1_Woman.jpg
IL_PPT_1-1.pptx
Support_PPT_1_Group.jpg
IL_PPT_1-2.pptx
IL_PPT_1-3.pptx

Define Presentation Software

Presentation software (also called presentation graphics software) is a computer program you use to organize and present information to others. Presentations are typically in the form of a slide show. Whether you are explaining a new product or moderating a meeting, presentation software can help you effectively communicate your ideas. You can use PowerPoint to create informational slides that you print or display on a monitor, share in real time on the web, or save as a video for others to watch. **CASE** *You need to start working on the global workforce presentation. Because you are only somewhat familiar with PowerPoint, you get to work exploring its capabilities. FIGURE 1-1 shows how a presentation looks printed as handouts. FIGURE 1-2 shows how the same presentation might look saved as a video.*

DETAILS

You can easily complete the following tasks using PowerPoint:

• **Enter and edit text easily**

  Text editing and formatting commands in PowerPoint are organized by the task you are performing at the time, so you can enter, edit, and format text information simply and efficiently to produce the best results in the least amount of time.

• **Change the appearance of information**

  PowerPoint has many effects that can transform the way text, graphics, and slides appear. By exploring some of these capabilities, you discover how easy it is to change the appearance of your presentation.

• **Organize and arrange information**

  Once you start using PowerPoint, you won't have to spend much time making sure your information is correct and in the right order. With PowerPoint, you can quickly and easily rearrange and modify text, graphics, and slides in your presentation.

• **Include information from other sources**

  Often, when you create presentations, you use information from a variety of sources. With PowerPoint, you can import text, photographs, videos, numerical data, and other information from files created in programs such as Adobe Photoshop, Microsoft Word, Microsoft Excel, and Microsoft Access. You can also import information from other PowerPoint presentations as well as graphic images from a variety of sources such as the Internet, storage devices, computers, a camera, or other graphics programs. Always be sure you have permission to use any work that you did not create yourself.

• **Present information in a variety of ways**

  With PowerPoint, you can present information using a variety of methods. For example, you can print handout pages or an outline of your presentation for audience members. You can display your presentation as an on-screen slide show using your computer, or if you are presenting to a large group, you can use a video projector and a large screen. If you want to reach an even wider audience, you can broadcast the presentation or upload it as a video to the Internet so people anywhere in the world can use a web browser to view your presentation.

• **Collaborate with others on a presentation**

  PowerPoint makes it easy to collaborate or share a presentation with colleagues and coworkers using the Internet. You can use your email program to send a presentation as an attachment to a colleague for feedback. If you have a number of people that need to work together on a presentation, you can save the presentation to a shared workspace such as a network drive or OneDrive so authorized users in your group with an Internet connection can access the presentation.

FIGURE 1-1: PowerPoint handout

Asier Romero/Shutterstock.com

FIGURE 1-2: Presentation saved as a video

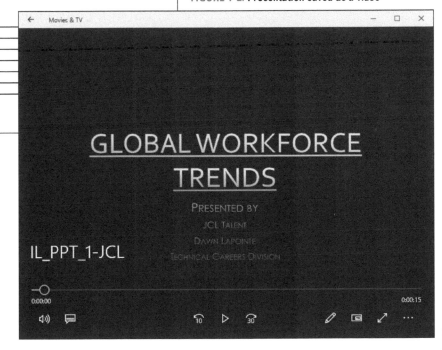

Using PowerPoint on a touch screen

You can use PowerPoint on a Windows computer with a touch-enabled monitor or any other compatible touch screen, such as a tablet. Using your fingers, you can use typical touch gestures to create, modify, and navigate presentations. To enable touch mode capabilities in PowerPoint, you need to add the Touch Mode button to the Quick Access Toolbar. Click the Customize Quick Access Toolbar button, click Touch/Mouse Mode, click the on the Quick Access Toolbar, then click Touch. In Touch mode, additional space is added around all of the buttons and icons in the Ribbon and the status bar to make them easier to touch. Common gestures that you can use in PowerPoint include double-tapping text to edit it and tapping a slide then dragging it to rearrange it in the presentation.

PowerPoint

Plan an Effective Presentation

**Learning
Outcome**
• Determine
presentation
content and
design

Before you create a presentation, you need to have a general idea of the information you want to communicate. PowerPoint is a powerful and flexible program that gives you the ability to start a presentation simply by entering the text of your message. If you have a specific design in mind that you want to use, you can start the presentation by working on the design. In most cases, you'll probably enter the text of your presentation into PowerPoint first and then tailor the design to the message and audience. When preparing your presentation, you need to keep in mind not only who you are giving it to, but also how you are presenting it. For example, if you are giving a presentation using a projector, you need to know what other equipment you will need, such as a sound system. **CASE** *Use the planning guidelines below to help plan an effective presentation.* **FIGURE 1-3** *illustrates a storyboard for a well-planned presentation.*

DETAILS

In planning a presentation, it is important to:

*   **Determine and outline the message you want to communicate**
    The more time you take developing the message and outline of your presentation, the better your presentation will be in the end. A presentation with a clear message that reads like a story and is illustrated with appropriate visual aids will have the greatest impact on your audience. Start the presentation by providing a general description of the global workforce trends. See **FIGURE 1-3**.

*   **Identify your audience and where and how you are giving the presentation**
    Audience and delivery location are major factors in the type of presentation you create. For example, a presentation you develop for a staff meeting that is held in a conference room would not necessarily need to be as sophisticated or detailed as a presentation that you develop for a large audience in an auditorium. Room lighting, natural light, screen position, and room layout all affect how the audience responds to your presentation. You might also broadcast your presentation over the Internet to several people who view the presentation on their computers in real time. This presentation will be broadcast over the Internet.

*   **Determine the type of output**
    Output choices for a presentation include black-and-white or color handouts for audience members, an on-screen slide show, a video, or an online broadcast. Consider the time demands and computer equipment availability as you decide which output types to produce. Because this presentation will be broadcast over the Internet, the default output settings work just fine.

*   **Determine the design**
    Visual appeal, graphics, and presentation design work together to communicate your message. You can choose one of the professionally designed themes that come with PowerPoint, modify one of these themes, or create one of your own. You decide to choose one of PowerPoint's design themes for your presentation.

FIGURE 1-3: Storyboard of the presentation

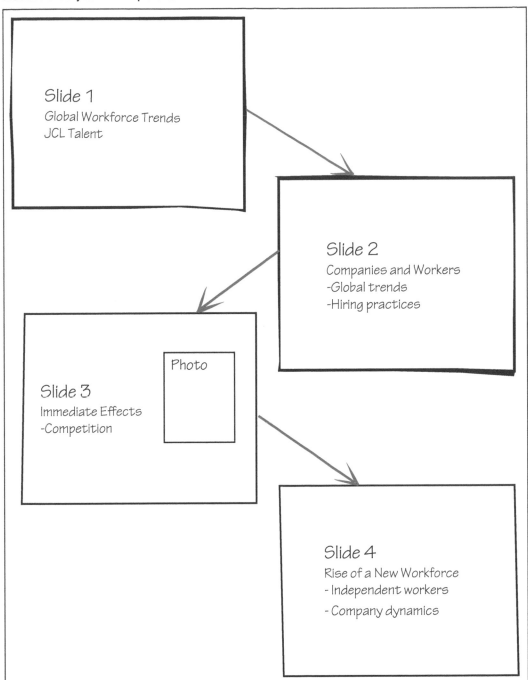

Understanding copyright

Intellectual property is any idea or creation of the human mind. Copyright law is a type of intellectual property law that protects works of authorship, including books, webpages, computer games, music, artwork, and photographs. Copyright protects the expression of an idea, but not the underlying facts or concepts. In other words, the general subject matter is not protected, but how you express it is, such as when several people photograph the same sunset. Copyright attaches to any original work of authorship as soon as it is created; you do not have to register it with the Copyright Office or display the copyright symbol, ©. Fair use is an exception to copyright and permits the public to use copyrighted material for certain purposes without obtaining prior consent from the owner. Determining whether fair use applies to a work depends on its purpose, the nature of the work, how much of the work you want to copy, and the effect on the work's value. Unauthorized use of protected work (such as downloading a photo or a song from the web) is known as copyright infringement and can lead to legal action.

Examine the PowerPoint Window

When you first start PowerPoint, you have the ability to choose what kind of presentation you want to use to start—a blank one, or one with a preformatted design. You can also open and work on an existing presentation. PowerPoint has different **views** that allow you to see your presentation in different forms. By default, the PowerPoint window opens in **Normal view**, which is the primary view that you use to write, edit, and design your presentation. Normal view is divided into areas called **panes**: the pane on the left, called the **Slides tab**, displays the slides of your presentation as small images, called **slide thumbnails**. The large pane is the Slide pane where you do most of your work on the slide. **CASE** ▶ *The PowerPoint window and the specific parts of Normal view are described below.*

STEPS

1. **sam** ↓ **Start** PowerPoint

   PowerPoint starts and the PowerPoint start screen opens, as shown in FIGURE 1-4.

2. **Click the** Blank Presentation slide thumbnail

   The PowerPoint window opens in Normal view, as shown in FIGURE 1-5.

DETAILS

Using Figure 1-5 as a guide, examine the elements of the PowerPoint window, then find and compare the elements described below:

- The **Ribbon** is a wide band spanning the top of the PowerPoint window that organizes all of PowerPoint's primary commands. Each set of primary commands is identified by a **tab**; for example, the Home tab is selected by default, as shown in FIGURE 1-5. Commands are further arranged into **groups** on the Ribbon based on their function. So, for example, text formatting commands such as Bold, Underline, and Italic are located on the Home tab, in the Font group.

- The Slides tab is to the left. You can navigate through the slides in your presentation by clicking the slide thumbnails. You can also add, delete, or rearrange slides using this pane.

- The **Slide pane** displays the current slide in your presentation.

- The **Quick Access Toolbar** provides access to common commands such as Save, Undo, Redo, and Start From Beginning. The Quick Access Toolbar is always visible no matter which Ribbon tab you select. Click the Customize Quick Access Toolbar button to add or remove buttons.

- The **View Shortcuts** buttons on the status bar allow you to switch quickly between PowerPoint views.

- The **Notes button** on the status bar opens the Notes pane and is used to enter text that references a slide's content. You can print these notes and refer to them when you make a presentation or use them as audience handouts. The Notes pane is not visible in Slide Show view.

- The **status bar**, located at the bottom of the PowerPoint window, shows messages about what you are doing and seeing in PowerPoint, including which slide you are viewing and the total number of slides. In addition, the status bar displays the Zoom slider controls, the Fit slide to current window button 🖼, and other functionality information.

- The **Zoom slider** on the lower-right corner of the status bar is used to zoom the slide in and out.

FIGURE 1-4: PowerPoint start screen

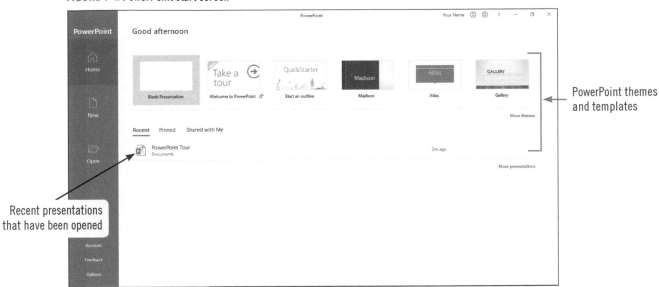

FIGURE 1-5: PowerPoint window in Normal view

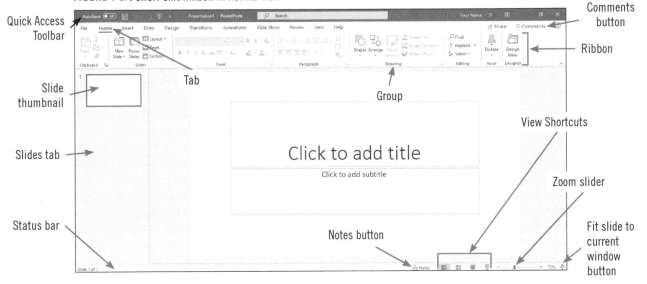

Creating a presentation using a template

PowerPoint offers you a variety of ways to create a presentation, including starting with a blank presentation, a theme, a template, or an existing presentation. A **template** is a type of presentation that contains design information on the slide master and often includes text and design suggestions for information you might want to include in the presentation. You have access to sample templates in PowerPoint and online at the Microsoft.com website. To create a presentation using a template, click the File tab on the Ribbon, click the New tab, locate the template, then click Create.

Enter Slide Text

Learning
Outcomes
• Enter slide text
• Change slide text

When you start a blank PowerPoint presentation, an empty title slide appears in Normal view. The title slide has two **text placeholders**—boxes with dotted borders—where you enter text. The top text placeholder on the title slide is the **title placeholder**, labeled "Click to add title." The bottom text placeholder on the title slide is the **subtitle text placeholder**, labeled "Click to add subtitle." To enter text in a placeholder, click the placeholder and then type your text. After you enter text in a placeholder, the placeholder becomes a text object. An **object** is any item on a slide that can be modified. Objects are the building blocks that make up a presentation slide. **CASE** ▶ *Begin working on your presentation by entering text on the title slide.*

STEPS

1. **Move the pointer ⬍ over the title placeholder labeled** Click to add title **in the Slide pane**

   The pointer changes to ⌶ when you move the pointer over the placeholder. In PowerPoint, the pointer often changes shape, depending on the task you are trying to accomplish.

2. **Click the** title placeholder **in the Slide pane**

   The **insertion point**, a blinking vertical line, indicates where your text appears when you type in the placeholder. A **selection box** with a dashed line border and **sizing handles** appears around the placeholder, indicating that it is selected and ready to accept text. When a placeholder or object is selected, you can change its shape or size by dragging one of the sizing handles. See **FIGURE 1-6**.

3. **Type** Global Workforce Trends

   PowerPoint center-aligns the title text within the title placeholder, which is now a text object. Notice the text also appears on the Slide 1 thumbnail on the Slides tab.

4. **Click the** subtitle text placeholder **in the Slide pane**

   The subtitle text placeholder is ready to accept text.

5. **Type** Presented by, **then press** ENTER

   The insertion point moves to the next line in the text object.

6. **Type** JCL Talent, **press** ENTER, **type** Dawn Lapointe, **press** ENTER, **type** Director, **press** ENTER, **then type** Technical Careers Division

   Notice the AutoFit Options button ⬍ appears near the text object. The AutoFit Options button on your screen indicates that PowerPoint has automatically decreased the font size of all the text in the text object so it fits inside the text object.

7. **Click the** AutoFit Options button ⬍, **then click** Stop Fitting Text to This Placeholder **on the shortcut menu**

   The text in the text object changes back to its original size and no longer fits inside the text object.

8. **In the subtitle text object, position ⌶ to the right of** Director, **drag left to select the whole word, press** BACKSPACE, **then click outside the text object in a blank area of the slide**

   The Director line of text is deleted and the AutoFit Options button menu closes, as shown in **FIGURE 1-7**. Clicking a blank area of the slide deselects all selected objects on the slide.

9. **Click the** File tab **on the Ribbon to open Backstage view, click** Save As, **click** Browse, **then save the presentation as** IL_PPT_1_JCL **in the location where you store your Data Files**

   In Backstage view, you have the option of saving your presentation to your computer or OneDrive. Notice that PowerPoint automatically entered the title of the presentation as the file name in the Save As dialog box.

FIGURE 1-6: **Title text placeholder selected**

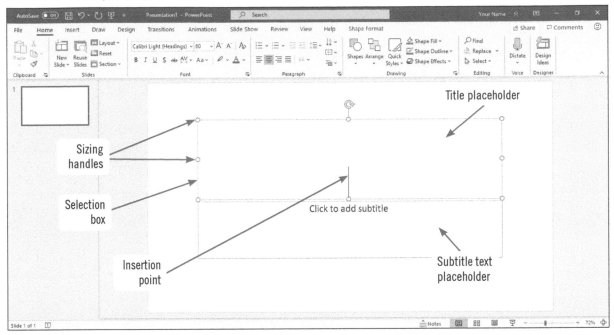

FIGURE 1-7: **Text on title slide**

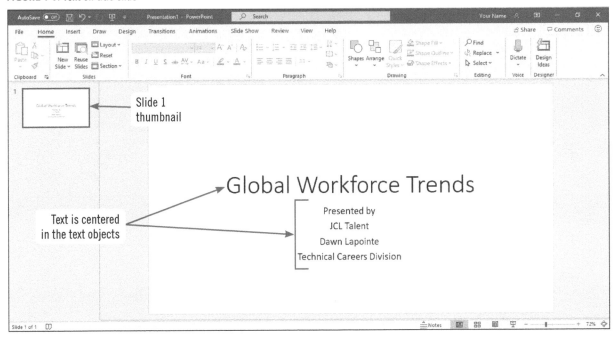

Inking a slide

In Normal view, you can add freehand pen and highlighter marks, also known as **inking**, to the slides of your presentation to emphasize information. To begin inking, go to the slide you want to mark up, click the Draw tab, then click one of the drawing tools in the Drawing Tools group. If you are using a touchscreen, you can use your finger or stylus to mark up a slide. To customize the thickness or color of your pen, click the down arrow on the selected pen. You can also click the Highlighter button in the Drawing Tools group to insert highlighter strokes on your slide. To erase inking on the slide, click the Eraser button in the Drawing Tools group, then click the ink or mark you want to erase.

PowerPoint

Add a New Slide

Learning
Outcomes
• Add a new slide
• Indent text levels
• Modify slide layout

Usually when you add a new slide to a presentation, you have an idea of what you want the slide to look like. For example, you may want to add a slide that has a title over bulleted text and a picture. To help you add a slide like this quickly and easily, PowerPoint provides many standard slide layouts. A **slide layout** contains text and object placeholders that are arranged in a specific way on the slide. You have already worked with the Title Slide layout in the previous lesson. In the event that a standard slide layout does not meet your needs, you can modify an existing slide layout or create a new, custom slide layout. **CASE** ▶ *To continue developing the presentation, you create a slide that explains the changing relationship between companies and workers.*

STEPS

1. **Click the** New Slide button **in the Slides group on the Home tab on the Ribbon**

   A new blank slide (now the current slide) appears as the second slide in your presentation, as shown in **FIGURE 1-8**. The new slide contains a title placeholder and a content placeholder. A **content placeholder** can be used to insert text or objects such as tables, charts, videos, or pictures. Notice the status bar indicates Slide 2 of 2 and the Slides tab now contains two slide thumbnails.

2. **Type** Relationship Between Companies and Workers, **then click the** bottom content placeholder

   The text you typed appears in the title placeholder, and the insertion point is now at the top of the bottom content placeholder.

3. **Type** Global trends, **then press** ENTER

   The insertion point appears directly below the text when you press ENTER, and a new first-level bullet automatically appears.

4. **Press** TAB

   The new first-level bullet is indented and becomes a second-level bullet.

QUICK TIP
You can also press
SHIFT+TAB to
decrease the
indent level.

5. **Type** Hiring practices since 2009, **press** ENTER, **then click the** Decrease List Level button ⊟ **in the Paragraph group**

   The Decrease List Level button changes the second-level bullet into a first-level bullet.

6. **Type** Reduction of full-time employees, **then click the** New Slide arrow **in the Slides group**

   The Office Theme layout gallery opens. Each slide layout is identified by a descriptive name.

7. **Click the** Two Content slide layout, **then type** Immediate Effects

   A new slide with a title placeholder and two content placeholders appears as the third slide. The text you typed is the title text for the slide.

8. **Click the left content placeholder, type** Independent workers—free agents, **press** ENTER, **click the** Increase List Level button ⊞, **type** Increase competition, **press** ENTER, **then type** Drive down costs

   The Increase List Level button moves the insertion point one level to the right.

9. **Click a blank area of the slide, then click the** Save button 🖫 **on the Quick Access Toolbar**

   The Save button saves all of the changes to the file. Compare your screen with **FIGURE 1-9**.

FIGURE 1-8: New blank slide in Normal view

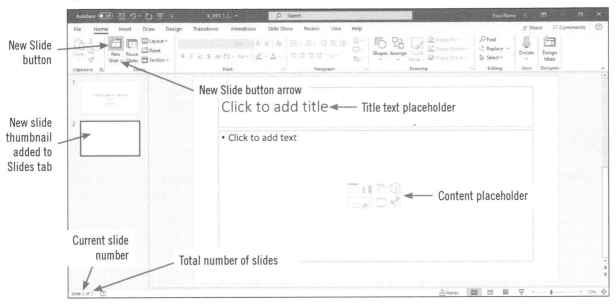

New Slide button

New slide thumbnail added to Slides tab

New Slide button arrow

Title text placeholder

Content placeholder

Current slide number

Total number of slides

FIGURE 1-9: New slide with Two Content slide layout

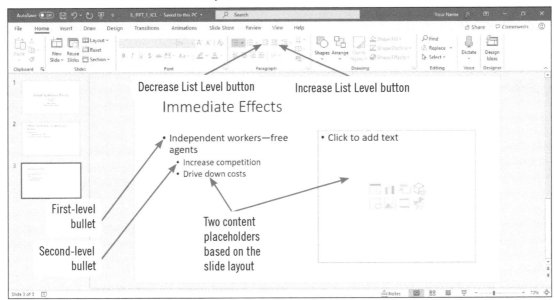

Decrease List Level button

Increase List Level button

First-level bullet

Second-level bullet

Two content placeholders based on the slide layout

Viewing your presentation in grayscale or black and white

Viewing your presentation in grayscale (using shades of gray) or pure black and white is very useful when you are printing a presentation on a black-and-white printer and you want to make sure your presentation prints correctly. To see how your color presentation looks in grayscale or black and white, click the View tab, then click either the Grayscale or Black and White button in the Color/Grayscale group. Depending on which button you select, the Grayscale or the Black and White tab appears, and the Ribbon displays different settings that you can customize. If you don't like the way an individual object looks in black and white or grayscale, you can change its color. Click the object while still in Grayscale or Black and White view, then choose an option in the Change Selected Object group on the Ribbon.

PowerPoint

Format Text

Once you have entered and edited the text in your presentation, you can modify the way the text looks to emphasize your message. Important text should be highlighted in some way to distinguish it from other text or objects on the slide. For example, if you have two text objects on the same slide, you could draw attention to one text object by changing its color, font, or size. **CASE** ▶ *You decide to format the text on two slides of the presentation.*

STEPS

1. **Click the** Slide 2 thumbnail **in the Slides tab, then double-click** Between **in the title text object**

   The word "Between" is selected, and a Mini toolbar appears above the text. The **Mini toolbar** contains basic text-formatting commands, such as bold and italic, and appears when you select text using the mouse. This toolbar makes it quick and easy to format text, especially when the Home tab is closed.

2. **Move** ⍾ **over the** Mini toolbar, **click the** Font Color arrow ⎣A⎦⌄, **then click the** Dark Red color box **in the Standard Colors row**

   The text changes color to dark red, as shown in **FIGURE 1-10**. When you click the Font Color arrow, the Font Color gallery appears showing the Theme Colors and Standard Colors. ScreenTips help identify font colors. Notice that the Font Color button on the Mini toolbar and the Font Color button in the Font group on the Home tab change color to reflect the new color choice, which is now the active color.

3. **Click the** Bold button ⎣B⎦ **in the Font group on the Ribbon, then click the** Italic button ⎣*I*⎦ **in the Font group**

   Changing the color and other formatting attributes of text helps emphasize it.

4. **Click the** Slide 1 thumbnail **in the Slides tab, select** Presented by, **click the** Font Size arrow ⎣11⎦⌄ **in the Mini toolbar, then click** 28

   The text increases in size to 28.

5. **Select the text** Global Workforce Trends **in the title object, then click the** Font arrow **in the Font group**

   A list of available fonts opens with Calibri Light, the current font used in the title text object, selected at the top of the list in the Theme Fonts section.

6. **Scroll down the alphabetical list, then click** Corbel **in the All Fonts section**

   The Corbel font replaces the original font in the title text object. Notice that as you move the pointer over the font names in the font list, the selected text on the slide displays a Live Preview of the available fonts.

7. **Click the** Underline button ⎣U⎦ **in the Font group, then click the** Increase Font Size button ⎣A˄⎦ **in the Font group**

   All of the text now displays an underline and increases in size to 66.

8. **Click a blank area of the slide outside the text object to deselect it, then save your work**

   Clicking a blank area of the slide deselects all objects that are selected. Compare your screen to **FIGURE 1-11**.

FIGURE 1-10: Selected word with Mini toolbar open

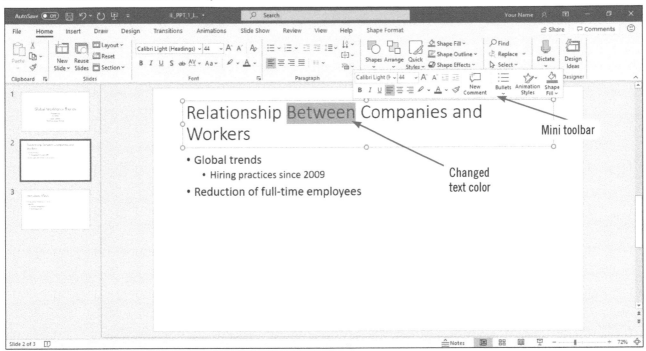

FIGURE 1-11: Formatted text

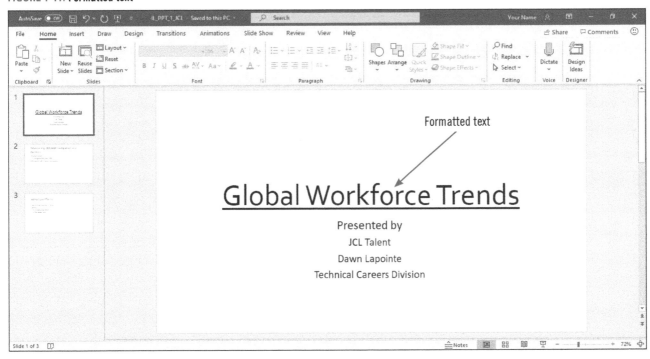

Adding bullets to paragraphs

In PowerPoint, paragraph text is often preceded by either a number or some kind of bullet. Common bullets include graphic images such as arrows, dots, or blocks. To add or change bullets, select the text or text object, click the Bullets arrow in the Paragraph group on the Ribbon, then select a bullet.

Creating a Presentation in PowerPoint

Apply a Design Theme

PowerPoint provides many design themes to help you quickly create a professional and contemporary-looking presentation. A **theme** includes a set of 12 coordinated colors for text, fill, line, and shadow, called **theme colors**; a set of fonts for titles and other text, called **theme fonts**; and a set of effects for lines and fills, called **theme effects** to create a cohesive look. In most cases, you would apply one theme to an entire presentation; you can, however, apply multiple themes to the same presentation. You can use a design theme as is, or you can alter individual elements of the theme as needed. Unless you need to use a specific design theme, such as a company theme or product design theme, it is faster and easier to use one of the themes supplied with PowerPoint. If you design a custom theme, you can save it to use in the future. **CASE** ▶ *You decide to change the default design theme in the presentation to a new one.*

STEPS

1. **Click the** Slide 1 thumbnail **on the Slides tab**

2. **Click the** Design tab **on the Ribbon, then point to the** Gallery theme **in the Themes group, as shown in** FIGURE 1-12
   The Design tab appears, and a Live Preview of the Gallery theme is displayed on the selected slide. A **Live Preview** allows you to see how your changes affect the slides before actually making the change. The Live Preview lasts about 1 minute, and then your slide reverts back to its original state. The first (far-left) theme thumbnail identifies the current theme applied to the presentation, in this case, the default design theme called the Office Theme.

3. **Slowly move your pointer** ⬚ **over the other design themes, then click the** Themes group down scroll arrow
   A Live Preview of the theme appears on the slide each time you pass your pointer over the theme thumbnails, and a ScreenTip identifies the theme names.

4. **Move** ⬚ **over the** design themes, **then click the** Wisp theme
   The Wisp design theme is applied to all the slides in the presentation and the Design Ideas pane opens. The Design Ideas pane provides additional customized design themes based on the current design theme applied to your presentation. Notice the new slide background color, graphic elements, fonts, and text color.

5. **Scroll down and back up the Design Ideas pane, then click the design at the top of the list**
   The presentation displays the suggested design theme. You decide this theme isn't right for the presentation.

6. **Click the** More button ⬚ **in the Themes group**
   The Themes gallery window opens. At the top of the gallery window in the This Presentation section is the current theme applied to the presentation. Notice that just the Slice theme is listed here because when you changed the theme, you replaced the default theme with the Slice theme. The Office section identifies all of the standard themes that come with PowerPoint.

7. **Right-click the** Mesh theme **in the Office section, then click** Apply to Selected Slides
   The Mesh theme is applied only to Slide 1. You like the Mesh theme better, and decide to apply it to all slides.

8. **Right-click the** Mesh theme **in the Themes group, then click** Apply to All Slides
   The Mesh theme is applied to all three slides. Preview the next slide in the presentation to see how it looks.

9. **Click the** Next Slide button ⬚ **at the bottom of the vertical scroll bar, click the** Close button ⬚ **in the Design Ideas pane, then save your changes**
   Compare your screen to FIGURE 1-13.

FIGURE 1-12: Slide showing a different design theme

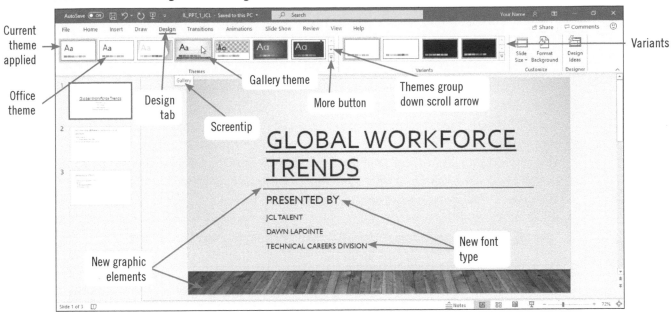

Current theme applied

Office theme

Design tab

Screentip

Gallery theme

More button

Themes group down scroll arrow

Variants

New graphic elements

New font type

FIGURE 1-13: Presentation with Mesh theme applied

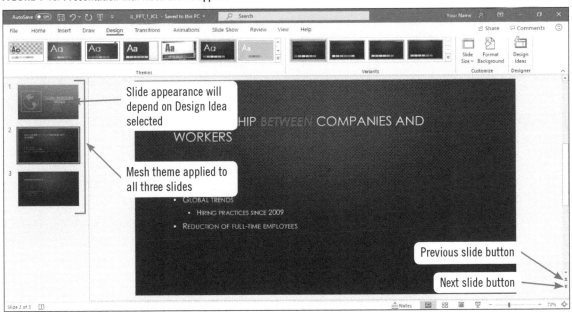

Slide appearance will depend on Design Idea selected

Mesh theme applied to all three slides

Previous slide button

Next slide button

Changing theme colors

You are not limited to using the standard theme colors PowerPoint provides; you can also modify theme colors or create your own custom theme. For example, you might want to incorporate your school's or company's colors on the slide background of the presentation. To change existing theme colors, click the Design tab on the Ribbon, click the More button in the Variants group, point to Colors then select a color theme. You also have the ability to create a new color theme from scratch by clicking the More button in the Variants group, pointing to Colors, then clicking Customize Colors. The Create New Theme Colors dialog box opens where you can select the theme colors you want and then save the color theme with a new name.

Compare Presentation Views

PowerPoint has six primary views: Normal view, Outline view, Slide Sorter view, Notes Page view, Slide Show view, and Reading view. Each PowerPoint view displays your presentation in a different way and is used for different purposes. Normal view is the primary editing view where you add text, graphics, and other elements to the slides. Outline view is the view you use to focus on the text of your presentation. Slide Sorter view is primarily used to rearrange slides; however, you can also add slide effects and design themes in this view. You use Notes Page view to type notes that are important for each slide. Slide Show view displays your presentation over the whole computer screen and is designed to show your presentation to an audience. Similar to Slide Show view, Reading view is designed to view your presentation on a computer screen. To move easily among the PowerPoint views, use the View Shortcuts buttons located on the status bar and the View tab on the Ribbon. TABLE 1-1 provides a brief description of the PowerPoint views. **CASE** *Examine some of the PowerPoint views, starting with Normal view.*

STEPS

1. **Click the** View tab **on the Ribbon, then click the** Slide Sorter button 🔲 **on the status bar**
   Slide Sorter view opens to display a thumbnail of each slide in the presentation in the window, as shown in FIGURE 1-14. You can examine the flow of your slides and drag any slide or group of slides to rearrange the order of the slides.

2. **Double-click the** Slide 1 thumbnail, **then click the** Notes button **on the status bar**
   The first slide appears in Normal view, and the Notes pane opens. The status bar controls at the bottom of the window make it easy to move between slides in this view. You can type notes in the Notes pane to guide your presentation.

3. **Click the** Slide Show button 🖵 **on the status bar**
   The first slide fills the entire screen now without the title bar and status bar. In this view, you can practice running through your slides as they would appear in a slide show.

4. **Click the** left mouse button **to advance to Slide 2, then click the** More slide show options button 🔘 **on the Slide Show toolbar**
   The slide show options menu opens.

5. **Click** Show Presenter View, **then click the** Pause the timer button ⏸ **above the slide, as shown in** FIGURE 1-15
   Presenter view is a view that you can use when showing a presentation through two monitors; one that you see as the presenter and one that your audience sees. The current slide appears on the left of your screen (which is the only object your audience sees), and the next slide in the presentation appears in the upper-right corner of the screen. Speaker notes, if you have any, appear in the lower-right corner. The timer you paused identifies how long the slide has been viewed by the audience.

6. **Click** 🔘, **click** Hide Presenter View, **then click the** left mouse button **to advance through the slide show until you see a black slide, then press** SPACEBAR
   At the end of a slide show, you return to Normal view and the last slide of the slide show, in this case, Slide 3.

7. **Click the** Home tab **on the Ribbon**

FIGURE 1-14: Slide Sorter view

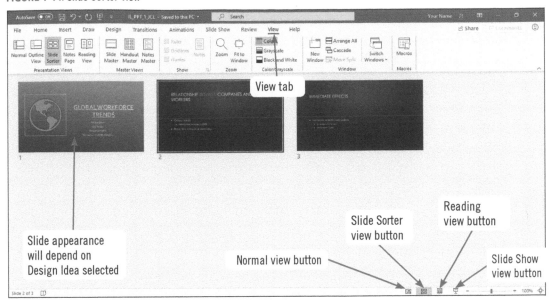

FIGURE 1-15: Slide 2 in Presenter view

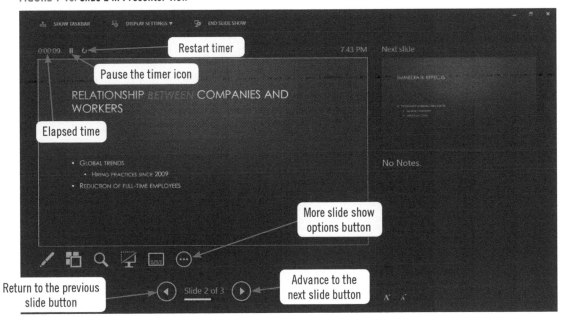

TABLE 1-1: PowerPoint views

view name	button	button name	displays
Normal	▣	Normal	The Slide pane and the Slides tab at the same time
Outline View	(no View Shortcuts button)		An outline of the presentation and the Slide pane at the same time
Slide Sorter	▤	Slide Sorter	Thumbnails of all slides
Slide Show	▽	Slide Show	Your presentation on the whole computer screen
Reading View	▦	Reading View	Your presentation in a large window on your computer screen
Notes Page	(no View Shortcuts button)		A reduced image of the current slide above a large text box

Creating a Presentation in PowerPoint

Insert and Resize a Picture

Learning
Outcomes
• Insert a picture
• Resize and move a
  picture

In PowerPoint, a **picture** is defined as a digital photograph, a piece of line art or clip art, or other artwork that is created in another program. PowerPoint gives you the ability to insert different types of pictures, including JPEG File Interchange Format and BMP Windows Bitmap files into a PowerPoint presentation. As with all objects in PowerPoint, you can format and resize inserted pictures to help them fit on the slide. You can resize pictures proportionally, which keeps changes to height and width relative to each other. You can also resize a picture non-proportionally, which allows the height and width to change independently from each other. **CASE** *Insert a stock picture given to you to use for this presentation. Once inserted, you resize it to best fit the slide.*

STEPS

QUICK TIP
You can also insert a picture by clicking the Pictures button in the Images group on the Insert tab.

1. **Click the** Slide 2 thumbnail **in the Slides tab, click the** Layout button **in the Slides group on the Ribbon, then click** Two Content
   The slide layout changes to the Two Content layout to accommodate a new picture.

2. **Click the** Pictures icon 🖻 **in the content placeholder on the slide, navigate to the location where you store your Data Files, select the picture file** Support_PPT_1_Woman.jpg, **then click** Insert
   The Insert Picture dialog box opens displaying the pictures available in the default Pictures folder. The newly inserted picture fills the content placeholder on the slide, and the Picture Format tab opens on the Ribbon. The Design Ideas pane also opens offering you design suggestions for the slide.

QUICK TIP
To select all the objects on a slide, click the Home tab on the Ribbon, click the Select arrow in the Editing group, then click Select All.

3. **Click the** Close button **in the Design Ideas pane, then place the pointer over the** middle-left sizing handle **on the picture**
   The pointer changes to ↦.

4. **Drag the** sizing handle **to the left as shown in** FIGURE 1-16, **then release the mouse button**
   Dragging any of the middle sizing handles resizes the picture non-proportionally, whereas dragging one of the corner sizing handles resizes the picture proportionally. The picture would look better if it was resized proportionally.

5. **Click the** Undo button **in the Quick Access Toolbar on the title bar**
   The picture reverts to its original size.

QUICK TIP
You can also resize a picture proportionally by entering specific height or width values in the Height or Width text boxes in the Size group on the Picture Format tab.

6. **Place the pointer over the** top-left sizing handle, **then drag to the left until the picture edge is just under the word "Between" in the title**
   The picture is now resized proportionally. To see a portion of a slide close up, you can zoom in.

7. **Drag the** Zoom slider ▮ **on the status bar to the right until the picture fills the screen**
   The selected picture fills the screen.

8. **Click the** Fit slide to current window button ⊕ **on the status bar, click a blank area of the slide, then save your work**
   The zoom setting returns to its previous position and the slide fits in the PowerPoint window. Compare your screen to FIGURE 1-17.

9. **Click the** File tab **on the Ribbon, then click** Close
   The presentation file closes.

FIGURE 1-16: Picture sized non-proportionally

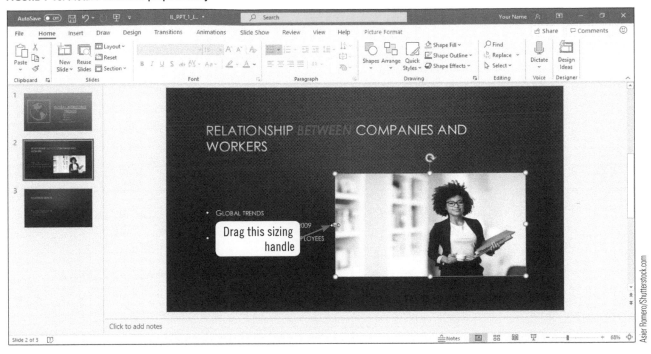

FIGURE 1-17: Picture sized proportionally

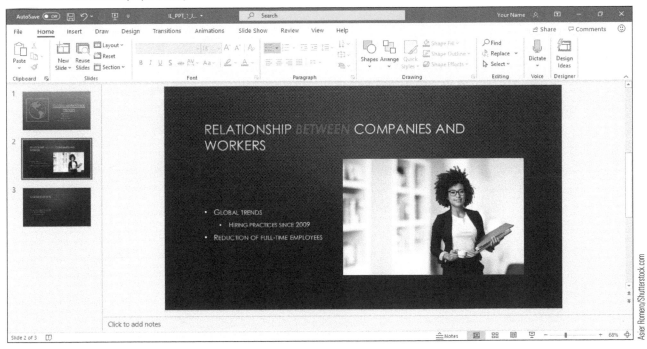

Check Spelling

Learning
Outcome
• Spell check a
  presentation

As your work on the presentation file nears completion, you need to review and proofread your slides thoroughly for errors. You can use the Spell Checker feature in PowerPoint to check for and correct spelling errors. This feature compares the spelling of all the words in your presentation against the words contained in the dictionary. You still must proofread your presentation for punctuation, grammar, and word-usage errors because the Spell Checker recognizes only misspelled and unknown words, not misused words. For example, the spell checker would not identify the word "last" as an error, even if you had intended to type the word "past." **CASE** ▷ *You've been given a presentation by a colleague to review.*

STEPS

1. **Open the presentation** IL_PPT_1-1.pptx **from the location where you store your Data Files, then save it as** IL_PPT_1_Interview

   A presentation with a new name appears in the PowerPoint window.

2. **Click the** Next Slide button ⤓ **at the bottom of the vertical scroll bar until Slide 4 appears**

   You notice some spelling errors and decide to check the spelling of the presentation.

3. **Click the** Previous Slide button ⤒ **at the bottom of the vertical scroll bar until Slide 1 appears, then click the** Review tab **on the Ribbon**

4. **Click the** Spelling button **in the Proofing group**

   PowerPoint begins to check the spelling in your presentation. When PowerPoint finds a misspelled word or a word that is not in its dictionary, the Spelling pane opens, as shown in **FIGURE 1-18**. In this case, the Spell Checker identifies a name on Slide 1, but it does not recognize that it's spelled correctly and suggests some replacement words.

5. **Click** Ignore Once **in the Spelling pane**

   PowerPoint ignores this instance of the word and continues to check the rest of the presentation for errors. PowerPoint finds the misspelled word "professional" on Slide 2.

6. **Click the** Change All button **in the Spelling pane**

   All instances of this misspelled word are corrected. The word "settings" on Slide 3 is also misspelled.

7. **Click the** Change button **in the Spelling pane**

   The misspelled word is corrected. When the Spell Checker finishes checking your presentation, the Spelling pane closes, and an alert box opens with a message stating the spelling check is complete.

8. **Click** OK **in the Alert box, then click the** Slide 4 thumbnail **in the Slides tab**

   The alert box closes.

9. **Drag the** Slide 4 thumbnail **between Slide 1 and Slide 2 in the Slides tab.**

   Slide 4 moves and becomes the second slide in the presentation. Compare your screen to **FIGURE 1-19**.

FIGURE 1-18: Window with Spelling pane open

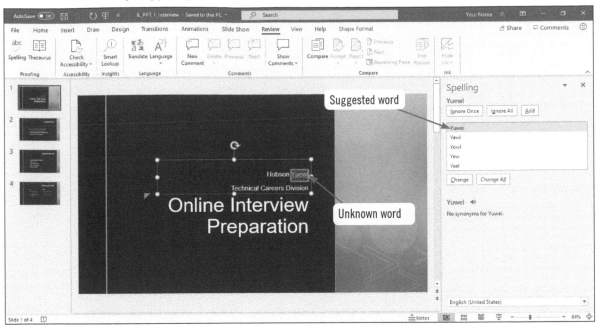

FIGURE 1-19: Moved slide

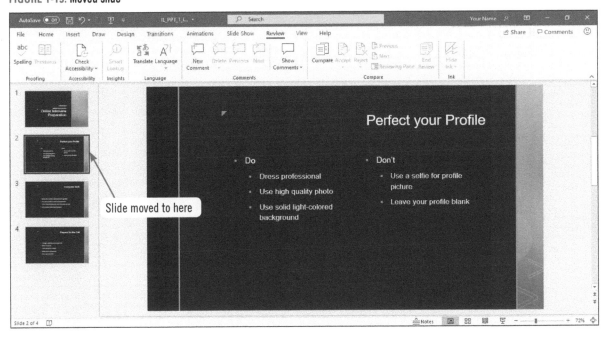

Checking spelling as you type

By default, PowerPoint checks your spelling as you type. If you type a word that is not in the dictionary, a wavy red line appears under it. To correct an error, right-click the misspelled word, then review the suggestions, which appear in the shortcut menu. You can select a suggestion, add the word you typed to your custom dictionary, or ignore it. To turn off automatic spell checking, click the File tab, then click Options to open the PowerPoint Options dialog box. Click Proofing in the left column, then click the Check spelling as you type check box to deselect it. To temporarily hide the wavy red lines, click the Hide spelling and grammar errors check box to select it. Contextual spelling in PowerPoint identifies common grammatically misused words; for example, if you type the word "their" and the correct word is "there," PowerPoint will identify the mistake and place a wavy red line under the word. To turn contextual spelling on or off, click Proofing in the PowerPoint Options dialog box, then click the Check grammar with spelling check box.

Creating a Presentation in PowerPoint

Print a PowerPoint Presentation

**Learning
Outcomes**
• Print a
  presentation
• Set print settings
• Modify color
  settings

You print your presentation when you want to review your work or when you have completed it and want a hard copy. Reviewing your presentation at different stages of development gives you a better perspective of the overall flow and feel of the presentation. You can also preview your presentation to see exactly how each slide looks before you print the presentation. When you are finished working on your presentation, even if it is not yet complete, you can close the presentation file and exit PowerPoint. **CASE** ▶ *You save and preview the presentation, then you print the slides and notes pages of the presentation so you can review them later. Before leaving for the day, you close the file and exit PowerPoint.*

STEPS

1. **Click the** Save button 🖫 **on the Quick Access Toolbar, click the** File tab **on the Ribbon, then click** Print

   The Print window opens, as shown in **FIGURE 1-20**. Notice the Preview pane on the right side of the window displays the first slide of the presentation. If you do not have a color printer, you will see a grayscale image of the slide.

2. **Click the** Next Page button ▶ **at the bottom of the Preview pane, then click** ▶ **again**

   The slides of the presentation appear in the Preview pane.

3. **Click the** Print button

   Each slide in the presentation prints.

4. **Click the** File tab **on the Ribbon, click** Print, **then click the** Full Page Slides button **in the Settings group**

   The Print Layout gallery opens. In this gallery you can specify what you want to print (slides, handouts, notes pages, or outline), as well as other print options. To save paper when you are reviewing your slides, you can print in handout format, which lets you print up to nine slides per page. The options you choose in the Print window remain there until you change them or close the presentation.

5. **Click** 3 Slides, **click the** Color button **in the Settings group, then click** Pure Black and White

   PowerPoint removes the color and displays the slides as thumbnails next to blank lines, as shown in **FIGURE 1-21**. Using the Handouts with three slides per page printing option is a great way to print your presentation when you want to provide a way for audience members to take notes. Printing pure black-and-white prints without any gray tones can save printer toner.

6. **Click the** Print button

   The presentation prints one page showing all the slides of the presentation as thumbnails next to blank lines.

7. **Click the** File tab **on the Ribbon, then click** Close

   If you have made changes to your presentation, a Microsoft PowerPoint alert box opens asking you if you want to save changes you have made to your presentation file.

8. **Click** Save, **if necessary, to close the alert box**

   Your presentation closes.

9. **sam▲ Click the** Close button ✕ **on the Title bar**

   The PowerPoint program closes, and you return to the Windows desktop.

FIGURE 1-20: Print window

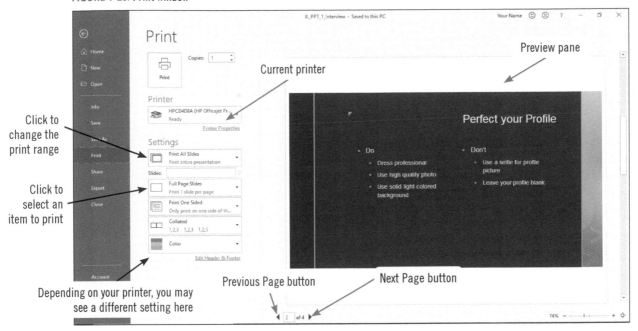

Current printer

Preview pane

Click to change the print range

Click to select an item to print

Depending on your printer, you may see a different setting here

Previous Page button

Next Page button

FIGURE 1-21: Print window with changed settings

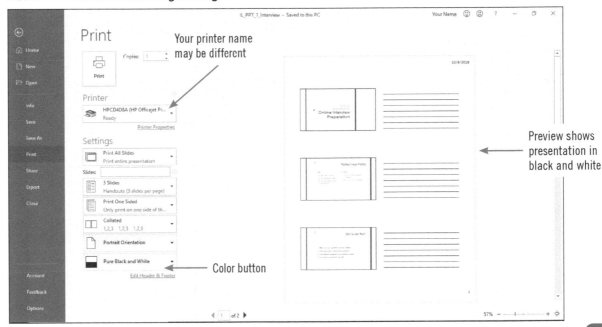

Your printer name may be different

Preview shows presentation in black and white

Color button

Office for the Web Apps

Some Office programs, PowerPoint for example, include the capability to incorporate feedback—called online collaboration—across the Internet or a company network. Using **cloud computing** (work done in a virtual environment), you can take advantage of web programs called Microsoft 365, which are simplified versions of the programs found in the Microsoft Office suite. Because these programs are online, they take up no computer disk space and are accessed using Microsoft OneDrive, a free service from Microsoft. Using Microsoft OneDrive, you and your colleagues can create and store documents in the "cloud" and make the documents available to whomever you grant access. To use Microsoft OneDrive, you need to create a free Microsoft account, which you obtain at the Microsoft website.

Practice

Skills Review

1. **Examine the PowerPoint window.**
   a. Start PowerPoint, if necessary then open a new blank presentation.
   b. Identify as many elements of the PowerPoint window as you can without referring to the lessons in this module.
   c. Be able to describe the purpose or function of each element.
   d. For any elements you cannot identify, refer to the lessons in this module.

2. **Enter slide text.**
   a. In the Slide pane in Normal view, enter the text **TC Insurance Services** in the title placeholder.
   b. In the subtitle text placeholder, enter **Company Security Division**.
   c. On the next line of the placeholder, enter your name.
   d. Deselect the text object.
   e. Save the presentation using the file name **IL_PPT_1_Analysis** to the location where you store your Data Files.

3. **Add a new slide.**
   a. Create a new slide using the Title and Content layout.
   b. Using **FIGURE 1-22**, enter text on the slide.
   c. Create another new slide.
   d. Using **FIGURE 1-23**, enter text on the slide.
   e. Save your changes.

4. **Format text.**
   a. Go to Slide 1, select the text TC Insurance Services, then move the pointer over the Mini toolbar.
   b. Click the Bold button, then click the Underline button.
   c. Select the text Company Security Division, click the Italic button, then click the Increase Font Size button.
   d. Go to Slide 2, select the word Accurately, click the Font Color arrow, then click Orange under Standard Colors.
   e. Go to Slide 3, select the word common in the third bullet point, click the Font Size arrow, then click 32.
   f. Click the Font button, click Algerian, then save your changes.

FIGURE 1-22

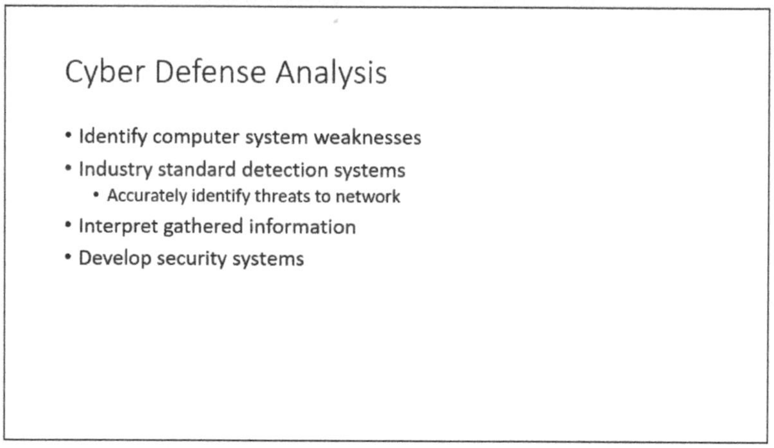

Cyber Defense Analysis

- Identify computer system weaknesses
- Industry standard detection systems
  - Accurately identify threats to network
- Interpret gathered information
- Develop security systems

FIGURE 1-23

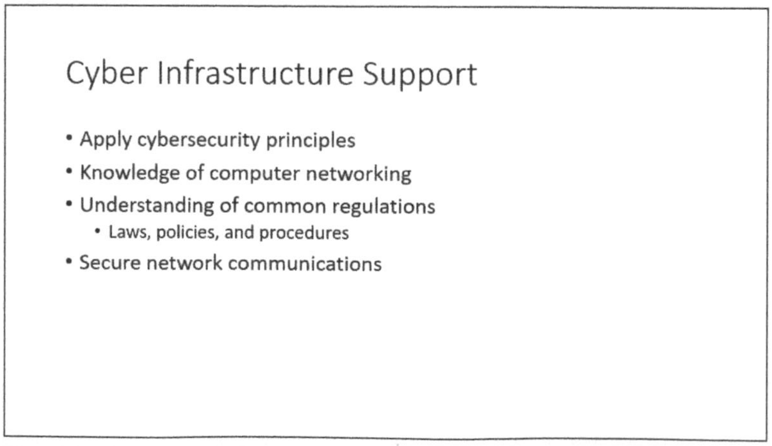

Cyber Infrastructure Support

- Apply cybersecurity principles
- Knowledge of computer networking
- Understanding of common regulations
  - Laws, policies, and procedures
- Secure network communications

Skills Review (continued)

5. Apply a design theme.

   a. Click the Design tab.

   b. Click the Themes group More button, then point to all of the themes.

   c. Locate the Madison theme, then apply it to the selected slide.

   d. Go to Slide 1, click the Themes group More button, locate the Ion Boardroom theme, then apply it to Slide 1.

   e. Apply the Ion Boardroom theme to all of the slides in the presentation.

   f. Click the first design in the Design Ideas pane, then close the Design Ideas pane.

   g. Use the Next Slide button to move to Slide 2, then save your changes.

6. Compare presentation views.

   a. Click the View tab, then click the Slide Sorter button in the Presentation Views group.

   b. Click the Normal button in the Presentation Views group, then click the Notes button on the status bar.

   c. Click the Notes button on the status bar, then click the Next Slide button.

   d. Click the Slide Show button on the status bar.

   e. Click the More slide show options button, click Show Presenter View, then click the Pause button.

   f. Click the More slide show options button, then click Hide Presenter View.

   g. Advance the slides until a black screen appears, then click to end the presentation.

   h. Save your changes.

7. Insert and resize a picture.

   a. Select Slide 2 in the Slides tab, then click the Home tab.

   b. Click the Layout button, change the slide layout to Two Content, then insert the picture **Support_PPT_1_Group.jpg** from the location where you store your Data Files.

   c. Close the Design Ideas pane, then drag the left-middle sizing handle to the left.

   d. Click the Undo button, then drag the bottom-left corner sizing handle down to the left to increase the picture size.

   e. Drag the Zoom slider on the status bar to the right until 100% appears next to the Zoom slider.

   f. Click the Fit slide to current window button on the status bar, save your changes, then close the presentation.

8. Check spelling.

   a. Open the presentation IL_PPT_1-2.pptx from the location where you store your Data Files, then save it as **IL_PPT_1_Emergency**.

   b. Click the Next Slide button at the bottom of the vertical scroll bar.

   c. Click the Previous Slide button at the bottom of the vertical scroll bar until Slide 1 appears, then click the Review tab.

   d. Click the Spelling button in the Proofing group. The word incident is misspelled on Slide 2.

   e. Make sure the word incident is selected in the Spelling pane, then click the Change All button. The word Responsibilities is also misspelled.

   f. Click the Change button in the Spelling pane. A correctly spelled abbreviation appears in the Spelling pane.

   g. Click the Ignore All button.

   h. Click OK in the alert box, then save your changes.

9. Print a PowerPoint presentation.

   a. Print all the slides as handouts, 3 Slides, in color.

   b. Close the file, saving your changes.

   c. Exit PowerPoint.

Independent Challenge 1

You work for Riverwalk Medical Clinic (RMC), a large medical facility in Cambridge, Massachusetts. You have been asked to put together a presentation on the hospital's internship program. The presentation will be used to recruit interns from local colleges.

a. Start PowerPoint, then open a new blank presentation.

b. In the title placeholder on Slide 1, type **Riverwalk Medical Clinic**.

c. In the subtitle placeholder, type **Medical Internship Program**, press ENTER, then type your name.

d. Underline the text Medical Internship Program, then italicize your name.

e. Save your presentation with the file name **IL_PPT_1_Intern** to the location where you store your Data Files.

f. Use FIGURE 1-24 and FIGURE 1-25 to add two more slides to your presentation then select Slide 1.

g. Apply the Wood Type design theme to the presentation, click the sixth design theme from the top in the Design Ideas pane, then close the Design Ideas pane.

h. On Slide 3 format the color, font type, and font size of the words Oral interview to Red, 24 pt, Arial Black.

i. Use the buttons on the View tab to switch between PowerPoint's views, then open and close Presenter View.

j. Print the presentation using handouts, 3 Slides, in black and white.

k. Save and close the file, then exit PowerPoint.

FIGURE 1-24

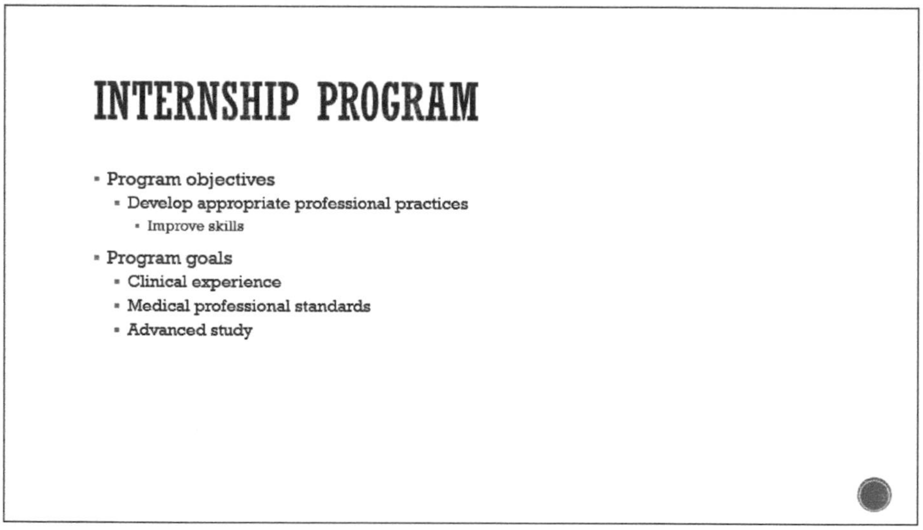

INTERNSHIP PROGRAM

- Program objectives
  - Develop appropriate professional practices
    - Improve skills
- Program goals
  - Clinical experience
  - Medical professional standards
  - Advanced study

FIGURE 1-25

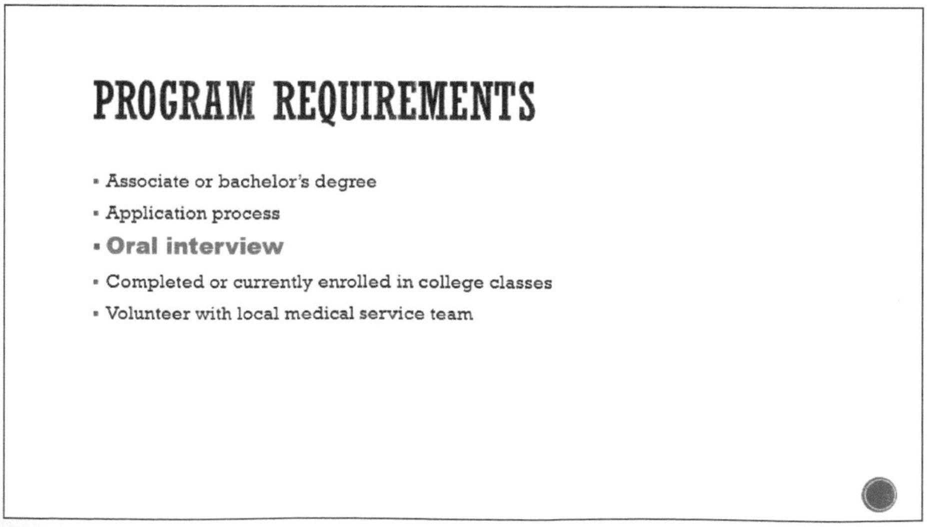

PROGRAM REQUIREMENTS

- Associate or bachelor's degree
- Application process
- **Oral interview**
- Completed or currently enrolled in college classes
- Volunteer with local medical service team

Independent Challenge 2

You are an assistant in the Computer Science Department at City College and you have been asked to create a presentation on a new course being offered on artificial intelligence (AI). AI is a fast-growing industry and the Computer Science Dept. wants to have relevant classes for students to better prepare them for future jobs. You have already started working on the presentation and now you add and resize a picture, add a design theme, and run a spell check.

a. Start PowerPoint, open the presentation IL_PPT_1-3.pptx from the location where you store your Data Files, and save it as **IL_PPT_1_AI400**.

b. Apply the Circuit design theme to all the slides, apply a design theme from the Design Ideas pane similar to one shown in **FIGURE 1-26**, then close the Design Ideas pane.

c. Spell check the presentation. There is a misspelled word on Slide 3.

d. Drag Slide 3 above Slide 2 in the Slides tab, then change the slide layout to Two Content.

e. Insert the picture **Support_PPT_1_ Group.jpg** from the location where you store your Data Files into the right content placeholder.

FIGURE 1-26

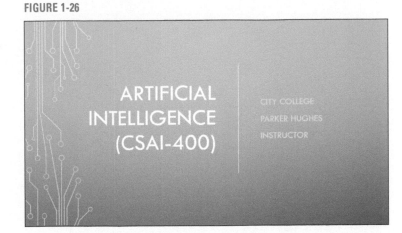

f. Resize the picture using a middle sizing handle, then undo the action by clicking the Undo button.

g. Resize the picture using a corner sizing handle, click the second design in the Design Ideas pane, then close the Design Ideas pane.

h. Switch views. Run through the slide show at least once.

i. Open and close Presenter view.

j. Close the presentation and exit PowerPoint.

Visual Workshop

Create the presentation shown in **FIGURE 1-27** and **FIGURE 1-28**. Make sure you include your name on the title slide. Save the presentation as **IL_PPT_1_Allesco** to the location where you store your Data Files. Print the slides.

FIGURE 1-27

FIGURE 1-28

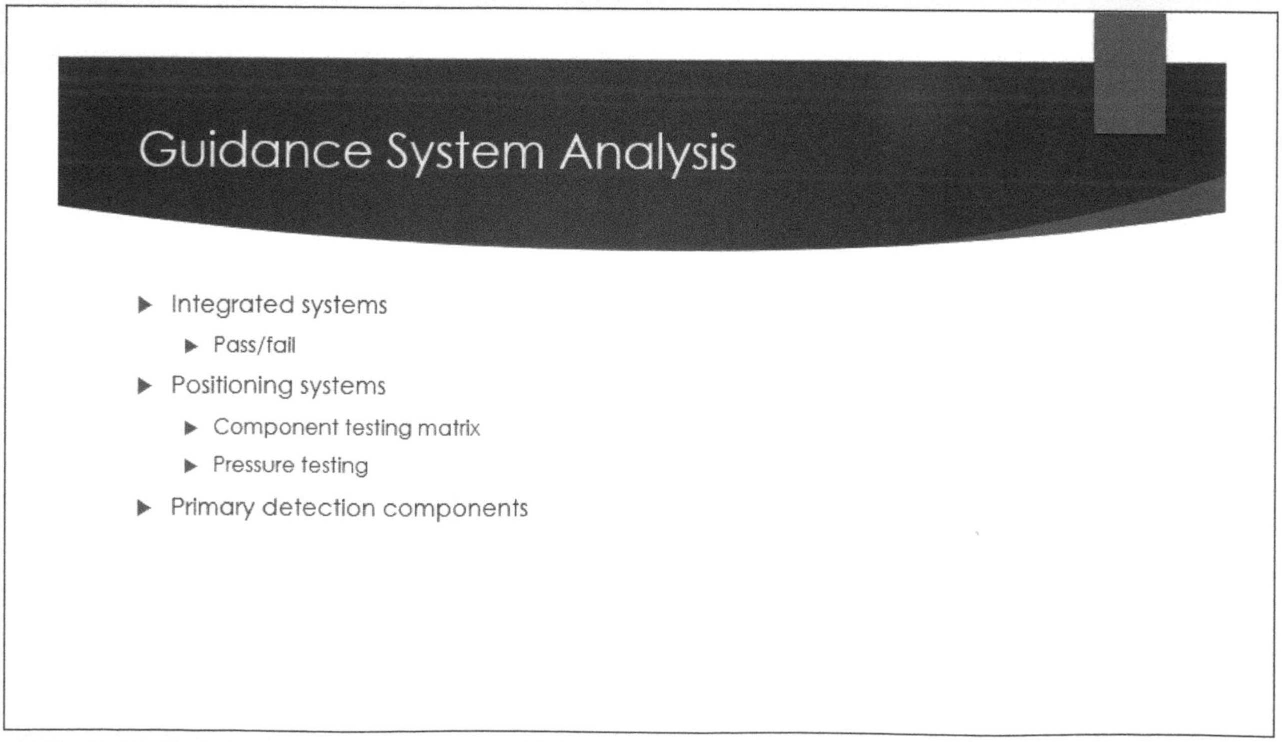

Creating a Presentation in PowerPoint

Modifying a Presentation

CASE You continue working on your global workforce presentation. In this module, you'll create a SmartArt graphic, draw and work with shapes, add slide footer information, and set slide transitions and timings in the presentation.

Module Objectives

After completing this module, you will be able to:

- Convert text to SmartArt
- Insert and style shapes
- Rotate and modify shapes
- Rearrange and merge shapes

- Edit and duplicate shapes
- Align and group objects
- Add slide footers
- Set slide transitions and timings

Files You Will Need

IL_PPT_2-1.pptx	IL_PPT_2-4.pptx
IL_PPT_2-2.pptx	IL_PPT_2-5.pptx
IL_PPT_2-3.pptx	

Convert Text to SmartArt

Learning
Outcomes
• Create a SmartArt
  graphic
• Modify the
  SmartArt design

Sometimes when you are working with text it just doesn't capture your attention. The ability to convert text to a SmartArt graphic provides a creative way to convey a message using text and graphics. A **SmartArt** graphic is a professional-quality diagram that graphically illustrates text. For example, you can show steps in a process or timeline, show proportional relationships, or show how parts relate to a whole. You can create a SmartArt graphic from scratch or create one by converting existing text you have entered on a slide. **CASE** *You want the presentation to appear visually dynamic, so you convert the text on Slide 4 to a SmartArt graphic.*

STEPS

1. **sam↓ Start PowerPoint, open the presentation** IL_PPT_2-1.PPTX **from the location where you store your Data Files, then save it as** IL_PPT_2_JCL

   A presentation with the new filename appears in the PowerPoint window.

2. **Click the** Slide 4 thumbnail **in the Slides tab, click** Service **in the text object, then click the** Convert to SmartArt Graphic button **in the Paragraph group**

   A gallery of SmartArt graphic layouts opens. As with many features in PowerPoint, you can preview how your text will look prior to applying the SmartArt graphic layout by using PowerPoint's Live Preview feature. You can review each SmartArt graphic layout and see how it changes the appearance of the text.

3. **Move** ↕ **over the** SmartArt graphic layouts **in the gallery**

   Notice how the text becomes part of the graphic and changes each time you move the pointer over a different graphic layout. SmartArt graphic names appear in ScreenTips.

   > **QUICK TIP**
   > To enter text using the Text pane, click the Text pane control ⟨ on the SmartArt graphic.

4. **Click the** Vertical Block List layout **in the SmartArt graphics gallery**

   A SmartArt graphic appears on the slide in place of the text object, and the SmartArt Design tab opens on the Ribbon, as shown in **FIGURE 2-1**. A SmartArt graphic consists of two parts: the SmartArt graphic and a Text pane where you type and edit text.

   > **QUICK TIP**
   > Text objects in the SmartArt graphic can be moved and edited like any other text object in PowerPoint.

5. **Click the** SmartArt Design tab **on the Ribbon, click the** More button ⥥ **in the Layouts group, click** More Layouts **to open the Choose a SmartArt Graphic dialog box, click** Pyramid, **click the** Pyramid List layout icon, **then click** OK

   The SmartArt graphic changes to the new graphic layout. You can change how the SmartArt graphic looks by applying a SmartArt Style. A **SmartArt Style** is a preset combination of simple and 3-D formatting options that follows the presentation theme.

6. **Move** ↕ **slowly over the styles in the SmartArt Styles group, then click the** More button ⥥ **in the SmartArt Styles group**

   A Live Preview of each style is displayed on the SmartArt graphic. The SmartArt styles are organized into sections; the top group offers suggestions for the best match for the document, and the bottom group shows you all the possible 3-D styles that are available.

   > **QUICK TIP**
   > Click the Convert button in the Reset group, then click Convert to Text to revert the SmartArt graphic to a standard text object.

7. **Move** ↕ **over the styles in the gallery, click** Inset **in the 3-D section, then click in a blank area of the slide outside the SmartArt graphic**

   Notice how the Inset style adds a shadow and an edge to achieve a 3-D effect. Compare your screen to **FIGURE 2-2**.

8. **Click the** Slide 4 thumbnail **in the Slides tab, then save your work**

FIGURE 2-1: Text converted to a Vertical Block List layout SmartArt graphic

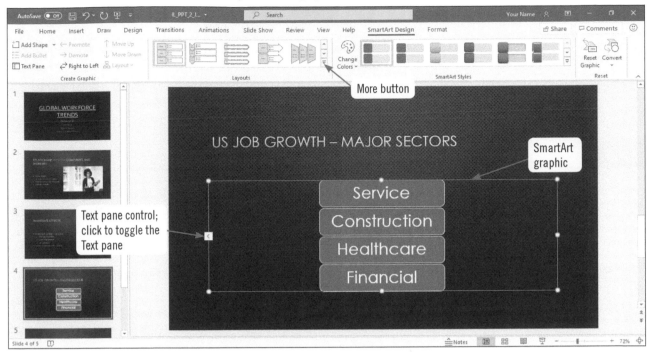

FIGURE 2-2: Final Pyramid List with Inset 3-D effect SmartArt graphic

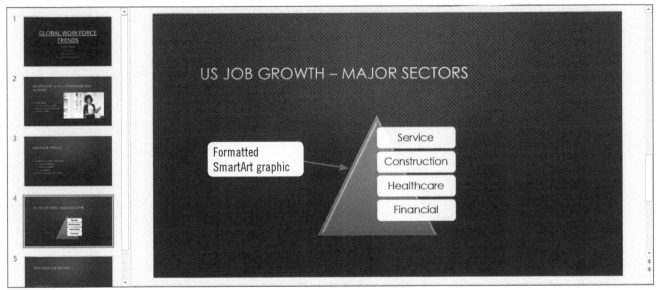

Entering and printing notes

You can add notes to your slides when there are certain facts you want to remember during a presentation or when there is additional information you want to hand out to your audience. Notes do not appear on the slides when you run a slide show. Use the Notes pane in Normal view or Notes Page view to enter notes for your slides. To open or close the Notes pane, click the Notes button on the status bar. To enter text notes on a slide, click in the Notes pane, then type the note. If you want to insert graphics as notes, you must use Notes Page view. To open Notes Page view, click the View tab on the Ribbon, then click the Notes Page button in the Presentation Views group. You can print your notes by clicking the File tab on the Ribbon to open Backstage view. Click Print, click the Full Page Slides list arrow in the Settings group (this button retains the last setting for what was printed previously so it might differ) to open the gallery, and then click Notes Pages. Once you verify your print settings, click the Print button. If you don't enter any notes in the Notes pane and print the notes pages, the slides print as large thumbnails with blank space below the thumbnails to handwrite notes.

Insert and Style Shapes

**Learning
Outcomes**
• Create a shape
• Modify a shape's
  style

In PowerPoint you can insert many different types of shapes, including lines, geometric figures, arrows, stars, callouts, and banners to enhance your presentation. You can modify many aspects of a shape, including its fill color, line color, and line style, as well as add shadows and 3-D effects. A quick way to alter the appearance of a shape is to apply a Quick Style. A **Quick Style** is a set of formatting options, including line style, fill color, and effects. **CASE** *You decide to draw some shapes on Slide 3 of your presentation that complement the slide content.*

STEPS

1. **Click the** Slide 3 thumbnail **on the Slides tab, click the** Shapes button **in the Drawing group, click the** Arrow: Pentagon button ▷ **in the Block Arrows section, then position** ╅ **in the blank area of Slide 3**

   ScreenTips help you identify the shapes.

2. **Press and hold** SHIFT, **drag** ╅ **down and to the right to create the shape, as shown in** FIGURE 2-3, **release the mouse button, then release** SHIFT

   A block arrow shape appears on the slide, filled with the default theme color. Pressing SHIFT while you create the object maintains the object proportions as you change its size. A **rotate handle**—circular arrow—appears on top of the shape, which you can drag to manually rotate the shape. A yellow-orange circle—called an **adjustment handle**—appears in the upper-right portion of the shape. Some shapes have an adjustment handle that can be moved to change the most prominent feature of an object, in this case the shape of the arrow.

3. **Drag the** adjustment handle **left over the middle sizing handle**

   The tip of the arrow changes shape.

4. **Click the** Shape Fill list arrow **in the Shape Styles group, then click** Orange, Accent 6

   An orange fill color is applied to the shape.

5. **Click the** Shape Outline list arrow **in the Shape Styles group, click** White, Text 1, **click the** Shape Outline list arrow **again, point to** Dashes, **then click the** Long Dash

   The shape outline changes to a long white dash. You also have the option of using a Quick Style to format a shape.

6. **Click the** ▾ **in the Shape Styles group, move** ⬚ **over the styles in the gallery to review the effects on the shape, then click** Intense Effect—Gold, Accent 4

   A gold Quick Style with coordinated gradient fill, line, and shadow color is applied to the shape.

7. **Click the** Shape Effects button **in the Shape Styles group, point to** Reflection, **move** ⬚ **over the effect options to review the effect on the shape, then click** Tight Reflection: Touching

   A short faded reflection of the shape appears below the shape, as shown in FIGURE 2-4.

8. **Click a blank area of the slide, then save your work**

   Clicking a blank area of the slide deselects all selected objects.

FIGURE 2-3: Arrow shape added to slide

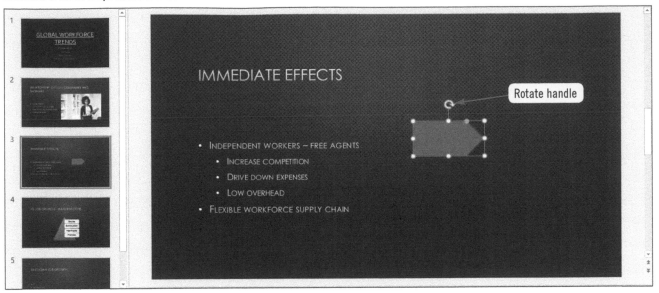

FIGURE 2-4: Styled arrow shape

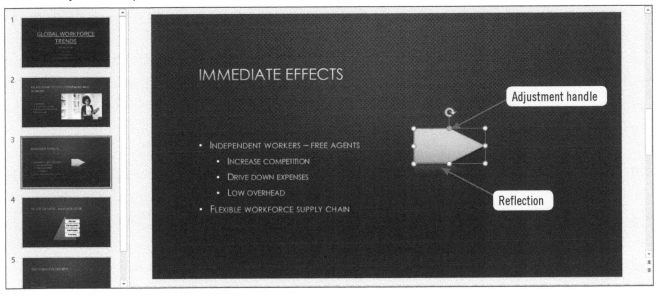

Using the Eyedropper to match colors

As you develop your presentation and work with different shapes and pictures, sometimes from other sources, there may be a certain color that is not in the theme colors of the presentation that you want to capture and apply to objects in your presentation. To capture a color on a specific slide, select any object on the slide, click any button arrow with a color feature, such as the Shape Fill button or the Shape Outline button in the Shape Styles group on the Shape Format tab, then click Eyedropper. Move the over the color you want to capture and pause, or hover. As you hover over a color, a Live Preview of the color appears and the RGB (Red Green Blue) values, called coordinates, appear in a ScreenTip. Click when you see the color you want to capture. The new color now appears in any color gallery under Recent Colors. If you decide not to capture a new color, press ESC to close the Eyedropper without making any change.

Rotate and Modify Shapes

Learning
Outcomes
• Rotate a shape
• Change a shape

Once you have created a shape, you have a number of formatting options available to you to enhance the shape. Some of these options include flipping and rotating the shape, which can radically change how the shape looks. Or, if a shape doesn't meet your needs, you can easily change to a different shape altogether. **CASE** *You continue to work on the shape on Slide 3.*

STEPS

> **QUICK TIP**
> To apply a picture fill to a shape, select the shape, click the Shape Fill button in the Shape Styles group on the Shape Format tab, click Picture, then locate and insert a picture.

1. **Select the** Block arrow shape **on Slide 3, if necessary click the** Shape Format tab **on the Ribbon, then click the** Rotate button **in the Arrange group**

   The Rotate menu appears with two rotate options and two flip options.

2. **Move ⟨⟩ over all of the options to review the effect on the shape, then click** Flip Horizontal

   Notice that the arrow tip is now pointing to the left with the rotate handle on top, indicating that the shape has flipped horizontally, or rotated 180 degrees, as shown in **FIGURE 2-5**.

3. **Click the** rotate handle **on the shape, then drag to the right until the shape is approximately 45 degrees from where it started**

   The shape is now pointing toward the top of the slide and the reflection is under the shape. You decide to rotate the shape by a specific amount.

4. **Click the** Undo button ⟲ **on the Quick Access Toolbar, click the** Rotate button, **then click** Rotate Right 90°

   The shape is now pointing up. It is 90 degrees from where it was just pointing and the rotate handle is to the right. It is easy to change the shape to any other shape in the shapes gallery.

5. **Click the** Edit Shape button **in the Insert Shapes group, point to** Change Shape **to open the shapes gallery, then click the** Frame button ▣ **in the Basic Shapes section**

   The block arrow shape changes to a frame shape. Notice that even though the shape has changed, it is still rotated 90 degrees from its original position and maintains the formatting changes you have already applied. You decide to rotate it back to its original position.

6. **Click the** Rotate button, **click** Rotate Left 90°, **click a blank area of the slide, then save your work**

   The shape is rotated back to its original position, as shown in **FIGURE 2-6**.

> **QUICK TIP**
> You can also use the Cut button in the Clipboard group on the Home tab to delete a slide.

7. **Right-click the** Slide 5 thumbnail **in the Slides tab**

   A shortcut menu appears with common slide commands. This slide is not needed, so you delete it from the presentation.

8. **Click** Delete Slide, **click the** Slide 3 thumbnail **in the Slides tab, then save your work**

   The fifth slide is deleted and Slide 3 appears in the Slide pane.

FIGURE 2-5: Flipped arrow shape

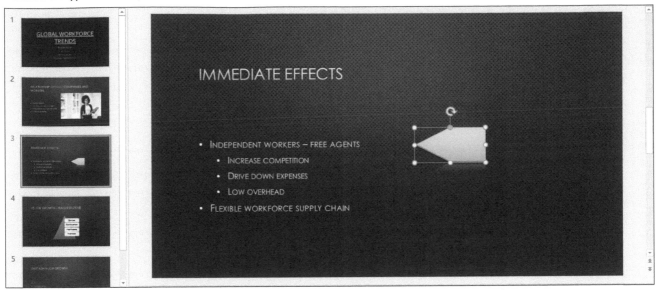

FIGURE 2-6: Frame shape

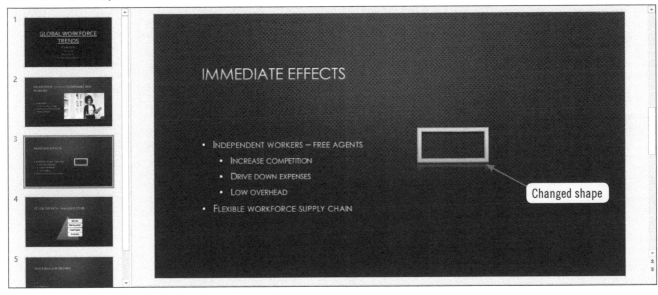

Aligning paragraph text

PowerPoint offers six ways to align paragraph text within a text object: Top, Middle, Bottom, Top Centered, Middle Centered, and Bottom Centered. To change paragraph text alignment, click the Home tab on the Ribbon, select the text you want to change, then click the Align Text button in the Paragraph group to open the Align Text menu. To see all the alignment options, click More Options in the Align Text menu, then click the Vertical alignment arrow.

Rearrange and Merge Shapes

Every object on a slide is placed, or stacked, on the slide in the order it was created, like a deck of cards placed one on top of another. Each object on a slide can be moved up or down in the stack depending on how you want the objects to look on the slide. **Merging** shapes, which combines multiple shapes together, provides you the potential to create unique geometric shapes not available in the shapes gallery. **CASE** *You create a pentagon shape on Slide 3, then merge it with the frame shape.*

STEPS

1. **Click** Independent **in the text object, position** ⬚ **over the** right-middle sizing handle, ⬚ **changes to** ⟷, **then drag the** sizing handle **to the left until the right border of the text object is next to the word "AGENTS" in the text object**

   The width of the text object decreases. When you position ⬚ over a sizing handle, it changes to ⟷. This pointer points in different directions depending on which sizing handle it is over.

2. **Click the** Shapes button **in the Drawing group, click the** Pentagon button ⬠ **in the Basic Shapes section, press and hold** SHIFT, **drag down and to the right to create the shape, then release** SHIFT

   Compare your screen to **FIGURE 2-7**. A pentagon shape appears on the slide, filled with the default theme color. You can move shapes by dragging them on the slide.

3. **Drag the** pentagon shape **over the frame shape, then use the Smart Guides that appear to position the pentagon shape in the center of the frame shape where the guides intersect**

   Smart Guides help you position objects relative to each other and determine equal distances between objects.

4. **Click the** Selection Pane button **in the Arrange group, then click the** Send Backward button ⬇ **in the Selection pane once**

   The Selection pane opens on the right side of the window showing the four objects on the slide and the order they are stacked on the slide. The Send Backward and Bring Forward buttons let you change the stacking order. The pentagon shape moves back one position in the stack behind the frame shape.

5. **Press** SHIFT, **click the** frame shape **on the slide, release** SHIFT **to select both shapes, click the** Merge Shapes button **in the Insert Shapes group, then point to** Union

   The two shapes appear to merge, or combine, to form one shape. The merged shape assumes the theme and formatting style of the pentagon shape because it was selected first.

6. **Move** ⬚ **over the other** merge shapes options **to review the effect on the shape, click a blank area of the slide, click the** pentagon shape, **then click the** Bring Forward button ⬆ **in the in the Selection pane once**

   Each merge option produces a different result. The pentagon shape moves back to the top of the stack. Now, you want to see what happens when you select the frame shape first before you merge the two shapes together.

7. **Click the** frame shape, **press** SHIFT, **click the** pentagon shape, **release** SHIFT, **click the** Shape Format tab **on the Ribbon, click the** Merge Shapes button **in the Insert Shapes group, then point to** Union

   The merged shape adopts the theme and formatting style of the frame shape.

8. **Point to each of the** merge shapes options, **then click** Subtract

   The two shapes merge into one shape. This merge option deletes the area of all shapes from the first shape you selected, so in this case the area of the pentagon shape is deleted from the frame shape. The merged shape is identified as a sequentially numbered Freeform in the Selection pane. See **FIGURE 2-8**.

9. **Click the** Selection Pane button **in the Arrange group, click a blank area of the slide, then save your work**

FIGURE 2-7: Pentagon shape added to slide

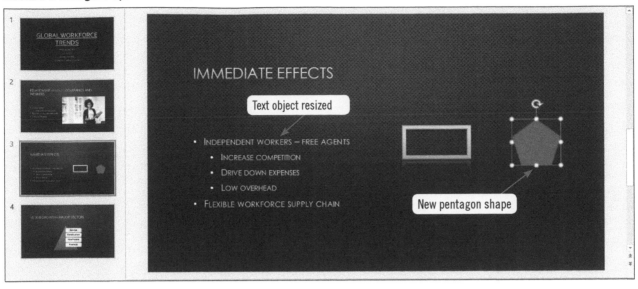

FIGURE 2-8: New Merged shape

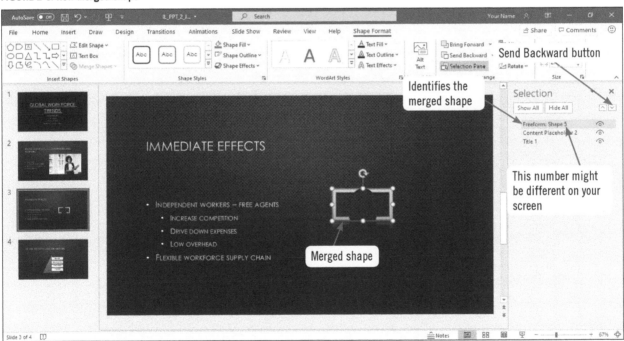

Changing the size and position of shapes

Usually when you resize a shape proportionally you can simply drag one of the corner sizing handles on the outside of the shape, but sometimes you may need to resize a shape more precisely. When you select a shape, the Shape Format tab appears on the Ribbon, offering you many different formatting options, including some sizing commands located in the Size group. The Width and Height commands in the Size group allow you to change the width and height of a shape. You also have the option to open the Format Shape pane, which allows you to change the size of a shape, as well as the rotation, scale, and position of a shape on the slide.

Edit and Duplicate Shapes

Once you have created a shape, you still have the ability to refine its basic characteristics, which helps change the size and appearance of the shape. For example, if you create a shape and it is too large, you can reduce its size by dragging any of its sizing handles. Most PowerPoint shapes can have text attached to them. All shapes can be moved and copied. To help you resize and move shapes and other objects precisely, PowerPoint has rulers you can add to the Slide pane. Rulers display the measurement system your computer uses, either inches or metric measurements. **CASE** ▶ *You want three identical frame shapes on Slide 3. You first add the ruler to the slide to help you change the size of the frame shape you've already created, then you make copies of it.*

STEPS

1. **Right-click a blank area of Slide 3, click** Ruler **on the shortcut menu, then click the edge of the** frame shape **to select it**

   Rulers appear on the left and top of the Slide pane. Unless the ruler has been changed to metric measurements, it is divided into inches with ½" and ⅛" marks. Notice the current location of the ⓚ is identified on both rulers by a small dotted red line.

2. **Drag the** middle-right sizing handle **on the frame shape to the right approximately ½", then release the mouse button**

   The frame shape is now slightly wider.

3. **Position** ⓚ **over the left edge of the selected** frame shape **so that it changes to** ⓚ**, then drag the** frame shape **to the 0.00 ruler position on the slide, as shown in** FIGURE 2-9 **using Smart Guides to position the shape**

   PowerPoint uses a series of evenly spaced horizontal and vertical lines—called **gridlines**—to align objects, which force objects to "snap" to the grid.

4. **Position** ⓚ **over the bottom part of the** frame shape, **then press and hold** CTRL

   The pointer changes to ⓚ, indicating that PowerPoint makes a copy of the shape when you drag the mouse.

5. **Holding** CTRL, **drag the** frame shape **down until the frame shape copy is in a blank area of the slide, release the mouse button, then release** CTRL

   An identical duplicate copy of the frame shape appears on the slide and Smart Guides appear above and below the shape as you drag the new shape, which helps you align shapes.

6. **With the** second frame shape **still selected, click the** Copy button ⬚ **in the Clipboard group, click the** Paste button, **then move the** new shape **to a blank area of the slide**

   You have duplicated the frame shape twice and now have three identical shapes on the slide.

7. **Click the** View tab **on the Ribbon, click the** Ruler **check box in the Show group, click the** Home tab, **then type** Growth

   The ruler closes, and the text you type appears in the selected frame shape and becomes a part of the shape. Now if you move or rotate the shape, the text moves with it. Compare your screen with FIGURE 2-10.

8. **Click the** middle frame shape, **type** Supply, **click the** top frame shape, **type** Trends, **click in a blank area of the slide, then save your work**

   All three frame shapes include text.

FIGURE 2-9: Merged shape moved on slide

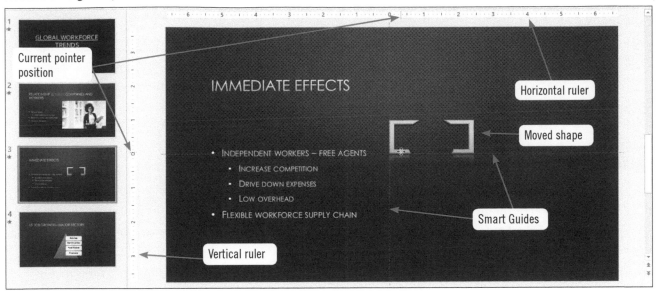

FIGURE 2-10: Duplicated shapes

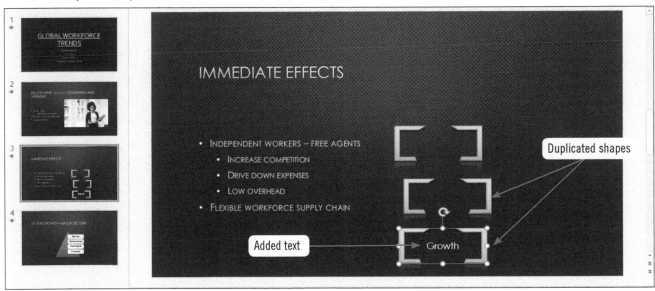

Editing points of a shape

If you want to customize the form (or outline) of any shape in the shapes gallery, you can modify its edit points. To display a shape's edit points, select the shape you want to modify, click the Shape Format tab on the Ribbon, click the Edit Shape button in the Insert Shapes group, then click Edit Points. Black edit points appear on the shape. To change the form of a shape, drag a black edit point. When you click a black edit point, white square edit points appear on either side of the black edit point, which allow you to change the curvature of a line between two black edit points. When you are finished with your custom shape, you can save it as a picture and reuse it in other presentations or other files. To save the shape as a picture, right-click the shape, then click Save as Picture.

Align and Group Objects

Learning
Outcomes
• Move shapes using
  guides
• Align and group
  shapes

After you are finished creating and modifying your objects, you can position them accurately on the slide to achieve the look you want. Using the Align commands in the Arrange group, you can align objects relative to each other by snapping them to the gridlines on a slide or to guides that you manually position on the slide. The Group command groups two or more objects into one object, which secures their relative position to each other and makes it easy to edit and move them. **CASE** ➤ *You are ready to position and group the frame shapes on Slide 3 to finish the slide.*

STEPS

1. **Right-click a blank area of the slide, point to the** Grid and Guides arrow **on the shortcut menu, then click** Gridlines

   Gridlines appear on the slide as a series of evenly spaced vertical and horizontal dotted lines. Gridlines can help you position objects on the slide.

2. **Drag the** Trends shape **until it snaps into place on a set of gridlines near its current position, click the** View tab, **then click the** Gridlines check box **to remove the gridlines**

   The shape snaps into place using gridlines.

3. **Right-click a blank area of the slide, point to** Grid and Guides arrow **on the shortcut menu, then click** Guides

   The guides appear as dotted lines on the slide and usually intersect at the center of the slide. Guides help you position objects precisely on the slide.

4. **Position** ↳ **over the** horizontal guide **in a blank area of the slide, notice the pointer change to** ⇻, **press and hold the mouse button until the pointer changes to a measurement guide box, then drag the** guide **up until the guide position box reads** 1.83

5. **Drag the** vertical guide **to the right until the guide position box reads** 1.83, **then drag the** Trends shape **so that the top and left edges of the shape touch the guides, as shown in** FIGURE 2-11

   The Trends shape attaches or "snaps" to the guides.

6. **Press and hold** SHIFT, **click the** Supply shape, **click the** Growth shape, **release** SHIFT, **then click the** Shape Format tab **on the Ribbon**

   All three frame shapes are now selected.

7. **Click the** Align button **in the Arrange group, then click** Align Right

   The two lower frame shapes move to the right and align with the top frame shape along their right edges.

8. **Click the** Align button, **click** Distribute Vertically, **click the** Group button **in the Arrange group, then click** Group

   The shapes are now distributed evenly among themselves and are grouped together to form one object without losing their individual attributes. Notice that the sizing handles and rotate handle now appear on the outer edge of the grouped object as shown in **FIGURE 2-12**, not around each individual object.

9. **Drag the** horizontal guide **to the middle of the slide until its guide position box reads** 0.00, **then drag the** vertical guide **to the middle of the slide until its guide position box reads** 0.00

10. **Click the** View tab **on the Ribbon, click the** Guides check box **in the Show group, click a blank area of the slide, then save your work**

    The guides are no longer displayed on the slide.

FIGURE 2-11: Repositioned shape

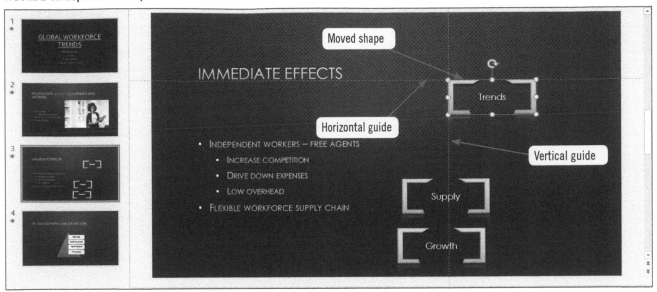

FIGURE 2-12: Grouped shapes

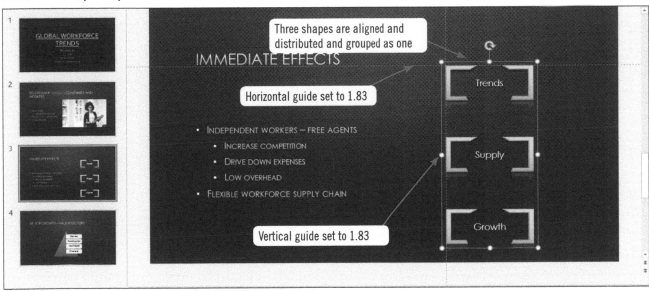

Distributing objects

There are two ways to distribute objects in PowerPoint: relative to each other and relative to the slide edge. If you choose to distribute objects relative to each other, PowerPoint evenly divides the empty space between all of the selected objects. When distributing objects in relation to the slide, PowerPoint evenly splits the empty space from slide edge to slide edge between the selected objects. To distribute objects relative to each other, click the Align button in the Arrange group on the Shape Format tab, then click Align Selected Objects. To distribute objects relative to the slide, click the Align button in the Arrange group on the Shape Format tab, then click Align to Slide.

Modifying a Presentation

Add Slide Footers

Footer text, such as a company, school, or product name, the slide number, or the date, can give your slides a professional look and make it easier for your audience to follow your presentation. Slides do not have headers. However, notes or handouts can include both header and footer text. You can review footer information that you apply to the slides in the PowerPoint views and when you print the slides. Notes and handouts header and footer text is visible when you print notes pages, handouts, and the outline. **CASE** ▶ *You add footer text that includes the date, slide number, and your name to the slides of the presentation to make it easier for the audience to follow.*

STEPS

1. **Click the** Insert tab **on the Ribbon, then click the** Header & Footer button **in the Text group**

   The Header and Footer dialog box opens, as shown in **FIGURE 2-13**. The Header and Footer dialog box has two tabs: a Slide tab and a Notes and Handouts tab. The Slide tab is selected. There are three types of footer text: Date and time, Slide number, and Footer. The bold rectangles in the Preview box identify the default position of the three types of footer text placeholders on the slides.

2. **Click the** Date and time check box **to select it**

   The date and time options are now available to select. The Update automatically date and time option button is selected by default. This option updates the date and time to the date and time set by your computer every time you open or print the file.

3. **Click the** Update automatically arrow, **then click the** fourth option **in the list**

   The month is spelled out in this option.

4. **Click the** Slide number check box, **click the** Footer check box, **click the** Footer text box, **then type your name**

   The Preview box now shows all three footer placeholders are selected.

5. **Click the** Don't show on title slide check box

   Selecting this check box prevents the footer information you entered in the Header and Footer dialog box from appearing on the title slide.

6. **Click** Apply to All

   The dialog box closes, and the footer information is applied to all of the slides in your presentation except the title slide. Compare your screen to **FIGURE 2-14**.

7. **Click the** Slide 1 thumbnail **in the Slides tab, then click the** Header & Footer button **in the Text group**

   The Header and Footer dialog box opens again.

8. **Click the** Don't show on title slide check box **to deselect it, click the** Footer check box, **then select the text in the Footer text box**

9. **Type** Always Looking Forward, **click** Apply, **then save your work**

   The text in the Footer text box appears on the title slide. Clicking Apply applies this footer information to just the current slide.

FIGURE 2-13: **Header and Footer dialog box**

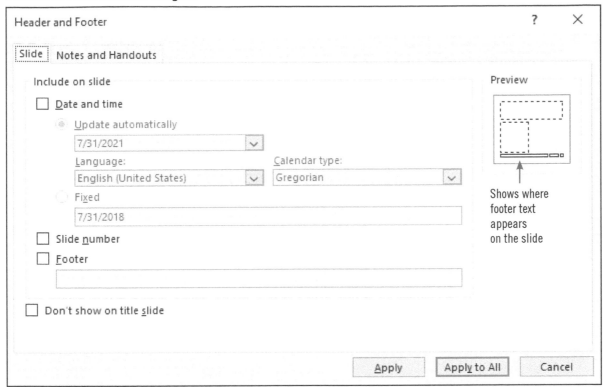

FIGURE 2-14: **Footer information added to presentation**

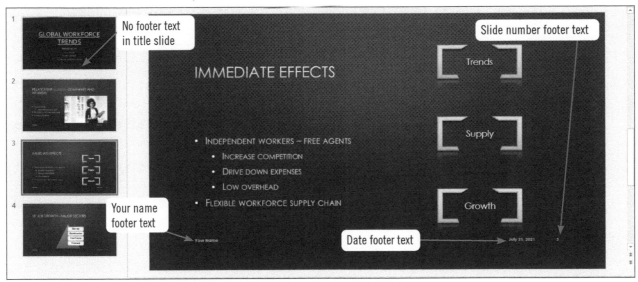

Creating superscript and subscript text

Superscript or subscript text is a number, figure, symbol, or letter that appears smaller than other text and is positioned above or below the normal line of text. A common superscript in the English language is the sign indicator next to a number, such as 1st or 2nd. Other examples of superscripts are the trademark symbol™ and the copyright symbol©. To create superscript text in PowerPoint, select the text, number, or symbol, then press CTRL SHIFT + at the same time. Probably the most familiar uses of subscript text are the numerals in chemical compounds and formulas, for example, H_2O and CO_2. To create subscript text, select the text, number, or symbol, then press CTRL = at the same time. To change superscript or subscript text back to normal text, select the text, then press CTRL SPACEBAR.

Set Slide Transitions and Timings

Learning Outcomes
- Apply and modify a transition
- Modify slide timings

In a slide show, you can determine how each slide advances in and out of view and how long each slide appears on the screen. **Slide transitions** are the visual and audio effects you apply to a slide that determine how each slide moves on and off the screen during the slide show. **Slide timing** refers to the amount of time a slide is visible on the screen. Typically, you set slide timings only if you want the presentation to automatically progress through the slides during a slide show. Each slide can have a different slide transition and different slide timing. **CASE** ▸ *You decide to set slide transitions and 7-second slide timings for all the slides.*

STEPS

1. **Click the** Transitions tab **on the Ribbon**

   Transitions are organized by type into three groups: Subtle, Exciting, and Dynamic Content.

2. **Click the** More button ▼ **in the Transition to This Slide group, then click** Page Curl **in the Exciting section**

   The new slide transition plays on the slide, and a transition icon ⭐ appears next to the slide thumbnail in the Slides tab as shown in **FIGURE 2-15**. You can change the direction and speed of the slide transition.

3. **Click the** Effect Options button **in the Transition to This Slide group, click** Double Right, **click the** Duration up arrow **in the Timing group until** 2.00 **appears, then click the** Preview button **in the Preview group**

   The Page Curl slide transition now plays double from the left on the slide for 2.00 seconds. You can apply this transition with the custom settings to all of the slides in the presentation.

4. **Click the** Apply To All button **in the Timing group, then click the** Slide Sorter button ▦ **on the status bar**

   All of the slides now have the customized Page Curl transition applied to them as identified by the transition icons located below each slide. You also have the ability to determine how slides progress during a slide show—either manually by mouse click or automatically by slide timing.

5. **Click the** On Mouse Click check box **under Advance Slide in the Timing group to clear the checkmark**

   When this option is selected, you have to click to manually advance slides during a slide show. Now, with this option disabled, you can set the slides to advance automatically after a specified amount of time.

6. **Click the** After up arrow **in the Timing group until** 00:07.00 **appears in the text box, then click the** Apply To All button

   The timing between slides is 7 seconds as indicated by the time under each slide thumbnail in **FIGURE 2-16**. When you run the slide show, each slide will remain on the screen for 7 seconds. You can override a slide's timing and speed up the slide show by using any of the manual advance slide commands.

7. **Click the** Slide Show button 🖵 **on the status bar**

   The slide show advances automatically. A new slide appears every 7 seconds using the Page Curl transition.

8. **sarf↑ When you see the black slide, press SPACEBAR, save your changes, submit your presentation to your instructor, then exit PowerPoint**

   The slide show ends, and you return to Slide Sorter view with Slide 4 selected.

FIGURE 2-15: Applied slide transition

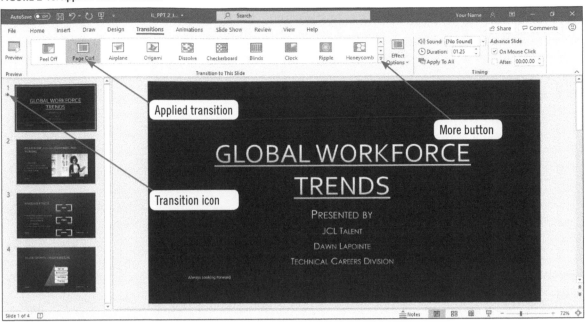

FIGURE 2-16: Slide Sorter view showing applied transition and timing

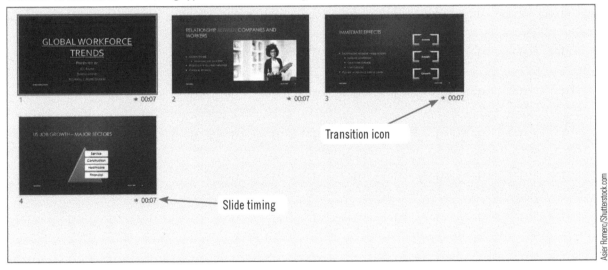

Inserting hyperlinks in a webpage

While creating a presentation there may be information on the Internet you want to reference or view during a slide show. Instead of re-creating the information in PowerPoint, you can insert a hyperlink on a slide that when clicked during a slide show will open the webpage directly from the Internet. To insert a hyperlink, select an object on the slide, such as a picture or text object, then click the Insert tab on the Ribbon. Click the Link button in the Links group to open the Insert Hyperlink dialog box. Click the Existing File or Web Page button in the link to section, then locate the webpage you want to link. Use the Address bar in the dialog box to insert the webpage address, then click OK. Now during a slide show, click the object with the hyperlink and you will view the linked webpage.

PowerPoint

Practice

Skills Review

1. Convert text to SmartArt.

a. Open the presentation IL_PPT_2-2.pptx from the location where you store your Data Files, then save it as **IL_PPT_2_Broker**. The completed presentation is shown in FIGURE 2-17.

b. Click the text object on Slide 2.

c. Click the Convert to SmartArt Graphic button, then apply the Basic Cycle graphic layout to the text object.

d. Click the More button in the Layouts group, click More Layouts, click Process in the Choose a SmartArt Graphic dialog box, click Continuous Block Process, then click OK.

e. Click the More button in the SmartArt Styles group, then apply the Metallic Scene style from the 3-D group to the graphic.

f. Click outside the SmartArt graphic in a blank part of the slide.

g. Save your changes.

FIGURE 2-17

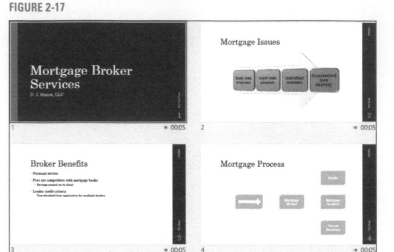

2. Insert and style shapes.

a. Go to Slide 5, click the More button in the Drawing group to open the Shapes gallery, click the Arrow: Right button in the Block Arrows section, then draw about a 1" shape in a blank area of the slide.

b. On the Shape Format tab, click the Shape Fill button in the Shape Styles group, click yellow under Standard Colors, click the Shape Outline button, point to Weight, then click 3 pt.

c. Click the More button in the Shape Styles group, then click Moderate Effect—Olive Green, Accent 3.

d. Click the Shape Effects button, point to Bevel, then click Angle.

e. Click the Undo list arrow in the title bar, click the Shape Effects button, then point to Glow.

f. Click Glow: 11 point; Olive Green, Accent color 3, then save your changes.

g. Drag the lower-left adjustment handle down slightly to adjust the width of the arrow shaft.

3. Rotate and modify shapes.

a. Click the arrow shape on the slide, click the Rotate button in the Arrange group, then click Flip Horizontal.

b. Drag the Rotate handle to the left until the arrow is pointing to the bottom of the slide, click the Undo list arrow, then click Rotate Object.

c. Click the Rotate button, then click Flip Horizontal.

d. Click the Edit Shape button in the Insert Shapes group, point to Change Shape, then click Arrow: Notched Right in the Block Arrows section.

e. Right-click the Slide 4 thumbnail in the Slides tab, click Delete Slide, then save your work.

4. Rearrange and merge shapes.

a. Click the green arrow shape on Slide 4, then click the Shape Format tab.

b. Drag the arrow shape over the top of the blank rectangle shape, center it on the rectangle shape using the SmartGuides, then adjust the shape if needed to make it fit in the space as shown in FIGURE 2-18.

Skills Review (continued)

c. Send the arrow shape back one level, press SHIFT, click the rectangle shape, then click the Merge Shapes button in the Insert Shapes group.

d. Point to each of the merge shapes options, click a blank area of the slide twice, then click the rectangle shape.

e. Send the rectangle shape back one level, then click a blank area of the slide.

f. Press SHIFT, click the arrow shape, click the rectangle shape, click the Merge Shapes button, click Combine, then save your work.

FIGURE 2-18

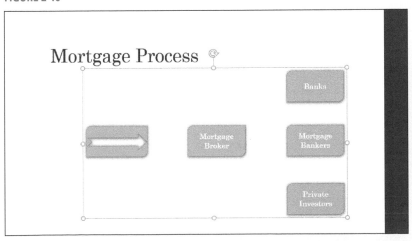

5. **Edit and duplicate shapes.**
   a. Show Rulers, select the Banks shape, then using CTRL make one copy of the shape.
   b. Using the ruler, move the new shape to approximately 3.5 (right of 0) on the horizontal ruler, then close the rulers.
   c. Click the new shape, click the Copy button in the Clipboard group, then click the Paste button in the Clipboard group.
   d. Move the new square shape to a blank area at the bottom of the slide, then select the text in the shape.
   e. Type **Private Investors**, select the text in the other new rectangle shape, then type **Mortgage Bankers**.
   f. Click the arrow shape, then drag the right-middle sizing handle to the right ¼".
   g. Click a blank area of the slide, add the gridlines to the Slide pane, then save your changes.

6. **Align and group objects.**
   a. Drag the Mortgage Broker rectangle shape down until its bottom edge snaps to a horizontal gridline, then click the Shape Format tab.
   b. Press SHIFT, click the arrow shape, click the Mortgage Bankers shape, release SHIFT, then click the Align button in the Arrange group.
   c. Click Align Middle, click the Align button, then click Distribute Horizontally.
   d. Hide the gridlines, display the guides, then move the vertical guide to the right until 3.00 appears.
   e. Move the Private Investors shape to the left until it is centered over the vertical guide, move the vertical guide back to 0.00, then hide the guides.
   f. Select the three rectangle shapes on the right, click the Align button, then click Align Right.
   g. Select all five square shapes, click the Group button in the Arrange group, click Group, then save your work. Your screen should look similar to **FIGURE 2-19**.

FIGURE 2-19

Skills Review (continued)

7. Add slide footers.

   a. Open the Header and Footer dialog box.

   b. On the Slide tab, click the Date and time check box to select it, then click the Fixed option button.

   c. Add the slide number to the footer, then type your name in the Footer text box.

   d. Apply the footer to all of the slides except the title slide.

   e. Click the Slide 1 thumbnail on the Slides tab, open the Header and Footer dialog box again, then click the Don't show on title slide check box.

   f. Click the Footer check box, then type your class name in the text box.

   g. Click the Slide number check box, click Apply, then save your changes.

8. Set slide transitions and timings.

   a. Go to Slide Sorter view, click the Slide 1 thumbnail, click the Transitions tab, then apply the Wind transition to the slide.

   b. Change the effect option to Left, change the duration to 2.75, then apply to all the slides.

   c. Change the slide timing to 5 seconds, then apply to all of the slides.

   d. Switch to Normal view, view the slide show, then save your work.

   e. Submit your presentation to your instructor, close the presentation, then exit PowerPoint.

Independent Challenge 1

Riverwalk Medical Clinic (RMC) is a large medical facility in Cambridge, Massachusetts. You have been asked to create a presentation on the latest emergency response procedures for a staff training later in the week.

   a. Start PowerPoint, open the presentation IL_PPT_2-3.pptx from the location where you store your Data Files, and save it as **IL_PPT_2_ERP**.

   b. On Slide 3 display the guides in the Slide pane, move the horizontal guide down to 2.00, then move the vertical guide left to 5.00.

   c. Drag the rectangle shape so its top and left edges snap into the guides, then move both guides back to 0.00 and hide the guides.

   d. Move the left adjustment handle on the rectangle shape slightly to the right to change the shape of the rectangle.

   e. Change the shape fill color to Rose, Accent 6, then change the shape outline to solid 1 ½-point black.

   f. Duplicate the shape twice, align the shapes along their bottom edges across the slide, distribute the space horizontally between the shapes, then group the shapes.

   g. Type **CPR** in the left shape, type **Airway kits** in the middle shape, then type **Crash cart** in the right shape.

   h. Apply the Reveal transition to all the slides with a 4.50 duration time.

   i Change the bulleted text on Slide 4 to the Trapezoid List SmartArt Graphic, then apply the Inset SmartArt style.

   j. Add your name and slide number as a footer on all the slides except the title slide, then save your changes. Your completed presentation might look similar to **FIGURE 2-20**.

   k. Submit your presentation to your instructor, close your presentation, then exit PowerPoint.

FIGURE 2-20

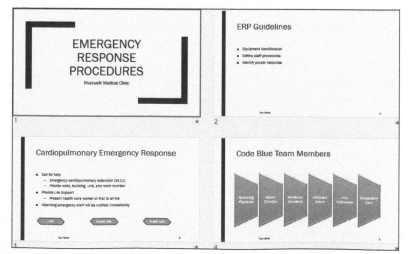

Independent Challenge 2

You are one of the assistants to the Career and Intern Program manager at Delvall Corp., a large engineering and manufacturing company. You have been asked by your manager to develop a new presentation outlining the details of the career and intern leadership program offered by Delvall. You continue working on the presentation you have already started.

a. Start PowerPoint, open the presentation IL_PPT_2-4.pptx from the location where you store your Data Files, and save it as **IL_PPT_2_Delvall**.

b. Go to Slide 4, show the rulers in the Slide pane, then drag the lower-right sizing handle on the shape down and to the right until the pointer reaches the 3 in the horizontal ruler.

c. Draw a 1" proportional chevron shape from the Block Arrows section of shapes. (*Hint*: to draw a specific size shape, position your pointer on the 0 of a ruler and drag until your pointer reaches the size you want on the ruler.)

d. Click the Shape Format tab, flip the shape horizontal, then drag the shape's rotate handle until the arrow is pointing up.

e. Select both shapes, then apply Intense Effect—Orange, Accent 2 from the Shape Styles group.

f. Apply the Preset 1 shape effect, then merge the two shapes together using the Union option, as shown in FIGURE 2-21.

g. Show gridlines in the Slide pane, drag the merged shape to the left until the shape's left and bottom edges are touching gridlines, then hide the gridlines.

h. Apply to all the slides the transition Random Bars with a duration of 2.00, then change the effect option to horizontal.

i. Delete Slide 2 from the presentation, add the slide number and your name as a footer on the slides, then save your changes.

j. Run a slide show, submit your presentation to your instructor, close your presentation, then exit PowerPoint.

FIGURE 2-21

Visual Workshop

Open the presentation IL_PPT_2-5.pptx from the location where you store your Data Files, and save it as **IL_PPT_2_LaSalle**. Create the presentation shown in **FIGURE 2-22** and **FIGURE 2-23**. Add today's date as the date on the title slide. Create and duplicate the merged shape, which is made with an Arrow: Bent-Up shape and a Rectangle: Rounded Corners shape. The shapes are 1 ½" proportional shapes with the Subtle Effect—Dark Purple, Accent 2 applied to them. (*Hint*: The arrow shape is rotated 90 degrees before it's merged with the square shape.) Set the horizontal guide to 3 and the vertical guide to 1, as shown in **FIGURE 2-22**. The SmartArt graphic in **FIGURE 2-23** is created with the Basic Matrix layout and has the Moderate Effect style applied to it. Review your slides in Slide Show view, then add your name as a footer to the slides. Submit your presentation to your instructor, save your changes, close the presentation, then exit PowerPoint.

FIGURE 2-22

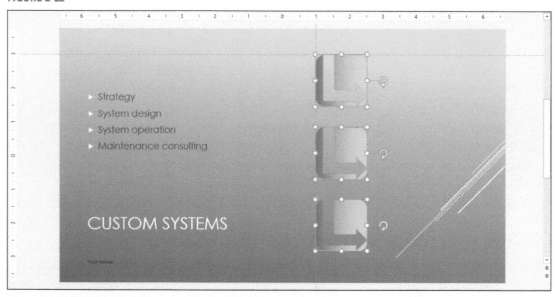

FIGURE 2-23

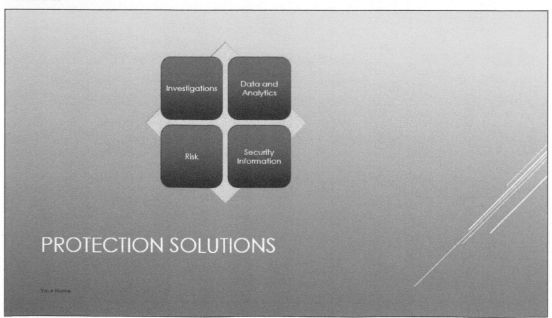

Inserting Objects into a Presentation

CASE > In this module, you continue working on the JCL Talent presentation by inserting and formatting a text box and then cropping and styling a picture. You also add visual elements into the presentation, including a chart, slides from another presentation, and a table. You format these objects using the powerful object-editing features in PowerPoint.

Module Objectives

After completing this module, you will be able to:

- Insert a text box
- Crop and style a picture
- Insert a chart
- Enter and edit chart data
- Insert slides from other presentations
- Insert a table
- Insert and format WordArt
- Animate objects
- Insert and edit digital video

Files You Will Need

IL_PPT_3-1.pptx

Support_PPT_3_Group.jpg

Support_PPT_3_Presentation.pptx

Support_PPT_3_Video.mp4

IL_PPT_3-2.pptx

Support_PPT_3_PMI.pptx

Support_PPT_3_Desk.mp4

IL_PPT_3-3.pptx

Support_PPT_3_ER.jpg

IL_PPT_3-4.pptx

Support_PPT_3_Invest.pptx

Support_PPT_3_Woman.jpg

Insert a Text Box

In most cases, you enter text on a slide using a title or content placeholder that is arranged on the slide based on a slide layout. Every so often you need additional text on a slide where the traditional place-holder does not place text. There are two types of text boxes: a text label, used for a small phrase where text doesn't automatically wrap inside the boundaries of a text box, and a word-processing box, used for a sentence or paragraph where the text wraps inside a text box. Either type of text box can be formatted and edited just like any other text object. **CASE** ▶ *You create a text box next to the SmartArt graphic on Slide 4, then edit and format the text.*

STEPS

1. **sam** ⬇ **Start PowerPoint, open the presentation** IL_PPT_3-1.pptx **from the location where you store your Data Files, then save it as** IL_PPT_3_JCL

2. **Click the** Slide 4 thumbnail **on the Slides tab, click the** Insert tab **on the Ribbon, then click the** Text Box button **in the Text group**
   The pointer changes to ↓.

3. **Move** ↓ **to the blank area to the left of the SmartArt object on the slide, then drag the pointer ＋ down and toward the right about 3" to create a text box**
   When you begin dragging, an outline of the text box appears, indicating the size of the text box you are drawing. After you release the mouse button, a blinking insertion point appears inside the text box, in this case a word-processing box, indicating that you can enter text.

4. **Type** Last year's growth increased over 25% in all areas
   Notice the text box increases in size as your text wraps to additional lines inside the text box. Your screen should look similar to **FIGURE 3-1**. After entering the text, you decide to edit the sentence.

5. **Drag** I **over the phrase** in all areas **to select it, position** ▷ **on top of the selected phrase, then press and hold the** left mouse button
   The pointer changes to ▷.

6. **Drag the selected words to the right of the word "growth", release the mouse button, then click to the left of the text box**
   A grey insertion line appears as you drag, indicating where PowerPoint places the text when you release the mouse button. The phrase "in all areas" moves after the word "growth". Notice there is no space between the words "growth" and "in" and the spelling error is identified by a red wavy underline.

7. **Right-click the** red underlined words **in the text box, then click** "growth in" **on the shortcut menu**
   Space is added between the two words in the text box.

8. **Move** I **to the edge of the text box, which changes to** ✣, **click the** text box border **(it changes to a solid line), then click the** Shape Format tab **on the Ribbon**

9. **Click the** Shape Fill list arrow **in the Shape Styles group, click the** Gold, Accent 4 color box, **click the** Shape Outline list arrow **in the Shape Styles group, point to** Weight, **then click** 4½ pt
   The text object is now filled with a gold color and has a thicker outline.

10. **Position** ✣ **over the text box edge, drag the** text box **to the Smart Guide on the slide as shown in** FIGURE 3-2, **then save your changes**

FIGURE 3-1: **New text object**

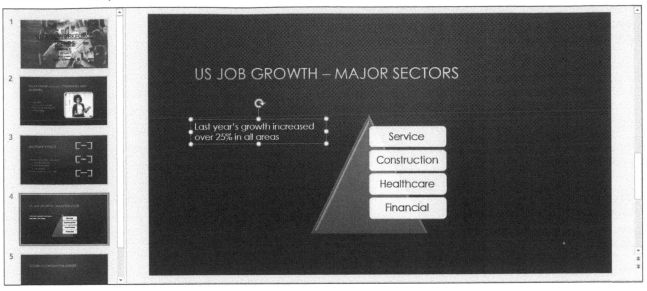

FIGURE 3-2: **Formatted text object**

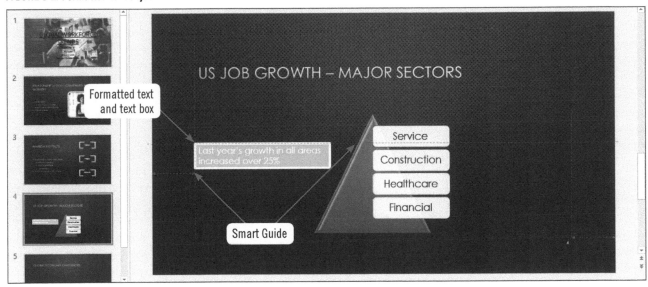

Changing text box defaults

You can change the default formatting characteristics of text boxes you create using the Text Box button on the Insert tab. To change the formatting defaults for text boxes, select an existing formatted text box, or create a new one and format it using any of the PowerPoint formatting commands. When you are ready to change the text box defaults of a text box that is not selected, press SHIFT, right-click the formatted text box, release SHIFT, then click Set as Default Text Box on the shortcut menu. Now, any text boxes you create will display the formatting characteristics of this formatted text box.

Inserting Objects into a Presentation

Crop and Style a Picture

Learning
Outcomes
• Crop a picture
• Apply a picture
  style
• Add effects to a
  picture
• Resize and move a
  picture

PowerPoint provides many editing tools that help you style a picture, such as transparency, sharpening or softening edges, color tone, and cropping. **Cropping** a picture hides a portion of the picture you don't want to see. The cropped portion of a picture is still available to you if you ever want to show that part of the picture again. **CASE** ▶ *In this lesson you crop and style a picture to best fit the slide, but first you format a picture you insert on the Slide Master.*

STEPS

QUICK TIP

You can also insert a picture without a content placeholder by clicking the Pictures button in the Images group on the Insert tab.

1. **Click the** Slide 1 thumbnail **in the Slides tab, right-click a blank area of the slide, then click** Format Background **on the shortcut menu**

   The Format Background pane opens.

2. **Click** Insert **in the Format Background pane, click** From a File **in the Insert Pictures dialog box, navigate to the location where you store your Data Files, select the picture file** Support_PPT_3_Group.jpg, **then click** Insert

   The picture fills the slide.

3. **Drag the** Transparency Slider **to 50%, then close the Format Background pane**

   The slide background picture on Slide 1 is more transparent.

4. **Click the** Slide 2 thumbnail **in the Slides tab, click the** picture, **then click the** Picture Format tab **on the Ribbon**

QUICK TIP

Click the Crop button list arrow to take advantage of other crop options, including cropping to a shape from the Shapes gallery and cropping to a common photo size or aspect ratio.

5. **Click the** Crop button **in the Size group, then place the pointer over the** middle-left cropping handle **on the picture**

   The pointer changes to ⊣. When the Crop button is active, cropping handles appear next to the sizing handles on the selected object.

6. **Drag the** middle of the picture **to the right as shown in** FIGURE 3-3, **release the mouse button, then press** ESC

   The picture would look better on the slide if it had a different color tone.

7. **Click the** Color button **in the Adjust group, then click** Temperature: 4700 K **in the Color Tone row**

   The options in the Color Tone row add more blue or orange to the picture, making it appear cooler or warmer.

QUICK TIP

If you have multiple pictures on a slide, you can align them using guides or Smart Guides.

8. **Click the** Corrections button **in the Adjust group, then click** Soften: 25% **in the Sharpen/Soften section**

   The picture is slightly unclear.

9. **Click the** More button ⊡ **in the Picture Styles group, then click** Metal Rounded Rectangle **(4th row)**

   The picture now has rounded corners with a metal-looking frame. Notice the picture has an adjustment handle that you can move.

10. **Drag the** picture **to the center of the blank area of the slide to the right of the text object, click a blank area on the slide, then save your changes**

    Compare your screen to FIGURE 3-4.

FIGURE 3-3: Using the cropping pointer to crop a picture

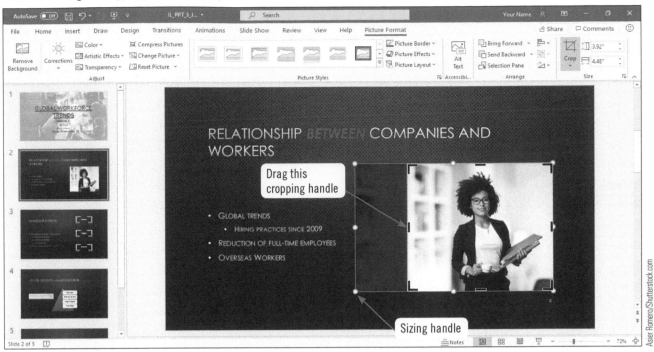

FIGURE 3-4: Cropped and styled picture

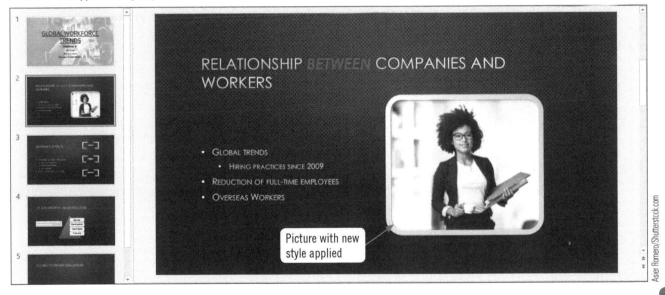

Inserting a screen recording

Using the Screen Recording button in the Media group on the Insert tab, you can record your computer screen with audio and insert the recording in a slide. For example, if you want to make a recording of an Internet video, locate and display the video on your computer screen. In PowerPoint on the slide where you want to insert the recording, click the Screen Recording button.

On the toolbar, click the Select Area button, drag a selection box around the video, click the Audio button if necessary, then click the Record button on the toolbar. Click the video play button. When finished recording, click Windows Logo+SHIFT+Q to stop recording. PowerPoint opens and the recording appears on your slide. Click the Play button to review your recording.

PowerPoint

Insert a Chart

Learning
Outcome
• Insert a new chart
  on a slide

Frequently, the best way to communicate numerical information is with a visual aid such as a chart. A **chart** is the graphical representation of numerical data. PowerPoint uses Excel to create charts. Every chart has a corresponding **worksheet** that contains the numerical data displayed by the chart. When you insert a chart object into PowerPoint, you are embedding it. An **embedded object** is one that is a part of your presentation (just like any other object you insert into PowerPoint) except that an embedded object's data source can be opened, in this case using Excel, for editing purposes. Changes you make to an embedded object in PowerPoint using the features in PowerPoint do not affect the data source. **CASE** ▷ *You insert a chart on a new slide.*

STEPS

QUICK TIP

Right-click a slide in
the Slides tab, then
click Duplicate Slide
to create an exact
copy of the slide.

1. **Click the** Slide 4 thumbnail **in the Slides tab, then press** ENTER

   Pressing ENTER adds a new slide to your presentation with the slide layout of the selected slide, in this case the Title and Content slide layout.

2. **Click the** Title placeholder, **type** Free Agency Trends, **then click the** Insert Chart icon 📊 **in the Content placeholder**

   The Insert Chart dialog box opens as shown in **FIGURE 3-5**. Each chart type includes several 2D and 3D styles. The Clustered Column chart is the default 2D chart style. For a brief explanation of common chart types, refer to **TABLE 3-1**.

QUICK TIP

You can also add a
chart to a slide by
clicking the Chart
button in the
Illustrations group
on the Insert tab.

3. **Click** OK

   The PowerPoint window displays a clustered column chart below a worksheet with sample data, as shown in **FIGURE 3-6**. The Chart Design tab on the Ribbon contains commands you use in PowerPoint to work with the chart. The worksheet consists of rows and columns. The intersection of a row and a column is called a **cell**. Cells are referred to by their row and column location; for example, the cell at the intersection of column A and row 1 is called cell A1. Each column and row of data in the worksheet is called a **data series**. Cells in column A and row 1 contain **data series labels** that identify the data or values in the column and row. "Category 1" is the data series label for the data in the second row, and "Series 1" is a data series label for the data in the second column. Cells below and to the right of the data series labels, in the shaded blue portion of the worksheet, contain the data values that are represented in the chart. Cells in row 1 appear in the chart **legend** and describe the data in the series. Each data series has corresponding **data series markers** in the chart, which are graphical representations such as bars, columns, or pie wedges. The boxes with the numbers along the left side of the worksheet are **row headings**, and the boxes with the letters along the top of the worksheet are **column headings**.

4. **Move the pointer over the worksheet, then click cell** C4

   The pointer changes to ⊕. Cell C4, containing the value 1.8, is the selected cell, which means it is now the **active cell**. The active cell has a thick green border around it.

5. **Click the** Close button ✕ **on the worksheet title bar, then click the** Quick Layout button **in the Chart Layouts group**

   The worksheet window closes, and the Quick Layout gallery opens.

6. **Move** ⌖ **over the layouts in the gallery, then click** Layout 9

   This new layout moves the legend to the right side of the chart and increases the size of the data series markers.

7. **Drag the chart straight up to center it on the slide**

8. **Click in a blank area of the slide to deselect the chart, then save your changes**

   The Chart Design tab is no longer active.

FIGURE 3-5: Insert Chart dialog box

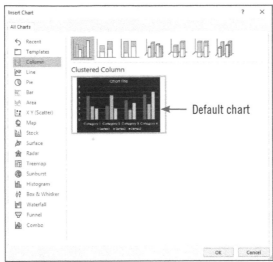

FIGURE 3-6: Worksheet open showing chart data

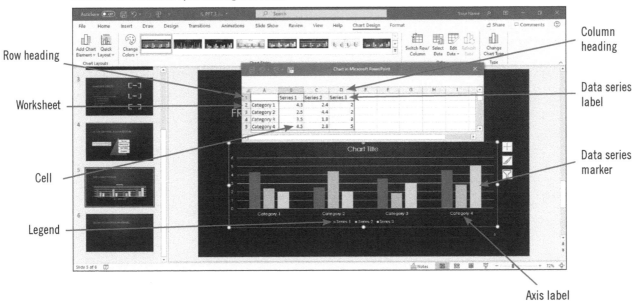

TABLE 3-1: Common chart types

chart type	icon looks like	use to
Column		Track values over time or across categories
Line		Track values over time
Pie		Compare individual values to the whole
Bar		Compare values in categories or over time
Area		Show contribution of each data series to the total over time
X Y (Scatter)		Compare pairs of values
Stock		Show stock market information or scientific data
Surface		Show value trends across two dimensions
Radar		Show changes in values in relation to a center point
Combo		Use multiple types of data markers to compare values

PowerPoint

Enter and Edit Chart Data

Learning
Outcomes
• Change chart data
  values and labels
• Format a chart

After you insert a chart into your presentation, you need to replace the sample information with the correct data. If you have the data you want to chart in an Excel worksheet, you can import it from Excel; otherwise, you can type the data into the worksheet on the slide. As you enter data and make other changes in the worksheet, the chart on the slide automatically reflects the new changes. **CASE** ▶ *You enter and format internal company data you have gathered comparing free agency trends over the last five years.*

STEPS

1. **Click the** chart object **on Slide 5, click the** Chart Design tab **on the Ribbon, then click the** Edit Data button **in the Data group**

   The chart is selected and the worksheet opens in a separate window. The information in the worksheet needs to be replaced with the correct data.

   QUICK TIP
   Click the chart in the PowerPoint window, then move your pointer over each bar in the chart to see the data source values.

2. **Click the** Series 1 cell, **type** Last 5 Yrs, **press** TAB, **type** Prev 10 Yrs, **press** TAB, **then type** Next 5 Yrs

   The data series labels you enter in the worksheet are displayed in the legend on the chart. Pressing TAB moves the active cell from left to right one cell at a time in a row. Pressing ENTER in the worksheet moves the active cell down one cell at a time in a column.

3. **Click the** Category 1 cell, **type** Decreased, **press** ENTER, **type** Stayed Same, **press** ENTER, **type** Increased Slightly, **press** ENTER, **type** Increased Dramatically, **then press** TAB

   These data series labels appear in the worksheet and along the bottom of the chart on the *x*-axis. The *x*-axis is the horizontal axis also referred to as the **category axis**, and the *y*-axis is the vertical axis also referred to as the **value axis**.

4. **Enter the data shown in** FIGURE 3-7 **to complete the worksheet, then click** cell E5

   Notice that the height of each column in the chart, as well as the values along the *y*-axis, adjust to reflect the numbers you typed. You have finished entering the data in the Excel worksheet.

5. **Click the** Close button ✕ **on the worksheet title bar, click the** Chart Title text box object **in the chart, click the** Home tab **on the Ribbon, then click the** A͘ Increase Font Size **button in the Font group**

   The worksheet window closes. The text in the Chart Title text box is larger.

   QUICK TIP
   You can also change the chart style by clicking a style option in the Chart Styles group on the Chart Design tab.

6. **Type** Global Changes, **click a blank area of the chart, then click the** Chart Styles button ✐ **to the right of the chart to open the Chart Styles gallery**

   The Chart Styles gallery opens on the left side of the chart with Style selected.

7. **Scroll down the gallery, click** Style 5, **click** Color **at the top of the Chart Styles gallery, then click the** Colorful Palette 2 **in the Colorful section**

   The new chart style and color give the column data markers a professional look as shown in FIGURE 3-8.

8. **Click a blank area on the slide, then save the presentation**

   The Chart Styles gallery closes.

FIGURE 3-7: Worksheet data for the chart

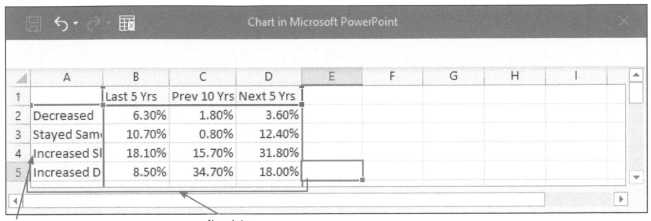

Text may not be visible
in the worksheet but
will appear in the chart

New data

FIGURE 3-8: Formatted chart

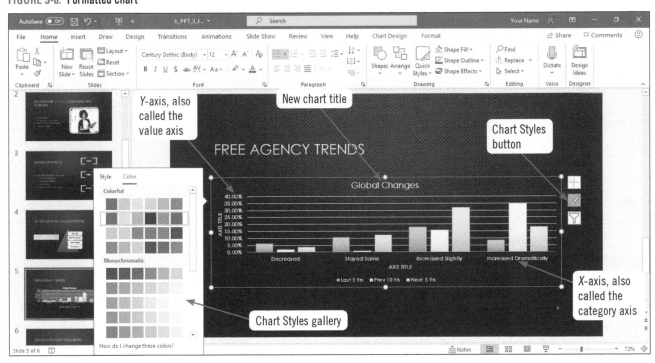

Adding a hyperlink to a chart

You can add a hyperlink to any object in PowerPoint, including a chart. Select that chart, click the Insert tab on the Ribbon, then click the Link button in the Links group. If you are linking to another file, click the Existing File or Web Page button, locate the file you want to link to the chart, then click OK. Or, if you want to link to another slide in the presentation, click the Place in This Document button, click the slide in the list, then click OK. Now, during a slide show you can click the chart to open the linked object. To remove the link, click the chart, click the Link button in the Links group, then click Remove Link.

Inserting Objects into a Presentation

Insert Slides from Other Presentations

To save time and energy, you can insert one or more slides you already created in other presentations into an existing presentation or the one you are currently working on. One way to share slides between presentations is to open an existing presentation, copy the slides you want to the Clipboard, then paste them into your open presentation. However, PowerPoint offers a simpler way to transfer slides directly between presentations. By using the Reuse Slides pane, you can insert slides from another presentation or a network location. Newly inserted slides automatically take on the theme of the open presentation, unless you decide to use slide formatting from the original source presentation. **CASE** *You decide to insert slides you created for another presentation into the JCL Talent presentation.*

STEPS

1. **Click the** Slide 2 thumbnail **in the Slides tab, then click the** Reuse Slides button **in the Slides group**

   The Reuse Slides pane opens on the right side of the presentation window and displays recently opened presentations.

2. **Click** Browse **in the Reuse Slides pane, navigate to the location where you store your Data Files, then double-click** Support_PPT_3_Presentation.pptx

   Slide thumbnails are displayed in the pane as shown in **FIGURE 3-9**. The slide thumbnails identify the slides in the **source presentation**, Support_PPT_3_Presentation.pptx.

   QUICK TIP
   To maintain the formatting and design of a reused slide, make sure the Use source formatting check box is selected.

3. **Click the** Use source formatting check box **in the Reuse Slides pane, then click the** Slide 1 thumbnail **in the Reuse Slides pane**

   The new slide appears in the Slides tab and Slide pane as the new Slide 3. Notice the new slide assumes the design style and formatting of your presentation, which is the **destination presentation**.

4. **Click the** Slide 3 thumbnail **in the Reuse Slides pane, then click the** Slide 2 thumbnail **in the Reuse Slides pane**

   The new Slides 4 and 5 assume the design style and formatting of the destination presentation.

5. **Click the** Reuse Slides pane Close button ![X]

   The Reuse Slides pane closes. You realize the last slide you inserted is not needed for this presentation.

   QUICK TIP
   To copy noncontiguous slides, open Slide Sorter view, click the first slide thumbnail, press and hold CTRL, click each additional slide thumbnail, release CTRL, then click the Copy button.

6. **Right-click the** Slide 5 thumbnail **in the Slides tab, then click** Delete Slide **in the shortcut menu**

   Slide 5 is deleted.

7. **Click the** ![Slide Sorter icon] Slide Sorter button **in the status bar, then drag** Slide 4 **to the right of Slide 2**

8. **Click the** ![Normal icon] Normal button **in the status bar, then save the presentation**

   Slide 4 becomes Slide 3. Compare your screen to **FIGURE 3-10**.

FIGURE 3-9: **Presentation window with Reuse Slides pane open**

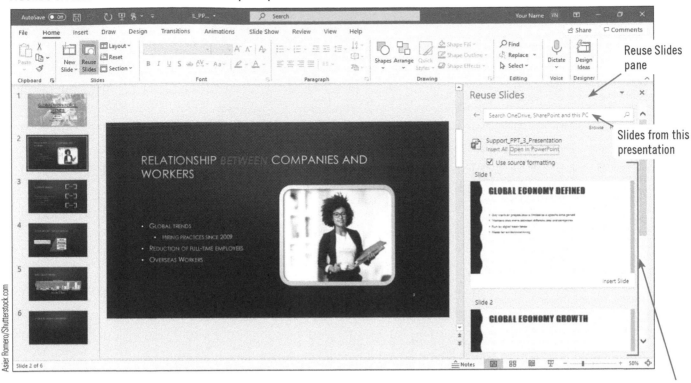

Reuse Slides pane

Slides from this presentation

Slide thumbnails

FIGURE 3-10: **New slides added to presentation**

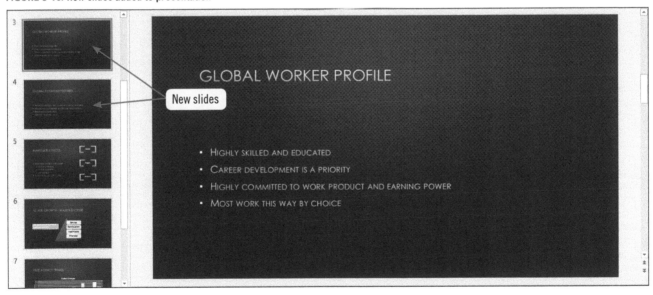

New slides

Working with multiple windows

Another way to work with information in multiple presentations is to arrange the presentation windows on your monitor so you see each window side by side. Open each presentation, click the View tab on the Ribbon in any presentation window, then click the Arrange All button in the Window group. Each presentation you have open is placed next to each other so you can easily drag, or transfer, information between the

presentations. If you are working with more than two open presentations, you can overlap the presentation windows on top of one another. Open all the presentations you want, then click the Cascade button in the Window group. Now you can easily jump from one presentation to another by clicking the presentation title bar or any part of the presentation window.

Inserting Objects into a Presentation

PowerPoint

Asier Romero/Shutterstock.com

Insert a Table

**Learning
Outcomes**
• Insert a table
• Add text to a table
• Change table size
and layout

As you create your presentation, you may have some information that would look best organized in rows and columns. For example, if you want to view related data side by side, a table is ideal for this type of information. Once you have created a table, two new tabs, the Table Design tab and the Layout tab, appear on the Ribbon. You can use the commands on the table tabs to apply color styles, change cell borders, add cell effects, add rows and columns to your table, adjust the size of cells, and align text in the cells. **CASE** ▶ *You decide a table best illustrates the challenges of using free agency workers.*

STEPS

1. **Click the** Slide 8 thumbnail **in the Slides tab, then click the** Insert Table icon ▦ **in the content placeholder**

   The Insert Table dialog box appears.

2. **Click the** Number of columns down arrow **until** 2 **appears, click the** Number of rows up arrow **twice until** 4 **appears, then click** OK

   A formatted table with two columns and four rows appears on the slide, and the Table Design tab opens on the Ribbon. The table has 8 cells and you realize you need more cells.

   QUICK TIP
   Press TAB when the insertion point is in the last cell of a table to insert a new row.

3. **Click the** Layout tab **on the Ribbon, then click the** Insert Below button **in the Rows & Columns group**

   A new row is added to the table below the current row.

4. **Click the** top-left cell **in the table, click the** Insert Left button **in the Rows & Columns group, then click the** top-left cell **again**

   The table has a new column to the left of the current column and the insertion point is in the first cell of the table ready to accept text.

5. **Type** Rank of Concerns, **press** TAB, **type** Free Agency Employer, **press** TAB, **type** Non-Free Agency Employer, **then press** TAB

   The text you typed appears in the top three cells of the table. Pressing TAB moves the insertion point to the next cell; pressing ENTER moves the insertion point to the next line in the same cell.

6. **Enter the rest of the table information shown in** FIGURE 3-11

   The table would look better if it were formatted differently.

   QUICK TIP
   Change the height or width of any table cell by dragging its borders.

7. **Click the** top-left cell **in the table, click the** Select button **in the Table group, click** Select Row, **then click the** Center button ▤ **in the Alignment group**

   The text in the top row is centered horizontally in each cell.

8. **Click the** Select button **in the Table group, click** Select Table, **click the** Table Design tab **on the Ribbon, click the** More button ▾ **in the Table Styles group, scroll to the bottom of the gallery, then click** Dark Style 2 - Accent 5/Accent 6

   The table color changes to reflect the table style you applied.

   QUICK TIP
   To change the cell color behind text, click the Shading list arrow in the Table Styles group, then choose a color.

9. **Click the** Effects button **in the Table Styles group, point to** Cell Bevel, **click** Divot **(3rd row), click a blank area of the slide, then save the presentation**

   The 3D effect makes the cells of the table stand out. Compare your screen with FIGURE 3-12.

FIGURE 3-11: Inserted table with data

FIGURE 3-12: Formatted table

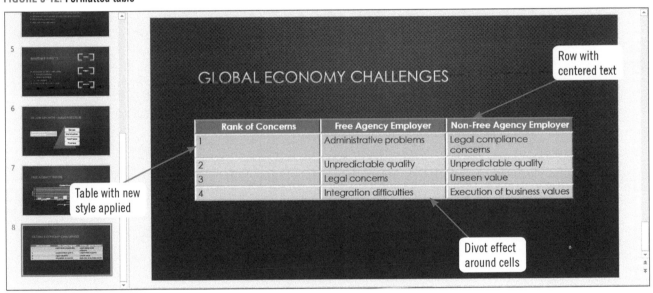

Setting permissions

In PowerPoint, you can set specific access permissions for people who review or edit your work so you have better control over your content. For example, you may want to give a user permission to edit or change your presentation but not allow them to print it. You can also restrict a user by permitting them to view the presentation without the ability to edit or print the presentation, or you can give the user full access or control of the presentation. To use this feature, you first access the information rights management services company. Then, to set user access permissions, click the File tab on the Ribbon, click Info, click the Protect Presentation button, point to Restrict Access, then click an appropriate option.

Insert and Format WordArt

As you work to create an interesting presentation, your goal should include making your slides visually appealing. Sometimes plain text can come across as dull and unexciting in a presentation. **WordArt** is a set of decorative text styles, or text effects, you can apply to any text object to help direct the attention of your audience to a certain piece of information. You can use WordArt in two different ways: you can apply a WordArt text style to an existing text object that converts the text into WordArt, or you can create a new WordArt object. The WordArt text styles and effects include text shadows, reflections, glows, bevels, 3D rotations, and transformations. **CASE** > *Create a new WordArt text object on Slide 3.*

STEPS

QUICK TIP
To convert any text
or text object to
WordArt, select the
text or text object,
click the Shape
Format tab on the
Ribbon, then click a
WordArt style option
in the WordArt
Styles group.

1. **Click the** Slide 3 thumbnail **in the Slides tab, click the** Insert tab **on the Ribbon, then click the** WordArt button **in the Text group**

   The WordArt gallery appears displaying 20 WordArt text styles.

2. **Click** Fill: Gold, Accent color 4; Soft Bevel **(first row)**

   A text object appears in the middle of the slide displaying sample text with the WordArt style you just selected. The Shape Format tab is open on the Ribbon.

3. **Click the edge of the** WordArt text object, **then when the pointer changes to** ⁺⬚, **drag the text object to the blank area at the bottom of the slide**

4. **Click the** More button ⏷ **in the WordArt Styles group, move** ⬚ **over all the WordArt styles in the gallery, then click** Fill: Tan, Accent color 3; Sharp Bevel

   The sample text in the WordArt text object changes to the new WordArt style.

5. **Drag to select the text** Your text here **in the WordArt text object, click the** Decrease Font Size button A˅ **in the Mini toolbar so that** 40 **appears in the Font Size text box, then type** Demand Drives Innovation

   The text, "Demand Drives Innovation" is on the slide as WordArt. Compare your screen to **FIGURE 3-13**.

QUICK TIP
To convert a WordArt
object to a SmartArt
object, right-click the
WordArt object,
point to Convert to
SmartArt on the
shortcut menu,
then click a
SmartArt layout.

6. **Select the text in the WordArt object, click the** Text Fill button **in the WordArt Styles group, then click** Tan, Accent 3, Darker 25%

   The WordArt color is darker.

7. **Click the** Text Outline button **in the WordArt Styles group, then click** White, Text 1

   The WordArt outline is now white.

8. **Click the** Text Effects button **in the WordArt Styles group, point to** 3-D Rotation, **then click** Perspective: Relaxed Moderately **in the Perspective section (second row)**

   The off-axis effect is applied to the text object. You are unsure of this effect and apply another one.

9. **Click the** Text Effects button, **point to** Transform, **then click** Triangle: Down **in the Warp section (first row)**

   The effect is applied to the text object.

10. **Press** SHIFT, **drag the** lower-right sizing handle **down ½ inch, release** SHIFT, **click a blank area of the slide, then save your work**

    The text object is proportionally larger. Compare your screen to **FIGURE 3-14**.

FIGURE 3-13: WordArt inserted on slide

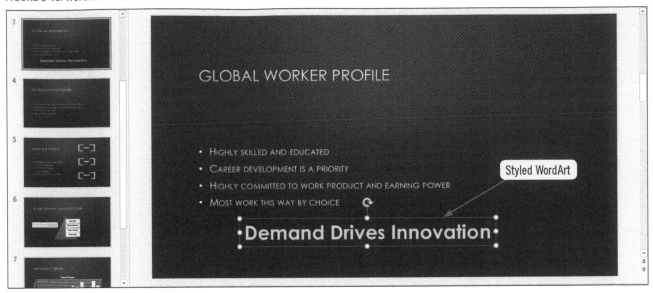

FIGURE 3-14: Formatted WordArt object

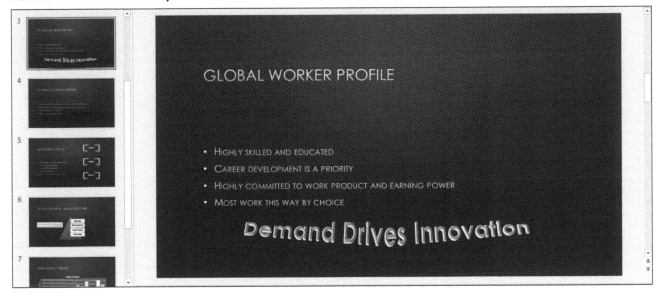

Animate Objects

Animations let you control how objects and text appear and move on the screen during a slide show and allow you to manage the flow of information and emphasize specific facts. You can animate text, pictures, sounds, hyperlinks, SmartArt diagrams, charts, and individual chart elements. Animations are organized into four categories: Entrance, Emphasis, Exit, and Motion Paths. The Entrance and Exit animations cause an object to enter or exit the slide with an effect. An Emphasis animation causes an object visible on the slide to have an effect, and a Motion Path animation causes an object to move on a specified path on the slide. **CASE** ▶ *You animate the text and graphics on several slides in the presentation.*

STEPS

1. **Click the** Slide 6 thumbnail **in the Slides tab, click the** Animations tab **on the Ribbon, then click the** SmartArt object

   Text as well as other objects, such as a shape or picture, can be animated during a slide show.

2. **Click the** More button ⊡ **in the Animation group, then click** Shape **in the Entrance section**

   A small numeral 1, called an animation tag 〔1〕, appears on the slide. **Animation tags** identify the order in which objects are animated during a slide show.

3. **Click the** Effect Options button **in the Animation group, click** All at Once, **click the** Effect Options button, **then click** Out

   Effect options are different for every animation, and some animations don't have effect options. All of the objects in the SmartArt animate together in an outward direction. Compare your screen to **FIGURE 3-15**.

4. **Click the** Slide Show button 🖵 **on the status bar, click your** mouse **once, then press** ESC
   The SmartArt object animates.

5. **Click the** Slide 4 thumbnail **in the Slides tab, click the** bulleted list text object, **then click** Fade **in the Animation group**

   The text object is animated with the Fade animation. Each line of text has an animation tag with each paragraph displaying a different number. Accordingly, each paragraph is animated separately.

6. **Click the** Effect Options button **in the Animation group, click** All at Once, **click the** Duration up arrow **in the Timing group until** 01.50 **appears, then click the** Preview button **in the Preview group**

   Notice the animation tags for each line of text in the text object now have the same numeral (1), indicating that each line of text animates at the same time.

7. **Click** Economy **in the title text object, click** ⊡ **in the Animation group, scroll down, then click** Arcs **in the Motion Paths section**

   A motion path object appears over the shapes object and identifies the direction and shape, or path, of the animation. When needed, you can move, resize, and change the direction of the motion path. Notice the numeral 2 animation tag next to the title text object indicating that it is animated *after* the bulleted list text object. Compare your screen to **FIGURE 3-16**.

8. **Click the** Move Earlier button **in the Timing group, click the** Slide Show tab **on the Ribbon, then click the** From Beginning button **in the Start Slide Show group**
   Slide 1 appears in Slide Show view.

9. **Press** SPACE **to advance the slides, when you see the black slide, press** ENTER, **then save your changes**

FIGURE 3-15: Animation applied to SmartArt object

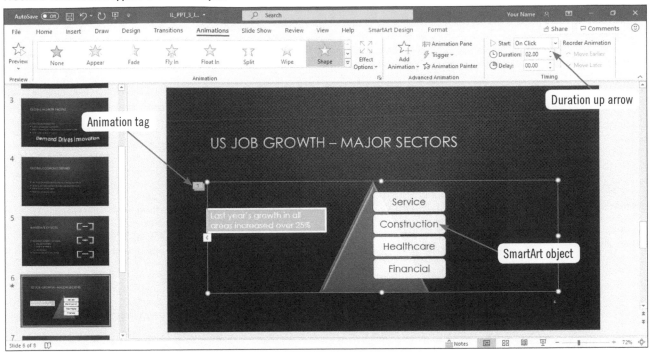

FIGURE 3-16: Motion path applied to title text object

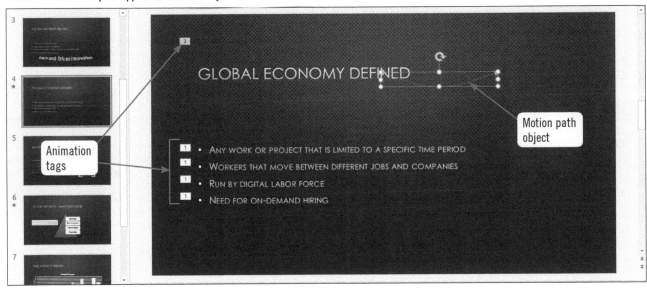

Attaching a sound to an animation

Text or objects that have animation applied can be customized further by attaching a sound for extra emphasis. First, select the animated object, then on the Animations tab, click the Animation Pane button in the Advanced Animation group. In the Animation Pane, click the animation you want to apply the sound to, click the Animation list arrow, then click Effect Options to open the animation effect's dialog box. In the Enhancements section, click the Sound list arrow, then choose a sound. Click OK when you are finished. Now, when you run the slide show, the sound you applied will play with the animation.

Inserting Objects into a Presentation

Insert and Edit Digital Video

Learning
Outcomes
• Link a video
• Add a bookmark

In your presentation, you may want to use special effects to illustrate a point or capture the attention of your audience. You can do this by inserting digital or animated video. **Digital video** is live action captured in digital format by a video camera. You can embed or link a digital video file from your hard drive or link a digital video file from a webpage on the Internet. **Animated video** contains multiple images that stream together or move to give the illusion of motion. If you need to edit the length of a video or add effects or background color to a video, you can use PowerPoint's video-editing tools to accomplish those and other basic editing tasks. **CASE** ➤ *You continue to develop your presentation by inserting and editing a video clip.*

STEPS

1. **Click the** Slide 4 thumbnail **in the Slides tab, click the** Home tab **on the Ribbon, right-click a blank area of the slide, point to** Layout **in the shortcut menu, then click** Two Content

   The slide layout changes and has two content placeholders.

2. **Click the** Insert Video icon ▣ **in the new Content placeholder, navigate to the location where you store your Data Files, click** Support_PPT_3_Video.mp4, **click the** Insert list arrow, **then click** Link to File

   The Support_PPT_3_Video.mp4 video clip displaying a black preview image is linked to the slide. By linking the digital video to the presentation, you do not increase the file size of the presentation, but remember, you need direct access to the location where the video file is stored in order to play it.

   QUICK TIP
   Adjust the volume of the video using the Mute/Unmute control on the video control timeline.

3. **Click the** Play/Pause button ▷ **in the video control bar**

   The short video plays through once but does not rewind to the beginning.

4. **Click the** Playback tab **on the Ribbon, click the** Rewind after Playing check box **in the Video Options group, then click the** Play button **in the Preview group**

   The video plays through once, and this time the video rewinds back to the beginning.

   QUICK TIP
   You can also add fade effects to the beginning and end of a video using the Fade Duration commands in the Editing group.

5. **Click the** video control timeline **at about** 00:06.00, **then click the** Add Bookmark button **in the Bookmarks group as shown in** FIGURE 3-17

   A yellow circle appears in the video control timeline, indicating the video has a bookmark. A **bookmark** can indicate a point of interest in a video; it can also be used to jump to a specific point in a video.

6. **Click the** Slide Show button ▣ **on the status bar, then click the mouse twice to view the animations on the slide**

   The text object animations play.

7. **Move** ▷ **over the video, the pointer changes to** 🖑, **then click the bookmark as shown in** FIGURE 3-18

   The video moves to the bookmarked frame.

8. **Click the** Play/Pause button ▷ **on the video**

   The video plays from the bookmarked frame to the end of the video and then rewinds to the beginning.

   QUICK TIP
   Click the Reset Design button in the Adjust group to remove all formatting changes you made to the video.

9. **Press** ESC, **click the** Video Format tab **on the Ribbon, click the** More button ▽ **in the Video Styles group, then click** Reflected Bevel Black **in the Intense section**

   A bevel effect is added to the video.

10. **sam** ↟ **Click a blank area of the slide, save your work, submit your presentation to your instructor, then exit PowerPoint**

FIGURE 3-17: Video clip inserted on the slide

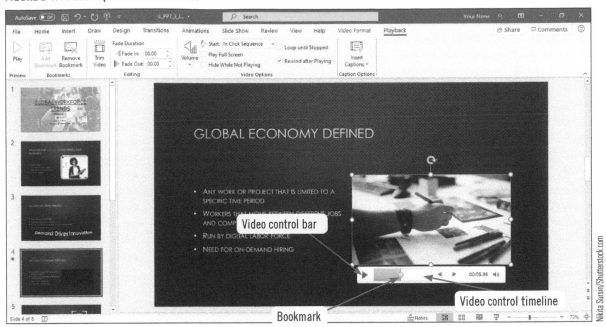

FIGURE 3-18: Video in Slide Show view with selected bookmark

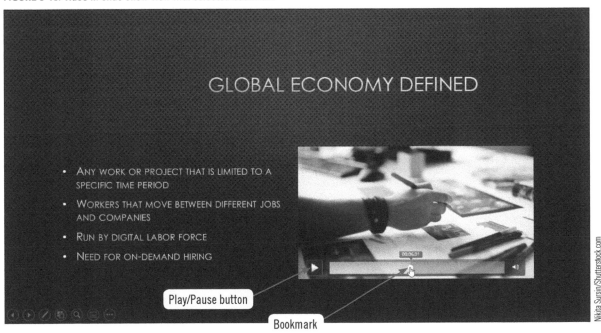

Saving a presentation as a video

You can save your PowerPoint presentation as a full-fidelity video, which incorporates all slide timings, transitions, animations, and narrations. The video can be distributed using a thumb drive, the Internet, or email. Depending on how you want to display your video, you have four resolution settings from which to choose: Ultra HD (4K), Full HD (1080p), HD (720p), and Standard (480p). The largest two settings, Ultra HD (3840 × 2160) and Full HD (1920 × 1080), are used for viewing on a computer monitor, projector, or other high-definition displays. The next setting, HD (1280 × 720), is used for uploading to the web or copying to a standard DVD. The smallest setting, Standard (852 × 480), is used on portable media players. To save your presentation as a video, click the File tab, click Export, click Create a Video, choose your settings, then click the Create Video button.

Inserting Objects into a Presentation

PowerPoint

Practice

Skills Review

1. Insert a text box.

a. Open IL_PPT_3-2.pptx from the location where you store your Data Files, then save it as **IL_PPT_3_Broker2**. You will work to create the completed presentation as shown in **FIGURE 3-19**.

FIGURE 3-19

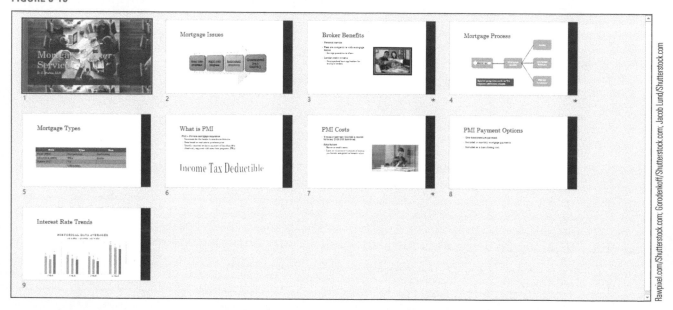

b. On Slide 4, insert a text box below the shapes, then type **Special programs require additional stages such as VA**

c. Move the words "such as VA" after the word "programs", then add space between words, as necessary.

d. Select the text object, then click the More button in the Shape Styles group on the Shape Format tab.

e. Click Moderate Effect – Purple, Accent 5, then resize the text box to fit the text on two lines by dragging its sizing handles, if necessary. The second line of text begins with the word "require".

f. Using Smart Guides, drag the text object so its right edge is centered on the slide and its bottom edge is aligned with the bottom edge of the bottom rectangle shape.

2. Crop and style a picture.

a. Select Slide 3 in the Slides tab, then crop the left side of the picture up to the right cup on the table in the background.

b. Drag the picture to the center of the blank area of the slide.

c. Click the Color button, then change the color tone to Temperature: 8800 K.

d. Click the Corrections button, then change the sharpness of the picture to Sharpen: 50%.

e. Change the picture style to Double Frame, Black.

f. Select Slide 1 in the Slides tab, open the Format Background task pane, then click the Picture or texture fill option button.

Skills Review (continued)

g. Click the Insert button in the task pane, click From a File, then insert the picture Support_PPT_3_Group.jpg from the location where you store your Data Files.

h. Click the Tile picture as texture check box in the task pane, close the Format Background pane, then save your changes.

3. **Insert a chart.**

  a. Create a new slide after Slide 5 with a Title and Content layout and title it **Interest Rate Trends**.

  b. Insert a Clustered Column chart, then close the worksheet.

  c. Drag the chart down the slide away from the title, then apply the Layout 3 quick layout to the chart.

4. **Enter and edit chart data.**

  a. Show the worksheet, enter the data shown in TABLE 3-2 into the worksheet, then close the worksheet.

  b. Type **Historical Data Averages** in the chart title text object then increase the font size of the chart title using the Increase Font Size button.

  c. Click the Chart Styles button next to the chart, then change the chart style to Style 2.

  d. Click Color in the Charts Styles gallery, then change the color to Colorful Palette 3 in the Colorful section.

  e. Close the Charts Styles gallery, then save your changes.

TABLE 3-2

	30 Yr FRM	15 Yr FRM	5/1 Yr ARM
1 Year	3.82	3.19	4.19
3 Year	4.20	3.36	3.14
5 Year	3.89	3.19	2.75
10 Year	6.32	5.79	5.45

5. **Insert slides from other presentations.**

  a. Go to Slide 5, then open the Reuse Slides pane.

  b. Open Support_PPT_3_PMI.pptx from the location where you store your Data Files, then click the Use source formatting check box.

  c. Insert the second slide thumbnail, insert the third slide thumbnail, then insert the first slide thumbnail.

  d. Close the Reuse Slides pane, then open the Slide Sorter view.

  e. Move Slide 8 between Slide 5 and Slide 6, switch to Normal view, then save your work.

6. **Insert a table.**

  a. Go to Slide 5, then insert a table with two columns and four rows.

  b. Add one more row and one more column to the table, then enter the information shown in TABLE 3-3.

  c. On the Table Design tab, change the table style to Themed Style 1 – Accent 5.

  d. On the Layout tab, select the top row, then center the text.

  e. Select the whole table, open the Table Design tab, click the Effects button, point to Cell Bevel, then apply the Soft Round effect.

  f. Move the table to the center of the blank area of the slide, then save your changes.

TABLE 3-3

Rate	Type	Size
Fixed (FRM)	Conventional	Conforming
Adjustable (ARM)	FHA	Jumbo
Hybrid (5/1)	VA	
	USDA/RHA	

7. **Insert and format WordArt.**

  a. Go to Slide 6, then insert a WordArt text object using the style Gradient Fill, Gray.

  b. Type **Income Tax Deductible**, apply the Transform text effect Inflate (sixth row in the Warp section) to the text object, then move the text object to the middle of the blank area of the slide.

  c. Apply the 3-D Rotation text effect Perspective: Relaxed Moderately (second row in the Perspective section).

  d. Change the text fill color to Dark Red, then change the text outline to Black, Text 1.

  e. Apply the WordArt style Fill: Black, Text color 1; Outline: White, Background color 1; Hard Shadow: Purple, Accent color 5.

  f. Increase the size of the WordArt object proportionally, view the slide in Slide Show view, then save your changes.

8. Animate objects.

   a. Go to Slide 4, click the Animations tab, then select the four black arrow lines on the slide. (*Hint*: Use SHIFT to select the shapes.)

   b. Apply the Wipe effect to the objects, click the Effect Options button, then apply the From Right effect.

   c. Change the animation duration to 01.00, then preview the animations.

   d. Click the Move Earlier button in the Timing group.

   e. Go to Slide 3, click the title text object, then apply the animation Brush Color in the Emphasis section.

   f. Click the Effect Options button, click Orange in Standard Colors, then open Slide Show view.

   g. Click through the animations on Slides 3 and 4, press ESC when you see Slide 5, then save your work.

9. Insert and edit digital video.

   a. Go to Slide 7, change the slide layout to Two Content, then click the Insert Video icon.

   b. Locate the file Support_PPT_3_Desk.mp4 from the location where you store your Data Files, click the Insert list arrow, then click Link to File.

   c. On the Playback tab, click the Rewind after Playing check box, then add a bookmark at about the 00:04.00 point on the video control timeline.

   d. Apply the video style Center Shadow Rectangle, then preview the video clip in Slide Show view.

   e. Switch to Normal view, then save your work.

   f. Submit your presentation to your instructor, close your presentation, then exit PowerPoint.

Independent Challenge 1

Riverwalk Medical Clinic (RMC), is a large medical facility in Cambridge, Massachusetts. You continue to work on a presentation on the latest emergency response procedures for a staff training later in the week.

   a. Start PowerPoint, open IL_PPT_3-3.pptx from the location where you store your Data Files, and save it as **IL_PPT_3_Riverwalk**. You will work to create the completed presentation as shown in **FIGURE 3-20**.

   b. Add your name and today's date to Slide 1 in the Subtitle text box.

   c. Go to Slide 4, change the slide layout to Two Content, click the Pictures icon in the content placeholder, then insert the file Support_PPT_3_ER.jpg from the location where you store your Data Files.

   d. Crop the right side of the picture up to the red emergency sign next to the entrance, apply the Drop Shadow Rectangle picture style to the picture, click the Color button, then change the color tone to Temperature: 5300 K.

FIGURE 3-20

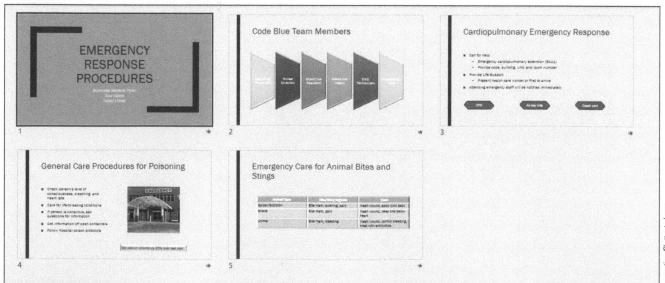

Independent Challenge 1 (continued)

e. Change the sharpness of the picture to Sharpen: 25%, then move the picture to the center of the blank area of the slide.

f. Insert a text box on the slide below the picture, type **ER walk-in volume up 20% over last year**, then change the text color to red.

g. Apply the shape style Colored Fill - Gold, Accent 2 to the text object, then apply the Preset 2 shape effect.

h. Go to Slide 5, create a new table, then enter the data in **TABLE 3-4**.

i. Apply the table style Medium Style 1 - Accent 2, apply the Round bevel effect, then center the text in the top row of the table.

j. Apply the Fly In animation to the SmartArt object on Slide 2, change the effect option to From Bottom-Right and the sequence to One by One, then change the duration to 01.00.

TABLE 3-4

Animal Type	Bite/Sting Signals	Care
Spider/Scorpion	Bite mark, swelling, pain	Wash wound, apply cold pack
Snake	Bite mark, pain	Wash wound, keep bite below heart
Animal	Bite mark, bleeding	Wash wound, control bleeding, treat with antibiotics

k. Add a Doors transition to all slides with a horizontal effect, and a duration time of 02.00.

l. View the final presentation in Slide Show view.

m. Save the presentation, submit the presentation to your instructor, close the file, then exit PowerPoint.

Independent Challenge 2

You are an associate at Myers Reed, a financial investment and management company, located in St. Louis, Missouri. One of your responsibilities is to create general presentations for use on the company website. As part of this presentation, you insert a chart, insert a video, add a WordArt object, and insert slides from another presentation. You finish the presentation by adding slide transitions and animations to the slides.

a. Open IL_PPT_3_4.pptx from the location where you store your Data Files, then save it as **IL_PPT_3_Reed**. You will work to create the completed presentation as shown in **FIGURE 3-21**.

b. Apply the Ion Design Theme, refer to Slide 1 in **FIGURE 3-21** and select the thumbnail in the Design Ideas task pane, then close the task pane.

FIGURE 3-21

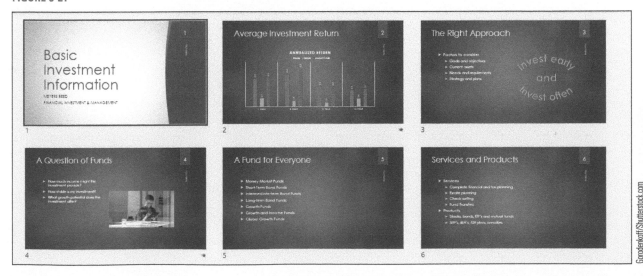

Gorodenkoff/Shutterstock.com

Independent Challenge 2 (continued)

c. Insert a clustered column chart on Slide 2, then enter the data in TABLE 3-5 into the worksheet.

d. Close the worksheet, format the chart using Style 2, change the color to Colorful Palette 3, then move the chart to the center of the blank area of the slide.

e. Type **Annualized Return** in the chart title text object, then decrease the font size to 20 point.

f. Open the Reuse Slides pane, open Support_PPT_3_Invest.pptx from the location where you store your Data Files, then insert Slides 2, 3, and 4.

TABLE 3-5

	Stocks	Bonds	Mutual Funds
1 Year	8.9	2.7	9.3
3 Year	10.3	1.8	11.9
5 Year	6.6	1.3	6.4
10 Year	5.2	2.5	5.7

g. Close the Reuse Slides pane, open Slide Sorter view, move Slide 5 between Slide 3 and Slide 4, then double-click Slide 3.

h. Insert a WordArt object using the Fill: Gold, Accent color 3; Sharp Bevel style, type **Invest early**, press ENTER, type **and**, press ENTER, then type **Invest often**.

i. Click the Text Effects button, point to Transform, apply the Button text effect from the Follow Path section, then move the WordArt object to a blank area of the slide.

j. Go to Slide 4, change the slide layout to Two Content, then link the video Support_PPT_3_Desk.mp4 from the location where you store your Data Files. (*Hint*: be sure to use the Link to File option when you link the video in this step.)

k. Insert a bookmark at about 00:03.00, rewind the video after playing, then apply the Center Shadow Rectangle video style.

l. Go to Slide 2, apply the animation Float In to the chart, apply the By Element in Category effect option, then set the duration to 01.50.

m. Apply the animation Random Bars to the slide title, then reorder the animation to first in the sequence.

n. Add your name and slide number as the footer on all of the slides, view the slide show, then save your work.

o. Submit the presentation to your instructor, close the presentation, then exit PowerPoint.

Visual Workshop

Create a one-slide presentation that looks like FIGURE 3-22. To complete this presentation, insert the picture file Support_PPT_3_Woman.jpg from the location where you store your Data Files to the slide background. Change the picture transparency to 30% and then format the text box with a 54-point, Orange, Accent 2 Calibri Light font and then apply a Tight Reflection: Touching text effect. Set the text object's top edge at 1.00 and its right edge on the slide center line. Add your name as footer text to the slide, save the presentation as **IL_PPT_3_Brookdale** to the location where you store your Data Files, then submit your presentation to your instructor.

FIGURE 3-22

Asier Romero/Shutterstock.com

Formatting Slide Masters and Backgrounds

CASE ▸ You have reviewed your work and are pleased with the slides you created so far for the JCL presentation. Now you are ready to add some enhancements to the slides that include formatting the slide masters, creating custom layouts, and working with themes. You finalize the presentation by using the proofing and language tools and then inspecting the presentation for any issues. You then use advanced slide show commands to view the presentation.

Module Objectives

After completing this module, you will be able to:

- Apply design themes
- Modify masters
- Create custom slide layouts
- Customize the background and theme
- Use slide show commands
- Use proofing and language tools
- Inspect a presentation

Files You Will Need

IL_PPT_4-1.pptx	Support_PPT_4_Group.jpg
IL_PPT_4-2.pptx	Support_PPT_4_AI.jpg
IL_PPT_4-3.pptx	Support_PPT_4_R2G_Logo.jpg
IL_PPT_4-4.pptx	Support_PPT_4_Logo.jpg

Apply Design Themes

Learning Outcomes
- Apply a theme Modify the design theme
- Crop a picture to a shape

A design theme uses coordinated theme colors, lines, fills, shadows, and effects to transform your presentation. You can apply a theme to the whole presentation or to selected slides. Each theme has at least four custom coordinated variants that provides you with additional color options and effects. Theme variants are subtle deviations from the original theme, usually with slight color or text changes. Another way to alter the look of a slide is to use the PowerPoint Designer and apply a layout from the Design Ideas pane. As you enter content on your slides, PowerPoint Designer detects objects, key terms, and concepts and then provides several slide layouts that best match your content. **CASE** ➤ *You decide to change the design theme and variant on one slide, then you use the PowerPoint Designer.*

STEPS

1. **sam ↓ Start PowerPoint, open the presentation IL_PPT_4-1.pptx from the location where you store your Data Files, save the presentation as IL_PPT_4_JCL, then click the Design tab on the Ribbon**

2. **Click the Slide 3 thumbnail on the Slides tab, click the More button ⊽ in the Themes group, then scroll to the bottom of the gallery**
   The Themes gallery opens.

QUICK TIP
One way to apply multiple themes to the same presentation is to click the Slide Sorter button on the status bar, select a slide or a group of slides, then click the theme.

3. **Right-click the View theme, then click Apply to Selected Slides**
   The new theme with a white background is applied to Slide 3.

4. **Slowly move your pointer ⌕ over the variants in the Variants group, then click the variant with the orange bar on the right side**
   The theme variant adds colored title text and background graphics to the slide, as shown in **FIGURE 4-1**. You can further modify the theme on Slide 3 by changing its color, font, or effects scheme.

5. **Click the ⊽ in the Variants group, point to Colors, then click Green**
   The title text color and background objects change color to reflect the new Green color scheme. Notice these changes only affect the design theme on Slide 3.

6. **Click the Slide 2 thumbnail on the Slides tab, then click the Design Ideas button in the Designer group**
   The Design Ideas pane opens. A list of slide layouts appears in the pane that the PowerPoint Designer identifies as being good matches for the content on Slide 2.

QUICK TIP
If Design Ideas is not active, and you are on the Internet, click the Turn on button in the Design Ideas pane.

7. **Locate and click the slide layout in the Design Ideas pane shown in FIGURE 4-2, then close the Design Ideas pane**
   Slide 2 changes to reflect the custom slide layout from the Design Ideas pane.

8. **Click the picture, click the Picture Format tab on the Ribbon, then click the Crop button arrow in the Size group**
   Pictures can be cropped to any shape found in the Shapes gallery.

9. **Point to Crop to Shape, click Flowchart: Document in the Flowchart section, then save your changes**

FIGURE 4-1: Slide showing a different design theme and variant

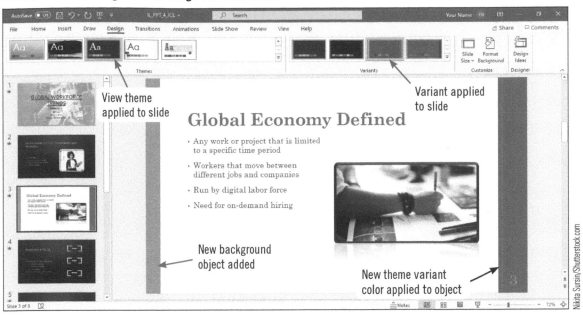

Nikita Sursin/Shutterstock.com

FIGURE 4-2: Slide 2 with new slide layout

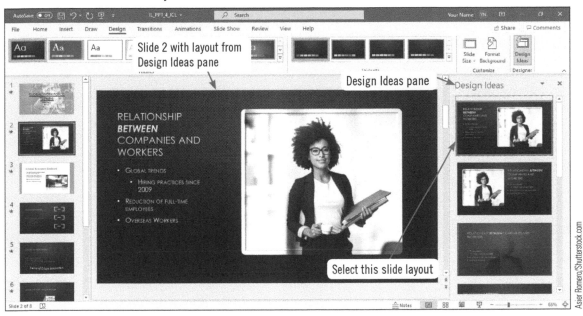

Asier Romero/Shutterstock.com

Customizing themes

You are not limited to using the standard themes PowerPoint provides; you can also modify a theme to create your own custom theme. For example, you might want to incorporate your school's or company's colors on the slide background of the presentation or be able to type using fonts your company uses for brand recognition. To change an existing theme, click the View tab on the Ribbon, then click one of the Master buttons in the Master Views group. Click the Colors button, the Fonts button, or the Effects button in the Background group to make changes to the theme, save this new theme for future use by clicking the Themes button in the Edit Theme group, then click Save Current Theme. You also have the ability to create a new font theme or color theme from scratch by clicking the Fonts button or the Colors button and then clicking Customize Fonts or Customize Colors. You work in the Create New Theme Fonts or Create New Theme Colors dialog box to define the custom theme fonts or colors.

Modify Masters

Learning Outcomes
- Navigate Slide Master view
- Change the Master background and theme fonts
- Add and modify a picture

Each presentation in PowerPoint has a set of **masters** that store information about the theme and slide layouts. Masters determine the position and size of text and content placeholders, fonts, slide background, color, and effects. There are three Master views: Slide Master view, Notes Master view, and Handout Master view. Changes made in Slide Master view are reflected on the slides in Normal view; changes made in Notes Master view are reflected in Notes Page view; and changes made in Handout Master view appear when you print your presentation using a handout printing option. The primary benefit to modifying a master is that you can make universal changes to your whole presentation instead of making individual repetitive changes to each of your slides. **CASE** *You decide to change the master background style and font scheme to modify the look of the whole presentation.*

STEPS

QUICK TIP

You can press and hold SHIFT and click the Normal button on the status bar to display the slide master.

1. **Click the** View tab **on the Ribbon, click the** Slide Master button **in the Master Views group, scroll to the top of the Master Thumbnails pane, then click the** Mesh Slide Master thumbnail **(first thumbnail)**

   The Slide Master view appears with the slide master displayed in the Slide pane, as shown in **FIGURE 4-3**. A new tab, the Slide Master tab, appears next to the Home tab on the Ribbon. The slide master is the Mesh theme slide master. Each theme comes with its own slide master. Each master text placeholder on the slide master identifies the font size, style, color, and position of text placeholders on the slides in Normal view. For example, for the Mesh theme, the Master title placeholder positioned at the top of the slide uses a white, 32-point, Century Gothic font. Slide titles use this font style and formatting. Each slide master comes with associated slide layouts located below the slide master in the Master Thumbnails pane. Slide layouts follow the information on the slide master, and changes you make are reflected in all the slide layouts.

2. **Click the** Title and Content Layout thumbnail **in the Master Thumbnails pane**

   A ScreenTip appears identifying the slide layout by name and lists if any slides in the presentation are using the layout. Slides 4–8 are using the Title and Content Layout.

QUICK TIP

You can make sure the current master remains with the presentation by clicking the Preserve button in the Edit Master group.

3. **Click the** Mesh Slide Master thumbnail, **click the** Background Styles button **in the Background group, then click the** Style 12 thumbnail

   This background style darkens the background and makes the white placeholder text stand out. By modifying the slide master thumbnail, every associated master slide layout is also changed.

4. **Click the** Fonts button **in the Background group, scroll down, then click** Cambria

   The fonts for title and body text change on every master slide layout in the presentation.

5. **Click the** Insert tab **on the Ribbon, click the** Pictures button **in the Images group, then click** This Device

   The Insert Picture dialog box opens.

6. **Select the picture file** Support_PPT_4_Logo.jpg **from the location where you store your Data Files, then click** Insert

   The JCL logo picture is placed on the slide master and will now appear on all slides in the presentation.

7. **Click** 2.45" **in the** Width text box **in the Size group, type** 1.00, **press ENTER, click the** Color button **in the Adjust group, then click** Orange, Accent color 6 Light **in the Recolor section**

   The logo changes color.

8. **Drag the** logo **to the lower-right corner to align with the footer placeholder, as shown in FIGURE 4-4, then save your changes**

FIGURE 4-3: Slide Master view

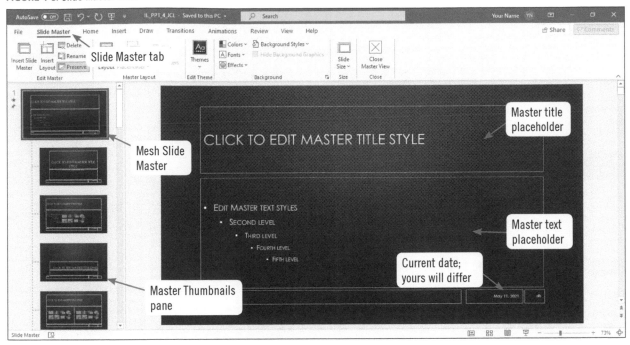

FIGURE 4-4: Customized slide master

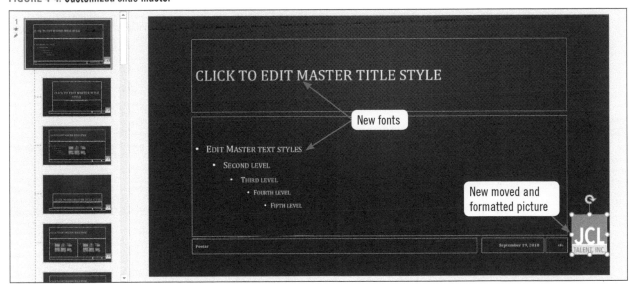

Understanding PowerPoint templates and themes

So what exactly is the difference between a PowerPoint template and a PowerPoint theme? A theme is a coordinated set of colors, fonts, and effects (such as shadows and reflections) that is used to modify the slide design of your presentation. For example, a theme is like the various colors a painter uses to paint the inside of a house where the walls are one color, the ceilings are a second color, and the window and door trim is a third color. A template, on the other hand, is a presentation that contains a theme and includes sample text about a specific subject matter, such as health and fitness. The sample text in a template provides you with the basic information that you can then use to modify the presentation with your own information. You can save any presentation as a template to use in the future by opening the Save As dialog box, then selecting PowerPoint Template in the Save as type text box. Your presentation is placed in the Custom Office Templates folder and can be accessed anytime.

Create Custom Slide Layouts

Learning
Outcomes
• Add a new slide
  master layout
• Create master
  placeholders

The standard slide layouts supplied in PowerPoint are adequate to design most of the slides for presentations that you will create. However, if you are consistently modifying a standard slide layout for presentations, having a custom slide layout that you created and saved would be helpful. To create a custom slide layout, you choose from eight different placeholders, including text, chart, and media placeholders. You draw the placeholder on the slide in Slide Master view; these then become a part of the presentation.

CASE ▶ *You decide to create a custom slide layout that displays picture thumbnails on the slide.*

STEPS

1. **Right-click a blank area of the** slide master **in the slide pane, point to the** Grid and Guides arrow, **click** Guides, **right-click the** slide master, **then click** Ruler
   The guides and rulers are displayed on the slide master.

   QUICK TIP
   To insert an additional slide master to use in your presentation, click the Insert Slide Master button in the Edit Master group.

2. **Click the** Insert Layout button **in the Edit Master group**
   A new slide layout is added to the presentation and appears in the Master Thumbnails pane with a title text placeholder and footer placeholders, as shown in **FIGURE 4-5**. The new slide layout contains all the slide background elements associated with the current theme. Notice the other slide master, which is the customized master for Slide 3 of the presentation.

3. **Click the** Insert Placeholder arrow **in the Master Layout group, then click** Picture
   The pointer changes to ┼ when moved over the slide layout.

4. **Position the pointer on the slide so** ┼ **is lined up on the** horizontal guide **at the 5 ½"**
   mark on the left side of the horizontal ruler and 0" on the vertical ruler
   As you move the pointer on the slide its position is identified on the rulers by red dotted lines.

5. **Drag** ┼ **to draw a box down and to the right until** ┼ **is lined up with the** 3 ½" **mark on the horizontal ruler and the** 2" **mark below 0 on the vertical ruler**
   You drew a 2" × 2" square picture placeholder on the slide. You can duplicate the placeholder.

   QUICK TIP
   To cut a content placeholder, right-click the placeholder, then click Cut in the shortcut menu.

6. **Click the** Home tab **on the Ribbon, click the** Copy button **in the Clipboard group, click the** Paste button **in the Clipboard group, then duplicate the picture placeholder two more times**
   There are four picture placeholders on the slide.

7. **Drag each** picture placeholder **using the horizontal guide to a position on the slide, as shown in** FIGURE 4-6, **then click the** Slide Master tab **on the Ribbon**
   The placeholders are arranged on the slide layout.

8. **Click the** Rename button **in the Edit Master group, select the default name, type** Picture, **click** Rename, **then position** ⌕ **over the** slide layout **in the Master Thumbnails pane**
   The new name of the custom slide layout appears in the ScreenTip. The new Picture layout will appear when you click the Layout button or the New Slide list button in the Slides group on the Home tab.

   QUICK TIP
   To rename a slide master, right-click the slide master in the Master Thumbnails pane, click Rename Master, then type a new name

9. **Right-click a blank area of the slide, click** Ruler, **right-click a blank area of the slide, point to the** Grid and Guides arrow, **then click** Guides

10. **Click the** Close Master View button **in the Close group, then save your changes**
    Slide 2 appears in Normal view.

FIGURE 4-5: New custom slide layout

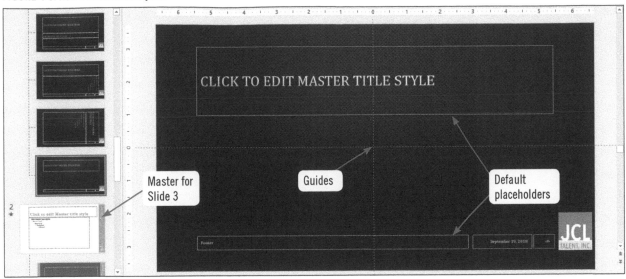

FIGURE 4-6: Custom slide layout with new placeholders

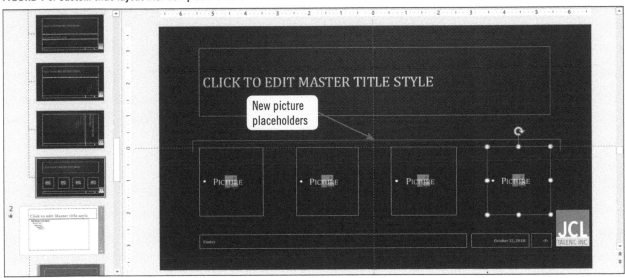

Restoring the slide master layout

If the slide master is missing a placeholder, open Slide Master view, then click the Master Layout button in the Master Layout group to reapply the placeholder. Clicking the Master Layout button opens the Master Layout dialog box, as shown in **FIGURE 4-7**. Click the placeholder check box to reapply the placeholder. To quickly apply or delete the title or footer placeholders on a slide master, click the Title or Footers check boxes in the Master Layout group on the Slide Master tab.

FIGURE 4-7: Master Layout dialog box

PowerPoint

Customize the Background and Theme

Learning
Outcomes
• Apply a slide
  background and
  change the style
• Modify
  presentation theme

Every slide in a PowerPoint presentation has a **background**, the area behind the text and graphics. You modify the background to enhance the slides using images and color. You can quickly change the background appearance by applying a background style, which is a set of color variations derived from the theme colors. Theme colors determine the colors for all slide elements in your presentation, including slide background, text and lines, shadows, fills, accents, and hyperlinks. Every PowerPoint theme has its own set of theme colors. See **TABLE 4-1** for a description of the theme colors. **CASE** ▶ *The JCL presentation can be improved with some design enhancements. You decide to modify the background of the slides by changing the theme colors and fonts.*

STEPS

1. **Click the** Design tab **on the Ribbon, then click the** Format Background button **in the Customize group**

   The Format Background pane opens displaying the Fill options. The Picture or texture fill option button is selected indicating the slide has a picture background.

2. **Click the** Slide 3 thumbnail **in the Slides tab, click the** Pattern fill option button, **then click the** Dotted: 25% pattern **(first row)**

   FIGURE 4-8 shows the new background on Slide 3 of the presentation. The new background style covers the slide behind the text and background graphics. **Background graphics** are objects placed on the slide master.

3. **Click the** Hide background graphics check box **in the Format Background pane**

   All the background objects, which include the colored shapes are hidden from view, and only the text objects, video object, and slide number remain visible.

4. **Click the** Hide background graphics check box, **then click the** Reset Background button **at the bottom of the Format Background pane**

   All the background objects and the solid fill slide background appear again as specified by the theme. The Reset Background button reverts the slide background to its original background, in this case a solid fill.

5. **Click the** Picture or texture fill option button, **click the** Texture button 🖼, **click** Canvas **(top row), then drag the** Transparency slider **until** 40% **is displayed in the text box**

   The new texture fills the slide background behind the background items.

6. **Click the** Gradient Fill option button

   A gradient fill now fills the slide background. PowerPoint splits the gradient background into four quadrants called **gradient stops** that can be individually customized.

7. **Click the** far-right gradient stop 4 of 4 🗓 **under Gradient stops, click the** Color button 🎨, **then click** Black, Text 1

   Changing the gradient stop color results in a shaded black color on the bottom of the slide. Compare your screen to **FIGURE 4-9**.

8. **Click the** Format Background pane Close button ✖, **then save your work**

FIGURE 4-8: **New background style applied**

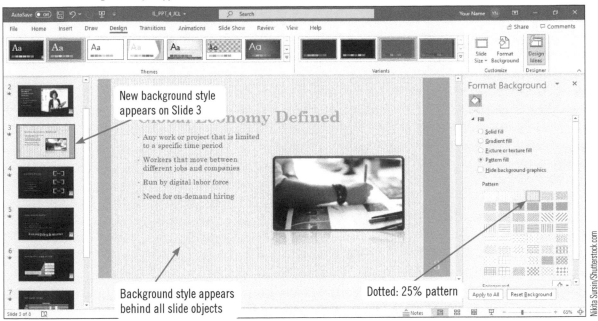

FIGURE 4-9: **Slide with gradient fill background**

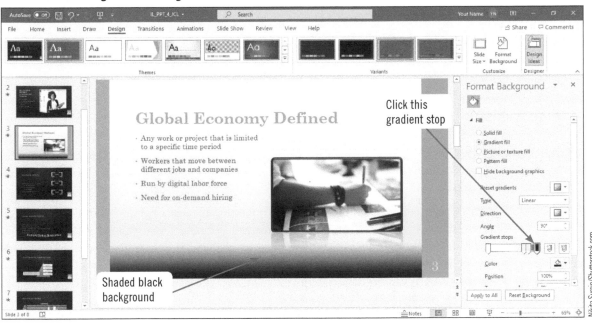

TABLE 4-1: **Theme colors**

color element	description
Text/Background colors	Contrasting colors for typed characters and the slide background
Accent colors	There are six accent colors used for shapes, drawn lines, and text; the shadow color for text and objects and the fill and outline color for shapes are all accent colors; all these colors contrast appropriately with background and text colors
Hyperlink color	Colors used for hyperlinks you insert
Followed Hyperlink color	Color used for hyperlinks after they have been clicked

Use Slide Show Commands

Learning Outcomes
• Preview a slide show
• Navigate a slide show
• Use slide show tools

With PowerPoint, Slide Show view is used primarily to deliver a presentation to an audience, either over the Internet using your computer or through a projector connected to your computer. As you've seen, Slide Show view fills your computer screen with the slides of the presentation, showing them one at a time. In Slide Show view, you can draw freehand pen or highlighter strokes, also known as **ink annotations**, on the slide or jump to other slides in the presentation. **CASE** *You run the slide show of the presentation and practice using some of the custom slide show options.*

STEPS

1. **Click the** Slide Show button ⬚ **on the status bar, then press** SPACEBAR, **watch the movie, then press** SPACEBAR **again**

   Slide 3 filled the screen first, and then Slide 4 appears. Pressing SPACEBAR or clicking the left mouse button is an easy way to move through a slide show. See **TABLE 4-2** for other basic slide show keyboard commands. You can easily navigate to other slides in the presentation during the slide show.

2. **Move** ⬚ **to the lower-left corner of the screen to display the Slide Show toolbar, click the** See all slides button ⬚, **then click the** Slide 2 thumbnail

   Slide 2 appears on the screen. With the Slide Show toolbar you can emphasize points in your presentation by drawing highlighter strokes on the slide during a slide show.

3. **Click the** Pen and laser pointer tools button ⬚, **on the Slide Show toolbar, then click** Highlighter

   The pointer changes to the highlighter pointer ⬚. You can use the highlighter anywhere on the slide.

4. **Drag** ⬚ **to highlight** Hiring practices since 2009 **and** Overseas workers **in the text object, then press** ESC

   Two lines of text are highlighted, as shown in **FIGURE 4-10**. While the ⬚ is visible, mouse clicks do not advance the slide show; however, you can still move to the next slide by pressing SPACEBAR or ENTER. Pressing ESC or CTRL+A while drawing with the highlighter or pen switches the pointer back to ⬚.

5. **Click the** More slide show options button ⬚ **on the Slide Show toolbar, click** Show Presenter View, **then click the** Pause the timer button ▐▐ **above the slide, as shown in** **FIGURE 4-11**

   Presenter view is a view that you can use when showing a presentation through two monitors; one that you see as the presenter and one that your audience sees. The current slide appears on the left of your screen (which is the only object your audience sees); the next slide in the presentation appears in the upper-right corner of the screen. If desired, you can black out the slide from view to prevent your audience from seeing it. Speaker notes, if you have any, appear in the lower-right corner. The timer you paused identifies how long the slide has been viewed by the audience.

6. **Click** ⬚ Black or unblack slide show, **click** ⬚, **click** ⬚, **click** Hide Presenter View, **then click the** Advance to the next slide button ⬚ **on the Slide Show toolbar**

   Slide 3 appears.

7. **Press** ENTER **to advance through the entire slide show until you see a black slide, then press** SPACEBAR

   If there are ink annotations on your slides, you have the option of saving them when you quit the slide show. Saved ink annotations appear as drawn objects in Normal view.

8. **Click** Discard, **then save the presentation**

   The highlight ink annotation is deleted on Slide 2, and Slide 8 appears in Normal view.

FIGURE 4-10: Slide 2 in Slide Show view with highlighter strokes

FIGURE 4-11: Slide 2 in Presenter view

TABLE 4-2: Basic Slide Show view keyboard commands

keyboard commands	description
ENTER, SPACEBAR, PGDN, N, DOWN ARROW, or RIGHT ARROW	Advances to the next slide
E	Erases the ink annotation drawing
HOME, END	Moves to the first or last slide in the slide show
UP ARROW, PGUP, or LEFT ARROW	Returns to the previous slide
S	Pauses the slide show when using automatic timings; press again to continue
B	Changes the screen to black; press again to return
ESC	Stops the slide show

Use Proofing and Language Tools

Learning
Outcomes
• Spell check a
  presentation
• Translate slide text

PowerPoint has a number of language tools, including the Spell Checker, which compares the spelling of all the words in your presentation against the words contained in the dictionary. The **proofing language** is the language used by the spelling checker that you can specify. PowerPoint also has a tool, called the Translator, that translates words or phrases from your default language into one of 60 different languages. And, as you develop content, if you are having trouble coming up with just the right word, PowerPoint has a comprehensive **thesaurus** that can help you. **CASE** *You're finished working on the presentation for now, so it's a good time to check spelling. You then experiment with language translation because the final presentation will be translated into different languages.*

STEPS

QUICK TIP

To display the Revisions pane to compare and combine changes with your current presentation and another presentation, click the Review tab, then click the Compare button in the Compare group to open the Revisions pane.

1. **Click the Slide 1 thumbnail in the Slides tab, click the Review tab on the Ribbon, then click the Spelling button in the Proofing group**

   PowerPoint begins to check the spelling in your presentation and opens the Spelling pane. The Spell Checker identifies a name on Slide 7, but it does not recognize that is spelled correctly and suggests some replacement words.

2. **Click Ignore All in the Spelling pane**

   PowerPoint ignores all instances of this name and continues to check the rest of the presentation for errors. When the Spell Checker finishes checking your presentation, the Spelling pane closes, and an alert box opens with a message stating the spelling check is complete.

3. **Click OK in the Alert box, then click the Slide 4 thumbnail in the Slides tab**

   The alert box closes. Now you experiment with the language translation feature.

4. **Click the Translate button in the Language group, then click Turn on if you need to turn on Intelligent Services**

   The Translator pane opens.

TROUBLE

Do not select the space past the word "overhead" in the third line.

5. **Select the three indented lines of text in the text object, click the To down arrow in the Translator pane, then click Catalan**

   A Catalan translation of the text appears in the Translator pane shown in **FIGURE 4-12**. You have the option of inserting the translated text directly onto your slide.

6. **Click the Insert button in the Translator pane, then close the Translator pane**

   The translated text is inserted into the text object in place of the original English text. Now you use the thesaurus on Slide 5.

QUICK TIP

You can also right-click a word, point to Synonyms in the shortcut menu, then choose a new word.

7. **Click the Slide 5 thumbnail in the Slides tab, select the word committed in the text object, then click the Thesaurus button in the Proofing group**

   The Thesaurus pane opens and displays a list of synonyms, as shown in **FIGURE 4-13**.

8. **Point to dedicated in the list of words, click the down arrow, then click Insert**

   The word "committed" is replaced with the word "dedicated."

9. **Close the Thesaurus pane, then save your work**

FIGURE 4-12: Translated text in the Translator pane

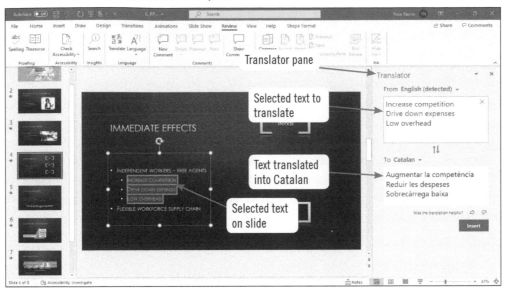

FIGURE 4-13: Window with open Thesaurus pane

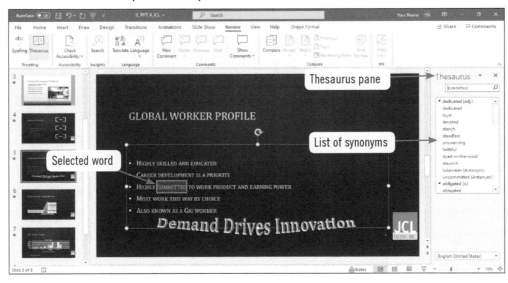

Rehearsing slide show timings

You can set different slide timings for each slide; for example, the title slide can appear for 20 seconds and the second slide for 1 minute. To set timings, click the Rehearse Timings button in the Set Up group on the Slide Show tab. Slide Show view opens and the Recording toolbar shown in **FIGURE 4-14** opens. It contains buttons to pause between slides and to advance to the next slide. After opening the Recording toolbar, you can practice giving your presentation by manually advancing each slide in the presentation. When you are finished, PowerPoint displays the total recorded time for the presentation and you have the option to save the recorded

timings. The next time you run the slide show, you can use the timings you rehearsed.

FIGURE 4-14: Recording toolbar

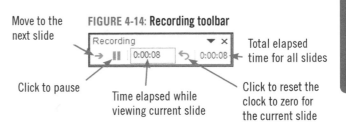

PowerPoint

Inspect a Presentation

Learning Outcomes
- Modify document properties
- Inspect and remove unwanted data

Reviewing your presentation can be an important step. You should not only find and fix errors, but also locate and delete confidential company or personal information and document properties you do not want to share with others. If you share presentations with others, especially over the Internet, it is a good idea to inspect the presentation file using the Document Inspector. The **Document Inspector** looks for hidden data and personal information that is stored in the file itself or in the document properties. Document properties, also known as **metadata**, include specific data about the presentation, such as the author's name, subject matter, title, who saved the file last, and when the file was created. Other types of information the Document Inspector can locate and remove include presentation notes, comments, ink annotations, invisible on-slide content, off-slide content, and custom XML data. **CASE** ▸ *You decide to view and add some document properties, inspect your presentation file, and learn about the Mark as Final command.*

STEPS

QUICK TIP
Click the Properties list button, then click Advanced Properties to open the Properties dialog box to see or change more document properties.

1. **Click the** File tab **on the Ribbon, click** Info **click the** Add a tag text box **in the Properties section, type** Changing international labor force, **then click the** Add a category text box
   This data provides some descriptive keywords for the presentation.

2. **Type** Industry review, **then click the** Show All Properties link
   The information you enter here about the presentation file can be used to identify and organize your file. The Show All Properties link displays all the file properties and those you can change. You now use the Document Inspector to search for information you might want to delete in the presentation.

QUICK TIP
If you need to save a presentation to run in an earlier version of PowerPoint, check for unsupported features using the Check Compatibility feature.

3. **Click the** Check for Issues button, **click** Inspect Document, **then click** Yes **to save the changes to the document**
   The Document Inspector dialog box opens. The Document Inspector searches the presentation file for 12 different types of information that you might want removed from the presentation before sharing it.

4. **Scroll down the dialog box, click any empty** check boxes, **then click** Inspect
   The presentation file is reviewed, and the results are shown in **FIGURE 4-15**. The Document Inspector found items having to do with document properties, which you just entered, task pane add-ins, and embedded documents which are the pictures in the file. You decide to leave all the document properties alone.

5. **Click** Close, **then click the** Protect Presentation button

6. **Click** Mark as Final, **then click** OK **in the alert box**
   An information alert box opens. Be sure to read the message to understand what happens to the file and how to recognize a marked-as-final presentation. You decide to complete this procedure.

7. **Click** OK, **click the** Home tab **on the Ribbon, then click anywhere in the title text object**
   When you select the title text object, the Ribbon closes automatically and an information alert box at the top of the window notes that the presentation is marked as final, making it a read-only file. Compare your screen to **FIGURE 4-16**. A **read-only** file is one that can't be edited or modified in any way. Anyone who has received a read-only presentation can only edit the presentation by changing its marked-as-final status. You still want to work on the presentation, so you remove the marked-as-final status.

8. **Click the** Edit Anyway button **in the information alert box, then save your changes**
   The Ribbon and all commands are active again, and the file can now be modified.

9. **sam⬆ Submit your presentation to your instructor, then exit PowerPoint**

FIGURE 4-15: Document Inspector dialog box

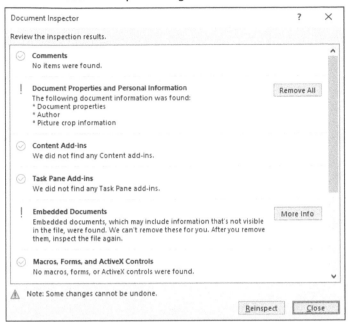

FIGURE 4-16: Marked as final presentation

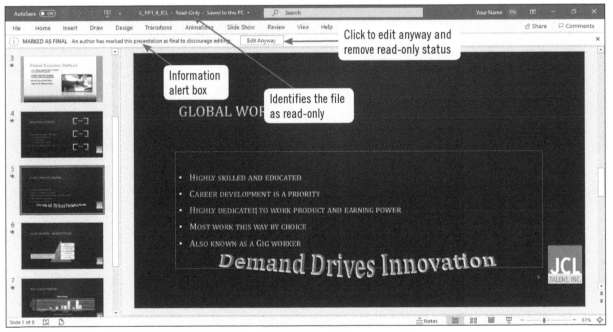

Practice

Skills Review

1. Apply design themes.

a. Open the presentation IL_PPT_4-2.pptx from the location where you store your Data Files, then save the presentation as **IL_PPT_4_Jenlan**. You will work to create the completed presentation, as shown in **FIGURE 4-17**.

b. Click the Slide 2 thumbnail in the Slides tab, then click the Design tab.

c. Click the Themes group More button, locate the Circuit theme, then apply it to the selected slide only.

d. Change the theme variant to the shaded black option.

e. Click the More button in the Variants group, point to Colors, then change the color scheme to Paper.

f. Go to Slide 3, then open the Design Ideas pane.

g. Apply the slide layout shown in **FIGURE 4-18**, then close the Design Ideas pane. If the layout does not appear, then choose another layout.

FIGURE 4-17: Completed presentation

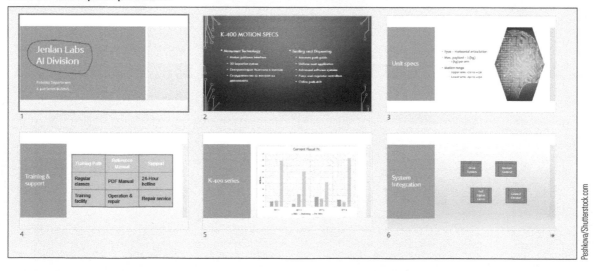

FIGURE 4-18

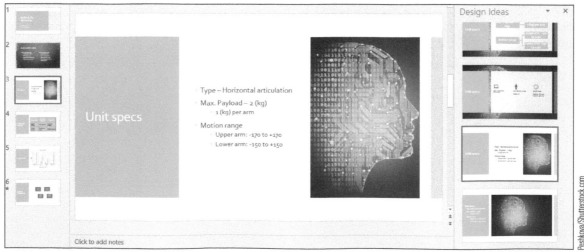

Formatting Slide Masters and Backgrounds

Skills Review (continued)

h. Click the picture, click the Picture Format tab, click the Crop button list arrow, then crop the picture to a Hexagon shape.

i. Save your changes.

2. Modify masters.

a. Open Slide Master view using the View tab, then click the Frame Slide Master thumbnail in the Master Thumbnails pane.

b. Change the background style to Style 9.

c. Change the theme fonts to Candara, then change the theme Colors to Blue Green.

d. Save your changes.

3. Create custom slide layouts.

a. Insert a new slide layout, then display the ruler and the guides.

b. Add a Content placeholder the same size as the blue shape. Use the guides and rulers to help you create the placeholder.

c. Add a Media placeholder, approximately 3.5" wide by 2.5" high, then use Copy and Paste to create a second placeholder.

d. Position and align the placeholders, as shown in FIGURE 4-19.

e. Name the custom slide layout **Media**, turn off guides, then close rulers.

f. Save your changes, then switch to Normal view.

FIGURE 4-19

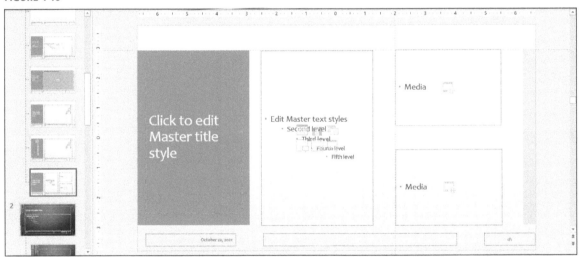

4. Customize the background and theme.

a. Go to Slide 6, then open the Format Background pane.

b. Click the Solid fill option button, then change the color to Aqua, Accent 1 Lighter 40%.

c. Change the color transparency to 40%, then click the Picture or texture fill option button.

d. Click the Texture button, then change the background to Blue tissue paper.

e. Click the Pattern fill option button, change the background to Small confetti, then click the Reset Background button at the bottom of the pane.

f. Click the Hide the background graphics check box, then click it again.

g. Select the Gradient fill option button, click the Preset gradients button, click Light Gradient - Accent 6 (top row), then close the Format Background pane.

Skills Review (continued)

5. Use slide show commands.

  a. Open Slide Show view, click the mouse twice, then go to Slide 1 using the See all slides button on the Slide Show toolbar.

  b. Use the Pen ink annotation tool to circle the slide title.

  c. Go to Slide 2, use the Highlighter to highlight any four points in the bulleted text on the slide, then press ESC.

  d. Open Presenter view, stop the timer, then click the Black or unblack slide show button twice.

  e. Advance the slides to Slide 6, then return to Slide 1.

  f. Hide Presenter view, advance through the slide show, save your ink and highlight annotations, then save your work.

6. Use proofing and language tools.

  a. Check the spelling of the document, and correct any misspelled words. There is one misspelled word in the presentation. Ignore any words that are correctly spelled but that the spell checker doesn't recognize. There is one word that spell checker does not recognize that is spelled correctly.

  b. On Slide 2, open the Translator pane.

  c. Select the last two bullet points in the left content placeholder, then change the To language in the Translator pane to Bulgarian.

  d. Click the Insert button in the Translator pane, then close the Translator pane.

  e. Go to Slide 3, right-click the word "Gesture" in the content placeholder, point to Synonyms, then click Motion.

  f. Save your changes.

7. Inspect a presentation.

  a. Go to the Info screen on the File tab, then in the Properties section, type information of your choosing in the Tags and Categories text fields.

  b. Open the Document Inspector dialog box.

  c. Make sure the Ink check box is selected, then inspect the presentation.

  d. Close the dialog box, then save your changes.

  e. Submit your presentation to your instructor, then close the presentation.

Independent Challenge 1

Riverwalk Medical Clinic (RMC) is a large medical facility in Cambridge, Massachusetts. You continue to work on a presentation on the latest emergency response procedures for a staff training later in the week.

  a. Open the file IL_PPT_4-3.pptx from the location where you store your Data Files, and save the presentation as **IL_PPT_4_Riverwalk**.

  b. Add the slide number and your name as the footer on all slides, except the title slide.

  c. Go to Slide 2, click the Design tab, then change the theme for the selected slide to Ion.

  d. If the Design Ideas pane is open, close it, then click the third variant from the left.

  e. Open the Slide Master view, click the Colors button, change the color scheme to Violet II, then change the background style to Style 3.

  f. Change the Font theme to Arial, then close the Slide Master view.

  g. Go to Slide 4, click the picture, click the Picture Format tab, then crop the picture to the Flowchart: Document shape.

  h. Go to Slide 5, click the Design Ideas button, select the first slide layout in the Design Ideas pane, then close the Design Ideas pane.

  i. Open Slide Show view, jump to Slide 1, then open Presenter view.

  j. Click the Pause the timer button, black the slide from view, make it appear again, then exit Presenter view.

  k. Proceed through the slide show to the end, then end the slide show.

Independent Challenge 1 (continued)

FIGURE 4-20

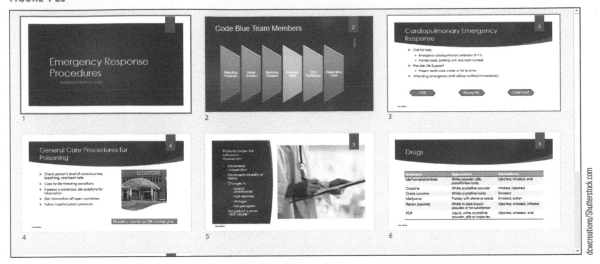

l. On Slide 5, right-click the word Alterations in the text object, point to Synonyms, then click the word Changes. An example of a finished presentation is shown in **FIGURE 4-20**.

m. Save your changes, submit your presentation to your instructor, close the presentation, then exit PowerPoint.

Independent Challenge 2

You are an associate at Global Systems, Inc., a manufacturer of civilian drone technology located in Santa Clara, California. Global Systems designs and manufactures personal drone systems largely used in the movie industry and in commercial business. You need to finish the work on a quarterly presentation that outlines the progress of the company's newest technologies by creating a custom slide layout, customizing the background, and using the Document Inspector.

a. Open the file IL_PPT_4-4.pptx from the location where you store your Data Files, and save the presentation as **IL_PPT_4_GSI**.

b. Go to Slide 2, then apply a gradient fill slide background using the Format Background pane.

c. Click the Preset gradients button, click Top Spotlight - Accent 3, then click the Hide background graphics check box.

d. Click the Hide background graphics check box again, then click the third gradient stop under Gradient stops.

e. Drag the Transparency slider to 40%, click Apply to All, then close the Format Background pane.

f. Open Slide Master view, insert a new slide layout, then create three 3" picture content placeholders.

g. On the vertical ruler, set a guide on the 1" mark above the 0, align the top edges of the placeholders on the guide, then distribute the placeholders horizontally.

h. Rename the new slide layout, **Picture**, close the Slide Master view, then open Slide Show view.

i. On Slide 3, use the highlighter to highlight two bullet points, move to Slide 4, use the pen to circle two bullet points, end the slide show, then save your annotations.

j. Run the Document Inspector with all the options selected, identify what items the Document Inspector finds, then close the Document Inspector dialog box.

k. Add your name and the slide number as a footer to all slides, check the spelling, fix any misspellings, close rulers and guides, then save your work.

l. Submit your presentation to your instructor, then close the presentation and exit PowerPoint.

PowerPoint

Visual Workshop

Create a presentation that looks like **FIGURE 4-21**, and **FIGURE 4-22**, which shows two slides with a specific slide layout. The theme used in this presentation is Berlin with a blue variant. Insert pictures **Support_PPT_4_Group.jpg** and **Support_PPT_4_AI.jpg** to the slides, then crop the first picture to the shape Rectangle: Diagonal Corners Rounded and the second picture to the shape Plaque. On the slide master, insert the picture **Support_PPT_4_R2G_Logo.jpg** to the Berlin Slide Master layout. Change the picture width to 1". Change the slide background of both slides to the Top Spotlight - Accent 1 preset gradient fill. Add your name as footer text to the slide, add slide number to the footer, save the presentation as **IL_PPT_4_R2G**, then submit your presentation to your instructor.

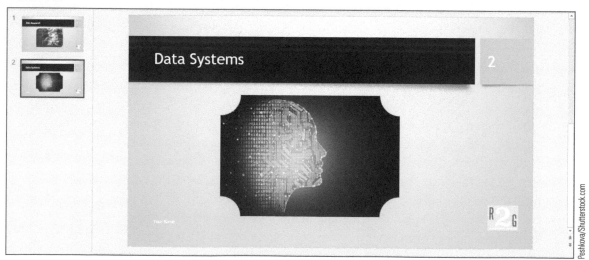

Working with Advanced Tools

CASE ▶ You continue working on the JCL Talent workforce trends presentation that details specific information on the labor force in the global economy. After receiving some initial feedback, you revise the presentation by formatting shapes, modifying pictures, customizing animations, using comments, customizing the master views, and combining reviewed presentations. You also add Zoom links to the presentation to facilitate navigation when you deliver the slide show.

Module Objectives

After completing this module, you will be able to:

- Use advanced formatting tools
- Insert and modify a picture
- Adjust and format text objects
- Customize animation effects

- Set advanced animation effects
- Use comments
- Combine reviewed presentations
- Insert Zoom links

Files You Will Need

IL_PPT_5-1.pptx
Support_PPT_5_Office_Group.jpg
Support_PPT_5_Review.pptx
IL_PPT_5-2.pptx

Support_PPT_5_TechRev.pptx
IL_PPT_5-3.pptx
IL_PPT_5-4.pptx
Support_PPT_5_Uganda.pptx

Use Advanced Formatting Tools

Learning Outcomes
- Apply 3D effects to objects
- Insert and modify connectors

With the advanced formatting tools available in PowerPoint, you can change the attributes of any object. You can format text and shapes using solid and texture fills, 3D effects, and shadows. To create a cohesive look on a slide with multiple objects, you can use the Format Painter to copy the attributes from one object and apply them to other objects. **CASE** ▶ *In this lesson, you draw and format a connector line on Slide 4 and then use the Format Painter to apply formatting to the connector line and to text on the slide.*

STEPS

1. **sam ↓** Start PowerPoint, open IL_PPT_5-1.pptx from the location where you store your Data Files, save the presentation as IL_PPT_5_JCL, then click Slide 4 in the Slides tab
   Slide 4 appears in the Slide pane.

2. **Click the** arrow connector, **click the** Shape Format tab **on the Ribbon, click the** More button ⊡ **in the Shape Styles group, then click** Intense Line - Accent 2
   A gray theme style is added to the double-arrow connector line.

3. **Click the** Shape Effects button **in the Shape Styles group, point to** Glow, **then click** Glow: 8 point; Orange, Accent color 6 **(last column, second row)**
   An orange glow color is applied to the arrow connector line.

4. **Click a blank area of the slide, click the** Shapes button **in the Drawing group, then click the** Line Arrow: Double button ⟍ **in the Lines section**

5. **Position** ✛ **on the** Supply shape connection site ◉ **as shown in** FIGURE 5-1, **press and hold the** left mouse button, **then drag** ✛ **to the right top-middle** ◉ **on the** Growth shape
   Green circle handles appear at each end of the connector line, indicating that it is attached to the two shapes. The connector line flows from the bottom left middle of the Supply shape to the top right middle of the Growth shape at a right diagonal.

6. **Click the** Home tab **on the Ribbon, click the** Trends to Supply connector arrow, **then click the** Format Painter button ⊠ **in the Clipboard group**
   The pointer changes to ⊠. The Format Painter tool "picks up," or copies, attributes of an object and pastes them on the next object you select.

7. **Position** ⊠ **over the** Supply to Growth connector arrow, **click the** connector arrow, **then click a blank area of the slide**
   Both connector lines are formatted using the same theme style and glow effect.

8. **Click** Trends, **click the** Shape Format tab **on the Ribbon, click the** Text Effects button **in the WordArt Styles group, point to** Glow, **then click** Glow: 18 point; Orange, Accent color 6
   The Trends text in the shape is formatted with an orange glow text effect.

QUICK TIP
You can also click ⊠ again to turn off the Format Painter.

9. **Click the** Home tab **on the Ribbon, double-click** ⊠ **in the Clipboard group, click** Supply, **click** Growth **in the rectangle shapes, then press** ESC
   Double-clicking the Format Painter button locks the Format Painter allowing you to apply the same formatting to multiple objects on the slide without having to reselect the tool.

10. **Click a blank area of the slide, then save your changes**
    Compare your screen with FIGURE 5-2.

FIGURE 5-1: Shape with connection sites displayed

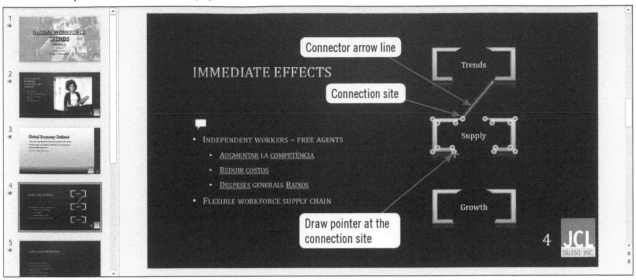

FIGURE 5-2: Formatted arrow connectors and shape text

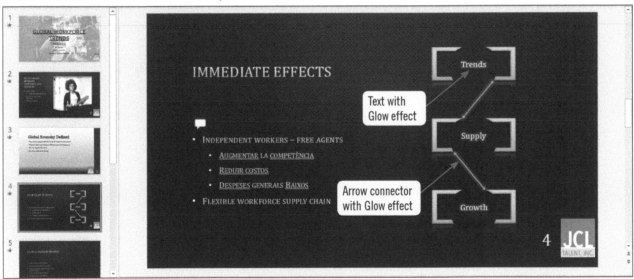

Creating columns in a text box

When the information you are working with fits better in a column format, you have the ability to format text into columns. Select the text object, click the Add or Remove Columns button in the Paragraph group on the Home tab, then click either One Column, Two Columns, Three Columns, or More Columns.

The More Columns option allows you to set up to 16 columns and customize the spacing between columns. You can display the ruler to set specific widths for the columns and further customize the columns.

Insert and Modify a Picture

Learning Outcomes
- Apply picture effects
- Recolor a picture
- Add Alt text to a picture

Inserting pictures and other media to your slides can dynamically enhance the message of your presentation. When working with pictures in PowerPoint, you have a number of design options you can use to format pictures in creative ways, including artistic effects, recoloring, and border styles. You can also add descriptive text to a picture that can help those who are visually impaired. These advanced picture-formatting features can dramatically change how a picture appears, and they can be useful when you are trying to match the picture to other content in the presentation. **CASE** ▶ *On Slide 5 you experiment with the picture tools and accessibility features in PowerPoint.*

STEPS

QUICK TIP

To compress a picture, select the picture, click the Compress Pictures button in the Adjust group, choose the options you want, then click OK.

1. **Click the** Slide 5 thumbnail **in the Slides tab, click the** Pictures icon 🖻 **in the content placeholder, navigate to the location where you store your Data Files, click** Support_PPT_5_Office_Group.jpg, **then click** Insert

    The picture fills the content placeholder and the Picture Format tab opens on the Ribbon.

2. **Click the** Picture Border button **in the Picture Styles group, point to** Weight, **then click** More Lines

    The Format Picture pane opens displaying border line style options.

3. **Click the** Solid line option button, **click the** Color button, **click** Orange, Accent 6 **in the Theme Colors section, click the** Width up arrow **until** 3 pt **appears, then click** ✖ **in the Format Picture pane**

    A three point orange border surrounds the picture.

4. **Click the** Artistic Effects button **in the Adjust group, point to each of the effect options to see how the picture changes, then click the** Pencil Sketch **(top row)**

    The picture has a pencil drawing quality now, as shown in **FIGURE 5-3**.

5. **Click the** Color button **in the Adjust group, point to each option to see how the picture changes, then click** Tan, Accent color 2 Dark **in the Recolor section**

    The picture is recolored with tan tones.

QUICK TIP

To make one color in a picture transparent, select the picture, click the Color button in the Adjust group, click Set Transparent Color, then click the color on the picture you want to make transparent.

6. **Click the** Picture Effects button **in the Picture Styles group, point to** Reflection, **point to each option to see how the picture changes, then click** Tight Reflection: Touching

    A reflection effect appears below the picture. Now edit the Alt text that was automatically generated for the picture using the Alt Text feature.

7. **Click the** Alt Text button **in the Accessibility group**

    The Alt Text pane opens. Use this pane to describe the picture for people who are visually impaired. Notice the automatically generated description of the picture.

8. **Click to the left of the word** people **in the text box, type** young, **press SPACEBAR, then click** ✖ **in the Alt Text pane**

    Text is edited and entered in the Alt Text pane providing a description of the picture.

9. **Click a blank area of the slide, then save your work**

    Compare your screen to **FIGURE 5-4**.

FIGURE 5-3: Pencil Sketch artistic effect applied to picture

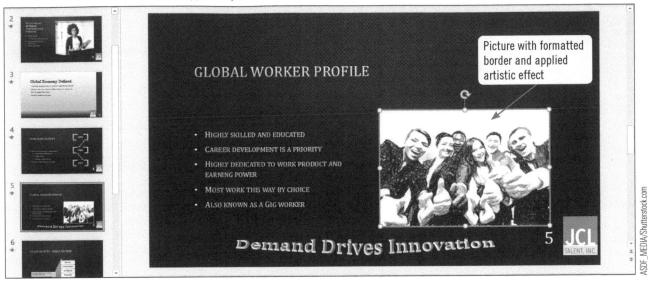

FIGURE 5-4: Color adjusted and reflection applied to picture

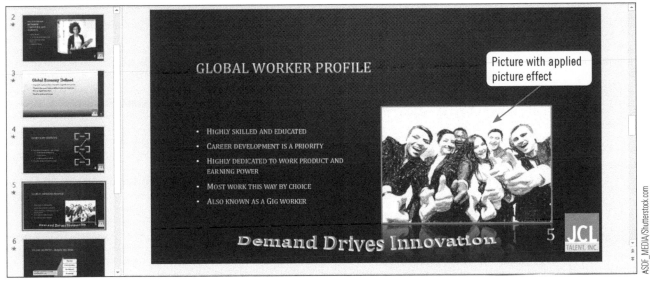

Using Paste Special

Paste Special is used to paste text or objects into PowerPoint using a specific format. For example, you may want to paste text as a picture or as plain text without formatting. Copy the text, or object, then in PowerPoint click the Home tab, click the Paste list arrow, click Paste Special, then select the appropriate format option. You can keep source formatting or apply the destination theme. You can also choose whether to embed or link an object or selected information from another program to PowerPoint using the Paste Special command. This technique is useful when you want to link part of an Excel worksheet or a chart from a workbook that contains both a worksheet and a chart. To link just the chart, open the Excel worksheet, then copy the chart. Leaving the Excel source file open, click the Paste list arrow, click Paste Special, click one of the Paste link options, then click OK.

Adjust and Format Text Objects

Learning Outcomes
- Change master text bullets
- Modify theme fonts

Having a consistent look in your presentation is important, so any changes you make to fonts or bullets, such as color or type, should be made to master text directly on the Slide Master. When you change a bullet type, you can use a character symbol, a picture, or an image that you have stored as a file. All text in PowerPoint is created within a text box that has space before and after lines of text or bullet points. You can modify this space between lines of text and paragraphs. **Paragraph spacing** is the space before and after paragraphs (bullet levels). **Leading** refers to the amount of space between lines of text within the same paragraph (bullet level). **CASE** *You decide to make a few formatting changes to the master text placeholder of your presentation.*

STEPS

1. **Press SHIFT, click the Normal button** 📧 **on the status bar, release SHIFT, then click the Mesh Slide Master thumbnail (first thumbnail) in the Master Thumbnails pane**
   Slide Master view appears with the slide master displayed in the Slide pane.

2. **Right-click** Edit Master Text Styles **in the master text placeholder, point to the** Numbering Arrow **on the shortcut menu, then click** 1. 2. 3.
   The bullet for the first level of the master text placeholder changes to a number. You decide to modify the bullets further.

QUICK TIP
To change a bullet to a picture bullet, click Picture in the Bullets and Numbering dialog box, navigate to the location of the picture then click the image.

3. **Right-click** Second Level **in the master text placeholder, point to the** Bullets Arrow **on the shortcut menu, then click** Bullets and Numbering
   The Bullets and Numbering dialog box opens. The Bulleted tab is selected; the Numbered tab is used to create sequentially numbered or lettered bullets.

4. **Click the** Hollow Square Bullets **option, click the** Size down arrow **until** 90 **appears, click the** Color button, **click** Orange, Accent 5, **then click** OK
   The style and color of the new bullet in the second level of the master text placeholder changes. The size of the bullet is decreased to 90% of the size of the second-level text.

5. **Right-click** Third Level **in the master text placeholder, point to the** Bullets Arrow **on the shortcut menu, click** Bullets and Numbering, **then click** Customize
   The Symbol dialog box opens.

QUICK TIP
To reset the bullet to the default symbol, click Reset in the Bullets and Numbering dialog box. Clicking Reset does not change the color or size back to their original default settings.

6. **Click the** Double Dagger symbol ‡, **click** OK, **then click** OK **again**
   All three new bullet symbols appear in the master text placeholder as shown in **FIGURE 5-5**.

7. **Click** 📧 **on the status bar, click the** Slide 2 thumbnail **in the Slides tab, click the** Global Trends text object, **move the pointer over the** text object border **until it changes to** ⬡, **then click the** border
   The text object is selected and surrounded by a solid line border.

8. **Click the** Line Spacing button ⬡ **in the Paragraph group, then click** 1.5
   The space or leading between lines of text within the same bullet point increases to 1.5.

9. **Click** ⬡ **in the Paragraph group, click** Line Spacing Options **to open the Paragraph dialog box, click the** Before up arrow **in the Spacing section until** 6 pt **appears, click the** After up arrow **in the Spacing section until** 18 pt **appears, click** OK, **then save your work**
   The spacing before and after each bullet on Slide 2 changes. Compare your screen to **FIGURE 5-6**.

FIGURE 5-5: New bullets applied to the Slide Master

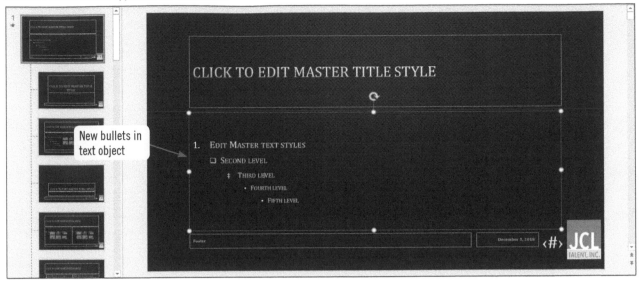

New bullets in text object

CLICK TO EDIT MASTER TITLE STYLE

1. EDIT MASTER TEXT STYLES
   ☐ SECOND LEVEL
       ‡ THIRD LEVEL
           • FOURTH LEVEL
               • FIFTH LEVEL

Footer   December 3, 2018   ‹#›

FIGURE 5-6: Text object with changed paragraph and line spacing

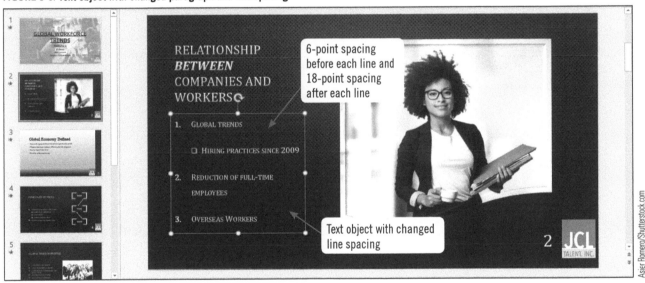

RELATIONSHIP
BETWEEN
COMPANIES AND
WORKERS

6-point spacing before each line and 18-point spacing after each line

1. GLOBAL TRENDS
   ☐ HIRING PRACTICES SINCE 2009
2. REDUCTION OF FULL-TIME EMPLOYEES
3. OVERSEAS WORKERS

Text object with changed line spacing

2

Asier Romero/Shutterstock.com

Changing text direction and margin space

Using the Text Direction button in the Paragraph group on the Home tab, you can change the direction of text and the margin space in a text object or shape. There are four text direction options available: Horizontal, Rotate all text 90°, Rotate all text 270°, and Stacked. The Horizontal option is the standard default text direction for all text in PowerPoint. The Rotate all text 90° text direction rotates text so it faces the right margin of a text object or shape. The Rotate all text 270° text direction rotates text so it faces the left margin of a text object or shape. The Stacked text direction stacks letters vertically on top of one another. Margins in a text object or shape determine the space between the edge of text and the edges of the text box. Click the Text Direction button, then click More Options to open the Format Shape pane. Four margin options are available to modify: Left margin, Right margin, Top margin, and Bottom margin.

PowerPoint

Customize Animation Effects

Learning
Outcomes
• Apply multiple
  animations to an
  object
• Change animation
  order

Animating objects allows you to control how information flows and how objects move on the slide during a slide show. The simplest way to animate an object is to apply a standard animation effect from the Animation group on the Animations tab. There are additional entrance, emphasis, exit, and motion path animation effects available through the menu at the bottom of the Animation gallery that you can apply to objects. You can customize effect options including starting time, direction, and speed. And when you want to copy animation settings from one object to another, you can use the Animation Painter. **CASE** ➤ *You decide to animate the shapes and connector lines you created on Slide 4.*

STEPS

1. **Click the** Slide 4 thumbnail **in the Slides tab, click the** Animations tab **on the Ribbon, click the** Growth shape, **click the** More button ⟱ **in the Animation group, then click** More Entrance Effects **at the bottom of the gallery**

   The Change Entrance Effect dialog box opens. Effects are grouped by categories: Basic, Subtle, Moderate, and Exciting.

2. **Click** Flip **in the Exciting section, click** OK, **click the** Duration up arrow **in the Timing group until** 01.50 **appears in the text box, then click the** Preview button **in the Preview group**

   The shape flips down the slide. An animation tag [1] appears next to the shape.

3. **Click the** Growth to Supply connector line, **click** Wipe **in the Animation group, click the** Growth shape, **click the** Add Animation button **in the Advanced Animation group, click** Teeter **in the Emphasis group, then click the** Preview button

   The Add Animation feature allows you to apply multiple animations to the same object. Notice the Animation tag 3 [3] appears beside [1], which indicates the shape now has two animations.

4. **Click the** Animation tag 2 [2] **on the slide, click the** Move Later button **in the Timing group, then click the** Preview button

   The animations for the shape now run consecutively before the animation for the connector line. Compare your screen to **FIGURE 5-7**.

5. **Click the** Growth shape, **double-click the** Animation Painter button **in the Advanced Animation group, click the** Supply shape, **click the** Trends shape, **then press** ESC

   When you use the Animation Painter all the animations and animation settings from the first shape are applied to the second and third shapes.

6. **Click the** Growth to Supply connector line, **click the** Delay up arrow **in the Timing group until** 00.50 **appears, then click the** Preview button

   The connector line's animation start time changes.

7. **With the connector line still selected, click the** Animation Painter button **in the Advanced Animation group, click the** Supply to Trends connector line, **then click the** Preview button

   Now both connector lines have the same animation and animation settings. The Supply to Trends connector line needs to play before the Trends shape.

8. **With the connector line still selected, click the** Move Earlier button twice **in the Timing group, click the** Preview button, **then save your changes**

   Compare your screen to **FIGURE 5-8**.

FIGURE 5-7: Animation effects applied to the objects

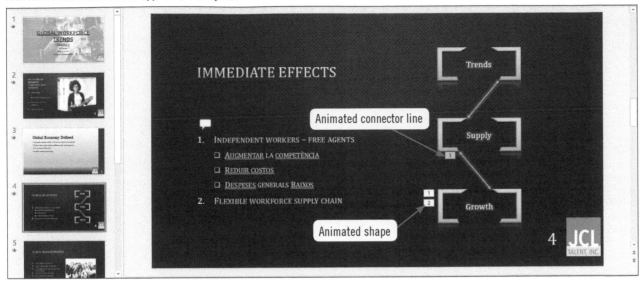

FIGURE 5-8: Completed animation effects

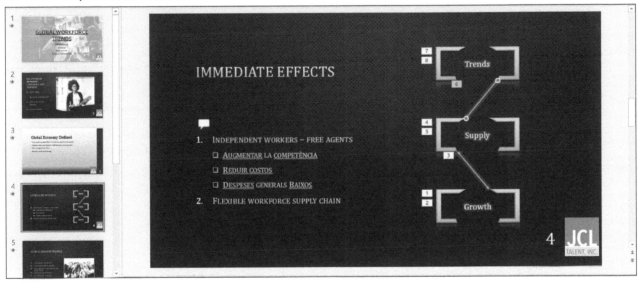

Understanding animation start timings

Each animated object on a slide has a starting time in relation to the other animated objects. There are three different starting time options: Start On Click, Start With Previous, and Start After Previous. The Start On Click timing option starts the animation effect when you click the mouse. The Start With Previous timing option begins the animation effect at the same time as the previous effect in the animation list, so two or more animation effects play at once. The Start After Previous timing option begins the animation immediately after the previous animation without clicking the mouse.

Set Advanced Animation Effects

Learning Outcomes
- Apply a motion path animation
- Add an animation trigger
- Add sound to an animation

Most of PowerPoint's animation effects are simple actions like float in or fade, but there are also more advanced motion path effects that bring objects to life. A motion path animation is a defined path, such as a straight line or a loop, or a customized path that you draw on the slide. You can also set a special condition, known as a **trigger**, that causes an animation to play after a specific action occurs, such as clicking a shape. Triggers are helpful when, for example, you want an animation to play after a video that is playing during a slide show reaches a bookmark. Triggers allow you be in control of your slide animations.

CASE ▶ *You add motion path animations, sound effects, and triggers to the SmartArt graphic on slide 6.*

STEPS

1. **Click the** Slide 6 thumbnail **in the Slides tab, click the** Animations tab **on the Ribbon, click the** SmartArt graphic, **then click the** None **in the Animations group**

   The animation is removed from the SmartArt graphic and it no longer displays an animation tag.

2. **Click the** More button ⊡ **in the Animation group, then click** Turns **in the Motion Paths section**

   The SmartArt graphic animates and a turn motion path object appears on the SmartArt graphic.

3. **Click the** Effect Options button **in the Animation group, click** Up, **right-click the** motion path line, **then click** Reverse Path Direction

   The SmartArt graphic now starts its animation up and moves down the slide in the reverse direction. Compare your screen to **FIGURE 5-9**.

4. **Click the** Trigger button **in the Advanced Animation group, point to** On Click of, **then click** TextBox 2

   The text box next to the SmartArt graphic is now the trigger for the SmartArt graphic animation.

5. **Click the** Slide Show view button 🖵 **in the status bar, move** ⬚ **over the text box, the pointer changes to** 🖑, **click the** text box, **watch the animation, then press** ESC

   Clicking the text box in Slide Show view triggers the motion path animation attached to the SmartArt graphic.

6. **Click the** title text object, **click** Fade **in the Animation group, click the** Animation Pane button **in the Advanced Animation group, then click the** Title 1 down arrow **shown in** FIGURE 5-10

   The animation will dim the text on the slide as part of the animation.

QUICK TIP
To set other timing options and advanced trigger options, click the Timing tab in the Fade dialog box.

7. **Click** Effect Options, **click the** After animation arrow **in the Fade dialog box, click the far right** color cell, **click the** Sound arrow, **scroll down the list, click** Chime, **then click** OK

   A chime sound now plays during the animation and the title text dims to an orange color when the animation finishes.

8. **Click the** Animation Pane Close button ✖, **click** 🖵 **on the status bar, click the** slide **twice, click the** text box, **press** ESC, **then save your changes**

   All the animations play during the slide show.

FIGURE 5-9: Motion path animation effect applied to SmartArt graphic

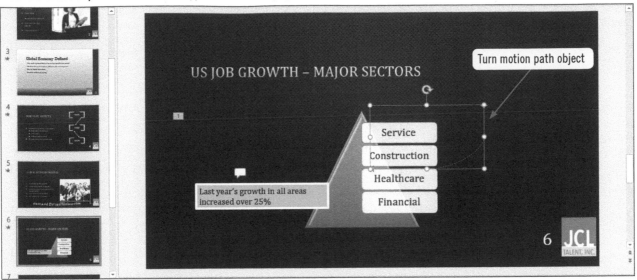

FIGURE 5-10: Slide with open Animation Pane

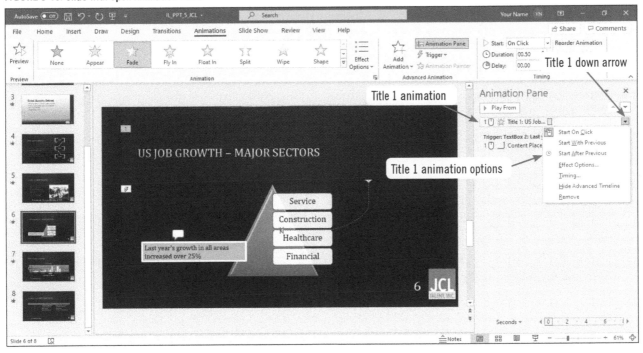

Animating objects with a custom motion path

Motion path animations provide you with a number of unique animations all of which follow a defined path, such as a loop, an arc, or a line. For a complete list of motion path animations click More Motion Paths at the bottom of the Animation gallery. If none of the defined motion paths provide the desired result, then you can draw a custom path. Custom motion paths can have both freeform and straight lines. Open the Animation gallery, then click Custom Path in the Motion Paths section. Drag ╋ to create a freeform motion path line or point and click ╋ to create a straight motion path line, then when you are finished, double-click the mouse. To change the route of the motion path, right-click the animation object, click Edit Points, then drag edit points as desired.

Use Comments

Learning Outcomes
• Add a new comment
• Review, reply to, and delete comments

When you need to review a presentation or when working with others on presentations, the Comments feature can be a useful tool to communicate ideas. Using comments to suggest changes or edits without disturbing the original content is an efficient way to collaborate on a presentation. Using the Comments Pane you can insert, reply, move between, and manage comments placed in the presentation by you or someone else. The Comments pane is easily accessible by clicking the Comments button on the Ribbon.

CASE ▶ *You review comments made by a colleague and add your own to the presentation.*

STEPS

QUICK TIP
To open the Comments pane when it is closed, click a comment icon on the slide.

1. **Click the** Comments button **on the Ribbon**

   The Comments icon indicates there is a comment on the slide. The Comments pane opens as shown in **FIGURE 5-11**. You can also access the Comments features through the Review tab on the Ribbon. You can insert new comments, move between comments, and reply to comments in the Comments pane.

2. **Click the** Reply text box **in the Comments pane, type** Verified by marketing dept., **then click the** Next button 🔁 **in the Comments pane**

   Your comment now appears in the Comments pane and a second Comment icon appears on the slide.

3. **Click the** Review tab **on the Ribbon, click the** Next button **in the Comments group until an alert box appears, then click** Continue **in the alert box**

   PowerPoint looks for comments from the beginning of the presentation and finds the comment on Slide 4.

QUICK TIP
To delete a comment, click the Delete button ✖ next to the comment in the Comments pane

4. **Click the** Reply text box **in the Comments pane, type** Not sure, **then click the** Comments pane Close button ✖

   A second Comment icon appears just behind the first Comment icon on the slide and the Comments pane closes.

5. **Click the** Show Comments arrow **in the Comments group, then click** Show Markup **to remove the checkmark**

   The comment icons are turned off or hidden from view. The Show Markup command is a **toggle command**, which means it has an on and an off position.

6. **Click the** Show Comments arrow **in the Comments group, click** Show Markup, **click the** Slide 5 thumbnail **in the Slides tab, then click the** New Comment button **in the Comments group**

   The Comment icons reappear on the slide and a new Comment icon appears on Slide 5 in the upper left corner. The Comments pane opens ready for you to enter a new comment.

7. **Type** Is this list complete?, **then click the** Previous button **in the Comments group**

   A new comment is placed on Slide 5 and Slide 4 appears with your previous comment open.

8. **Click** Not sure **in the Comment text box, then type** Yes, Spanish and French

   The comment is edited as shown in **FIGURE 5-12**.

9. **Click the** Comments button **on the Ribbon to close the Comments pane, then save your work**

FIGURE 5-11: Slide with open Comments pane

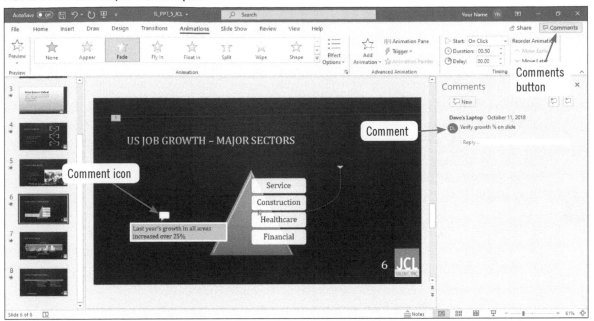

FIGURE 5-12: Edited comment in Comments pane

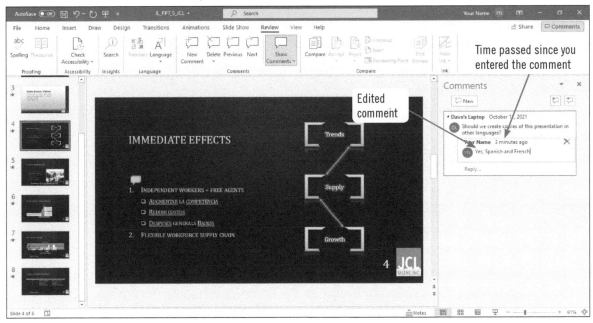

Replacing text and fonts

As you review your presentation, you may decide to replace certain text or fonts throughout the entire presentation using the Replace command. Text can be a word, phrase, or sentence. To replace specific text, click the Home tab on the Ribbon, then click the Replace button in the Editing group. In the Replace dialog box, enter the text you want to replace, then enter the text you want to use as its replacement.

You can also use the Replace command to replace one font for another. Simply click the Replace button list arrow in the Editing group, then click Replace Fonts to open the Replace Font dialog box. Finally, if you just want to find a word in your presentation, click the Find button in the Editing group, enter the word you want to find in the Find dialog box, then click Find Next.

Working with Advanced Tools

Combine Reviewed Presentations

Learning
Outcomes
• Accept or reject
  changes from a
  reviewer
• Add and rename a
  section

After a reviewer completes reviewing your presentation and sends it back, you can merge the changes in the reviewer's presentation into your original presentation using the Compare command. You can accept or reject individual changes, changes by slides, changes by reviewer if there is more than one reviewer, or all changes to the presentation. **CASE** *You sent the presentation to a colleague who has reviewed the presentation and sent it back to you. You are now ready to combine the reviewed presentation with your original one.*

STEPS

1. **Click the** Slide 1 thumbnail **in the Slides tab, click the** Review tab **on the Ribbon, then click the** Compare button **in the Compare group**

   The Choose File to Merge with Current Presentation dialog box opens.

2. **Navigate to the location where you store your Data Files, click** Support_PPT_5_Review.pptx, **then click** Merge

   The reviewed presentation is merged with your original one, and the Revisions pane opens showing the reviewer's changes. Slide 2 is selected because it is the first slide with a change as shown in **FIGURE 5-13**.

3. **Click the** All changes to Content Placeholder 2 check box, **then review the changes in the text object**

   The change icon and both check boxes now have check marks indicating the changes are accepted.

4. **Click the** Next button **in the Compare group, read the suggested changes, then click** SLIDES **in the Revisions pane**

   Choosing the Slides option in the Revisions pane allows you to see changes the reviewer made to your original slide.

5. **Click the** Accept button arrow **in the Compare group, click** Accept All Changes to This Slide, **then click the** Next button **in the Compare group**

   All the changes on Slide 3 are accepted and Slide 5 appears with more changes.

6. **Click the** Your Name check box **in the Revisions pane, click the** Reject button arrow **in the Compare group, then click** Reject All Changes to This Slide

   The changes to the text object are rejected.

7. **Click the** Next button **twice in the Compare group, click** Cancel **in the message dialog box, click the** End Review button **in the Compare group, then click** Yes **in the message dialog box**

   The Revisions pane closes and applied changes are made. To help organize your presentation, you decide to create a section.

8. **Click the** Slide 1 thumbnail **in the Slides tab, click the** Home tab **on the Ribbon, click the** Section button **in the Slides group, then click** Add Section

   A section heading appears in the Slides tab above the Slide 1 thumbnail as shown in **FIGURE 5-14**.

9. **Type** Intro **in the Rename Section dialog box, click** Rename, **then save your work**

   The new section name appears in the Slides tab above Slide 1.

FIGURE 5-13: Open Revisions pane showing reviewer's changes

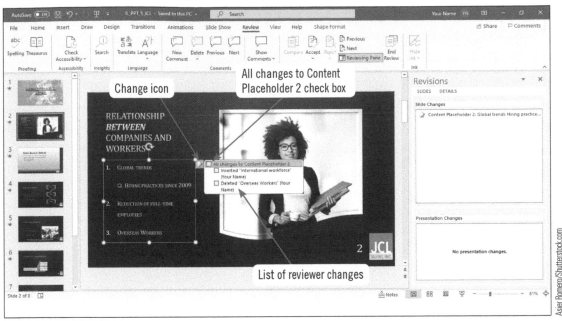

Asier Romero/Shutterstock.com

FIGURE 5-14: Slides tab showing new section

Rawpixel.com/Shutterstock.com

Changing page setup

When you need to customize the size of the slides in your presentation, you can do so using the Slide Size command in the Customize group on the Design tab. Click the Slide Size button to change the slide size to Widescreen (16:9) or Standard (4:3), or click Custom Slide Size to open the Slide Size dialog box. In the Slide Size dialog box, you can change the width and height of the slides to 13 different settings, including On-screen Show, Letter Paper, 35mm Slides, and Banner. You can also set a custom slide size by specifying the height and width of the slides.

Working with Advanced Tools

Insert Zoom Links

Learning
Outcomes
• Insert a Slide
Zoom
• Insert Summary
Zoom

If you want to creatively present information in a non-linear way during a slide show, you can create a Zoom. A **Zoom** is a link that allows you to jump to specific slides or sections during a slide show. Zoom gives you the ability to navigate anywhere in the presentation. You can also create a **Summary Zoom**, which organizes your presentation into sections and adds a new slide to the beginning of the presentation that displays all the sections. Using the Summary Zoom slide during a slide show you can skip around or revisit specific information as you like. **CASE** *In this lesson you create Zoom links to a slide and a section and then create a Summary Zoom, which adds a new section to the presentation.*

STEPS

1. **Click the** Slide 3 thumbnail **in the Slides tab, click the** Insert tab **on the Ribbon, click the** Zoom button **in the Links group, then click** Slide Zoom

   The Insert Slide Zoom dialog box opens with the eight slides in the presentation displayed as thumbnails.

2. **Click the** Slide 8 thumbnail, **then click** Insert

   A Zoom link of Slide 8 appears on the slide as shown in **FIGURE 5-15**. This thumbnail is the link that you click during a slide show to jump to Slide 8.

3. **Drag the** Zoom link **to the lower center of the slide, click the** Zoom tab **on the Ribbon, then click the** Return to Zoom check box **in the Zoom Options group**

   A Zoom link is created between Slides 3 and 8.

4. **Click the** Slide Show button 🖵 **on the status bar, click the** Slide 8 Zoom link, **press** ENTER, **then press** ESC

   The Zoom link jumps you from Slide 3 to Slide 8 and back again.

5. **Click the** Insert tab **on the Ribbon, click the** Zoom button **in the Links group, then click** Summary Zoom

   The Insert Summary Zoom dialog box opens with the Slide 1 thumbnail selected.

6. **Click the** Slide 4 thumbnail, **click the** Slide 7 thumbnail, **then click** Insert

   Each slide thumbnail selected in the Insert Summary Zoom dialog box creates a new section. A new summary slide with each section Zoom link is displayed in the Slide pane. Compare your screen to **FIGURE 5-16**.

7. **Click** 🖵 **on the status bar, click the** Slide 2 Zoom link, **press** ENTER **until the summary slide appears again, then press** ESC

   You viewed the slides in the Intro section and then jumped back to the summary slide.

8. **Click** 🖵 **on the status bar, watch the** Slide 5 and the Slide 8 Zoom links, **then press** ESC **to return to Normal view**

9. **Click the** Intro Collapse Section arrow ◢ **in the Slides tab, right-click** Intro **in the Slides tab, click** Move Section Up, **then click a blank area of the slide**

   The Intro section and associated slides move up above the Summary Section.

10. **sam** ↑ Save your work, submit your presentation to your instructor, then exit **PowerPoint**

FIGURE 5-15: Slide showing new Zoom slide

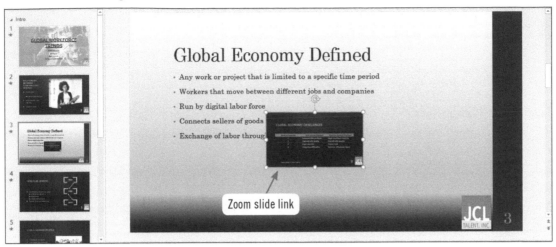

Zoom slide link

FIGURE 5-16: New Summary Section slide

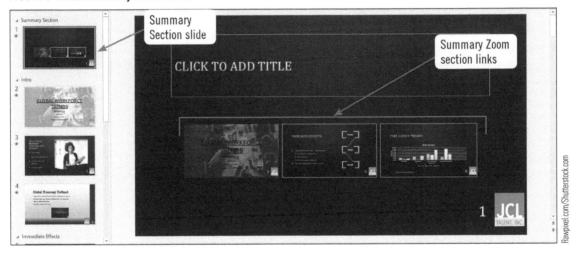

Summary Section slide

Summary Zoom section links

Rawpixel.com/Shutterstock.com

Dictating text on a slide

If you have a microphone and the Dictate feature is available in the Voice group on the Home tab, you can dictate text in text objects. Click in a text object where you want to begin dictating, click the Dictate button in the Voice group, then speak clearly into the microphone. When you are finished speaking, click the Dictate button again to turn off the feature. Using specific words and phrases, such as "comma" or "period," you can add punctuation to your text. Finally, if you want to dictate text in another (supported) language, click the Dictate button arrow, then select a language.

Practice

Skills Review

1. Use advanced formatting tools.

  a. Start PowerPoint and open the presentation IL_PPT_5-2.pptx from the location where you store your Data Files, then save it as **IL_PPT_5_Powell**.

  b. Go to Slide 3, click the Shapes button in the Drawing group, right-click the Connector: Elbow icon in the Lines section, then click Lock Drawing Mode.

  c. Position the pointer over the left connection site on the Plant shape, then drag down to the top connection site on the Distribution Centers shape.

  d. Position the pointer over the right connection site on the Plant shape, drag to the top connection site on the Consumer Sales shape, then press ESC.

  e. Click the orange dotted line, click the Home tab, double-click the Format Painter button in the Clipboard group, click both elbow connector lines, then press ESC.

  f. Double-click the text Plant in the circle shape, click the Shape Format tab, click the Text Effects button in the WordArt Styles group, point to Glow, then click Glow: 18 point; Gold, Accent color 3.

  g. Click the Home tab, double-click the Format Painter button in the Clipboard group, click the text Distribution, Centers, Consumer, and Sales in each of the remaining shapes, then press ESC.

  h. Click a blank area of the slide, then save the presentation.

2. Insert and modify a picture.

  a. Go to Slide 5, click the picture, click the Picture Format tab, click the Picture Border button in the Picture Styles group, then click Orange under Standard Colors.

  b. Click the Picture Border button, point to Weight, then click 4½ pt.

  c. Click the Picture Effects button in the Picture Styles group, point to Shadow, click Perspective: Upper Left under Perspective.

  d. Click the Artistic Effects button in the Adjust group, then click Cement (fourth row).

  e. Click the Color button in the Adjust group, then click Aqua, Accent color 1 Dark under Recolor.

  f. Click the Alt Text button in the Accessibility group, type **Picture of face as digital circuits**, close the Alt Text pane, then save your changes.

3. Adjust and format text objects.

  a. Go to Slide 2, click the View tab, click the Slide Master button in the Master Views group, then click the Headlines Slide Master slide in the Master Thumbnails pane.

  b. Right-click the Second level text, point to the Numbering arrow, then click 1) 2) 3).

  c. Right-click Edit Master text styles, point to the Bullets arrow, then click Bullets and Numbering.

  d. Click Arrow Bullets, click the Size up arrow until 110 appears in the text box, click the Color button, click Aqua, Accent 1 in the Theme Colors section, then click OK.

  e. Right-click Third level, point to the Bullets arrow, click Bullets and Numbering, then click Customize.

  f. Click the Fraction Slash symbol, click OK, then click OK again.

  g. Close Slide Master view, right-click Baltimore, click Paragraph, click the Before down arrow until 0 pt appears, click the After up arrow until 6 pt appears, then click OK.

  h. Click Philadelphia, click the Home tab, click the Line Spacing button in the Paragraph group, then click 1.5.

  i. Save your changes.

Skills Review (continued)

4. Customize animation effects.

   a. Go to Slide 3.

   b. Click the Animations tab, click the Plant shape, click the More button in the Animation group, then click Shape in the Entrance section.

   c. Select the left elbow connector, click the More button in the Animation group, click More Entrance Effects, apply the Strips animation, click OK, then click the Duration up arrow until 1.00 appears.

   d. Click the left elbow arrow connector, click the Animation Painter button, then click the right elbow connector.

   e. Click the Effects Options button, click Right Down, then click the Preview button.

   f. Select the Distribution Centers shape, apply the Shape animation, click the Effect Options button in the Animation group, then click Diamond.

   g. Click the Move Earlier button in the Timing group, then click the Preview button.

   h. Use the Animation Painter to apply the Distribution Centers shape animation to the Consumer Sales shape, then click the Preview button.

   i. Select the dotted line between the Distribution Centers shape and the Consumer Sales shape, click Split in the Animation group, click the Delay button up arrow until 01.00 appears, then click the Duration up arrow until 01.00 appears.

   j. Click the Add Animation button, click Split, change the Effect Options to Vertical Out, click the Preview button, then save your changes.

5. Set advanced animation effects.

   a. Go to Slide 5, click the title text, apply the Swivel animation, then click the Animation Pane button in the Advanced Animation group.

   b. Click the Rectangle 2 animation down arrow in the Animation Pane, click Effect Options, click the After animation arrow, click the far right purple color, then click OK.

   c. Select the picture, click None in Animation group, click the More button in the Animation group, scroll down if necessary, then click Shapes in the Motion Paths section.

   d. Click the Effect Options button in the Animation group, then click Reverse Path Direction under Path.

   e. Click the Content Placeholder animation arrow in the Animation Pane, click Effect Options, click the Sound list arrow, scroll down, click Whoosh, then click OK.

   f. Close the Animation Pane, click the Trigger button in the Advanced Animation group, point to On Click of, then click Text Placeholder 4.

   g. Click the Slide Show button in the status bar, click the text object to trigger the picture animation, click through the title text object animation, then press ESC.

   h. Click a blank area of the slide, then save your changes.

6. Use comments.

   a. Go to Slide 1, click the Review tab, then click the Show Comments button in the Comments group.

   b. Click the Next button in the Comments pane, reply to the comment by typing **We should ask Brian**, click the Next button in the Comments pane until Slide 3 appears, then type **Thank you** in the comment Reply text box.

   c. Click the Previous button in the Comments pane until Slide 2 appears, select the text box with your comment, then type **or Jeri** at the end of your comment in the text box.

   d. Click the New button in the Comments pane, type **Can you check on distribution?**, click the Next button in the Comments group until Slide 4 appears.

   e. Click the Delete button in the Comments group, close the Comments pane, then go to Slide 3.

   f. Click the comment icon, click the Show Comments arrow in the Comments group, click Show Markup, click the Show Comments arrow again, then click Show Markup.

   g. Save your work.

Skills Review (continued)

7. Combine reviewed presentations.

    a. Go to Slide 1, click the Review tab, click the Compare button in the Compare group, navigate to the location where you store your Data Files, click **Support_PPT 5_TechRev.pptx**, then click **Merge**.

    b. Click the Accept arrow in the Compare group, then click Accept All Changes to This Slide.

    c. Click the Reject arrow in the Compare group, click Reject All Changes to This Slide, then click the Next button in the Compare group until Slide 3 appears.

    d. Click the Inserted "Direct" check box on the Consumer Sales shape, then click the Next button in the Compare group, then end the review.

    e. Go to Slide 1, click the Home tab, click the Section button in the Slides group, then click Add Section.

    f. Type **Intro Slide**, click Rename, then save your work.

8. Insert Zoom links.

    a. Go to Slide 2, click the Insert tab, click the Zoom button in the Links group, then click Slide Zoom.

    b. Click the Slide 4 thumbnail, click Insert, click the Zoom tab, then click the Return to Zoom check box in the Zoom Options group.

    c. Drag the Zoom link to the left just under the slide title, click the Slide Show button on the status bar, click the Zoom link, click again, then press ESC.

    d. Click the Insert tab, click the Zoom button in the Links group, then click Summary Zoom.

    e. Click the Slide 2 thumbnail, click the Slide 4 thumbnail, then click Insert.

    f. Scroll down the Slides tab, right-click the Quarterly Sales Report section in the Slides tab, then click Move Section Up.

    g. Go to Slide 1, then click the Slide Show button on the status bar.

    h. Click each section Zoom link, then press ESC when you are finished. Be sure to click through animations in each section Zoom link and the animation trigger on Latest Technology slide.

    i. Click the Intro Slide section Collapse Section arrow in the Slides tab, click the Intro Slide section Expand Section arrow in the Slides tab, then save your work.

    j. Submit your presentation to your instructor, close the presentation, then exit PowerPoint.

Independent Challenge 1

Riverwalk Medical Clinic (RMC), is a large medical facility in Cambridge Massachusetts. You continue to work on a presentation on the latest emergency response procedures for a staff training later in the week.

    a. Open the presentation IL_PPT_5-3.pptx from the location where you store your Data Files, then save it as **IL_PPT_5_RiverwalkMC**.

    b. Go to Slide 3, draw two Connector: Curved Double-Arrows (one between the left and the middle shape and one between the middle and the right shape).

    c. Select the left arrow, click the Shape Format tab, apply the Intense Line - Accent 2 style, then use the Format Painter to apply the new style to the right arrow.

    d. Select the text "CPR" in the left shape, click the Shape Format tab, then apply the text effect Glow: 18 point; Gold, Accent color 1.

    e. Use the Format Painter to apply the text effect in the CPR shape to the text in the other two shapes. (*Hint*: double-click the Format Painter to apply formatting to more than one item.)

    f. Go to Slide 5, apply a 3 pt Gold, Accent 1 picture border to the picture, then apply a Grayscale color to the picture.

    g. Apply the Round bevel picture effect to the picture, then apply the artistic effect Mosaic Bubbles to the picture.

    h. Click the Alt Text button, type **A picture containing a doctor** (some existing text may be present in the Alt Text pane, if so edit the text), then close the Alt Text pane.

    i. Insert three comments on the slides, use the Next and Previous buttons in the Comments group to move between comments, then edit one of your comments.

Independent Challenge 1 (continued)

j. Use the Show Comments button in the Comments group to hide comments and then show comments.

k. Insert a Zoom link on Slide 3 to Slide 7, move the Zoom link to a blank area of the slide, apply the option Return to Zoom to the link, then in Slide Show view watch the link.

l. Go to Slide 1, open the Insert Summary Zoom dialog box, click the Slide 3 thumbnail and the Slide 6 thumbnail, click Insert, then in the Slides tab move the Summary Section up.

m. Rename the Default Section in the Slides tab to Intro Slides, then collapse the Intro Slides section.

n. Save the presentation, then submit your presentation to your instructor.

o. Close the presentation and exit PowerPoint.

Independent Challenge 2

You are an assistant at International Solutions Inc., a company that works with government agencies in countries throughout the world to solve basic infrastructure problems, such as potable drinking water or agriculture production. You continue working on a presentation that you have been developing for an upcoming meeting with a delegation from Uganda.

a. Open the presentation IL_PPT_5-4.pptx from the location where you store your Data Files, then save it as **IL_PPT_5_Solutions**.

b. Open Slide Master view, click the Parcel Slide Master thumbnail, change the bullet in the first-level indent level to an arrow bullet 95% of text size, then change the bullet color to Aqua, Accent 1.

c. Change the second-level bullet to the a. b. c. bullet format, change the third-level bullet to the Double Dagger symbol, then close Slide Master view.

d. Go to Slide 9, press SHIFT, click anywhere in the text object, release SHIFT, click the Home tab, then apply a 2.0 line spacing to the text object.

e. Go to Slide 6, drag to select the four second-level bullet points, right-click the selected text, click Paragraph, then change the paragraph before spacing to 18 pt and the paragraph after spacing to 12 pt.

f. Go to Slide 5, click the Animations tab, remove the animation applied to the SmartArt graphic, then apply the Arcs motion path animation to the graphic.

g. Apply a 01.00 delay to the SmartArt graphic animation, add the Teeter animation as a second animation to the SmartArt graphic, then apply a trigger to the animation using the slide number placeholder.

h. Apply a Fade animation to the title text object, apply a dim after animation effect with a red color, then move the title text object animation so it happens first.

i. Use the Animation Painter to apply the title text object animation to all the slides in the presentation, except Slide 1.

j. Click the Review tab, merge your presentation with the presentation Support_PPT_5_Uganda.pptx, then accept all changes on Slide 2.

k. Use the Next button to move to the next change on Slide 6, accept the change on the slide, reject the change, then end your review.

l. Create one section, rename the new section, save the presentation, then submit your presentation to your instructor.

m. Close the presentation and exit PowerPoint.

Visual Workshop

Create a new presentation with slides that looks like the examples in FIGURE 5-17 and FIGURE 5-18. Locate and insert the picture Support_PPT_5_Office_Group.jpg on Slide 1. Close the Design Ideas pane if it opens. Then format the picture with a Rose, Accent 6, Darker 25% border that is 3 pt wide. Apply the picture effect Glow: 18 point; Rose, Accent color 6 to the picture. Review the Alt text that was applied and make any edits you believe are appropriate. On Slide 2 draw the shapes, format them with the shape style Moderate Effect—Rose, Accent 6, then apply a Tight Reflection: 8 point offset. Between shapes draw connector arrows using the Connector: Elbow Arrow, format them with the Single Arrow—Dark 1 shape style, then change the weight of the arrows to 3 pt. Use the Format Painter to apply the formatting objects. Add your name to the slide footer, then save the presentation as **IL_PPT_5_Process**. Submit your presentation to your instructor, then exit PowerPoint.

FIGURE 5-17

FIGURE 5-18

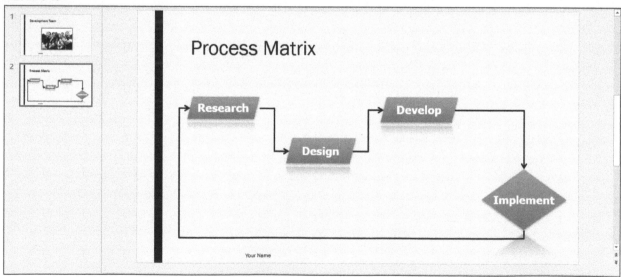

Enhancing Charts and Tables

CASE In this module, you continue to work on the global workforce project presentation for JCL Talent. You will focus on the slides that include charts and tables. You customize the chart layout, format chart elements, and create a custom table. To present the work done by the finance team, you embed an Excel chart, and then you link an Excel worksheet to the presentation so the presentation will always have the most recent data.

Module Objectives

After completing this module, you will be able to:

- Insert text from Microsoft Word
- Change chart design and style
- Customize a chart
- Modify chart elements
- Embed an Excel chart
- Link an Excel worksheet
- Create a custom table
- Modify data in a table
- Add effects to table data

Files You Will Need

IL_PPT_6-1.pptx
Support_PPT_6_Outline.docx
Support_PPT_6_International.xlsx
Support_PPT_6_Account.xlsx
IL_PPT_6-2.pptx
Support_PPT_6_Alpine.docx
Support_PPT_6_Chart.xlsx

Support_PPT_6_Balance.xlsx
IL_PPT_6-3.pptx
Support_PPT_6_EMS.docx
IL_PPT_6-4.pptx
Support_PPT_6_G1.xlsx
Support_PPT_6_G2.xlsx
Support_PPT_6_Trac.xlsx

Insert Text from Microsoft Word

Learning Outcomes
- Create slides using Outline view
- Move and delete slides

It is easy to insert documents saved in Microsoft Word format (.docx), Rich Text Format (.rtf), plain text format (.txt), and HTML format (.htm) into a PowerPoint presentation. If you have an outline saved in a document file, you can import it into PowerPoint to create a new presentation or create additional slides in an existing presentation. When you import a document into a presentation, PowerPoint creates an outline structure based on the styles in the document. For example, a Heading 1 style in the Word document becomes a slide title, and a Heading 2 style becomes the first level of text in a bulleted list. If you insert a plain text format document into a presentation, PowerPoint creates an outline based on the tabs at the beginning of the document's paragraphs. Paragraphs without tabs become slide titles, and paragraphs with one tab indent become first-level text in bulleted lists. **CASE** *You have a Microsoft Word document with information that you want to insert into your presentation.*

STEPS

QUICK TIP
While in Normal view you can click the Normal button in the status bar to display the Notes pane and Outline view.

1. **sam⬇ Start PowerPoint, open the presentation** IL_PPT_6-1.pptx **from the location where you store your Data Files, save it as** IL_PPT_6_JCL, **click the** View tab **on the Ribbon, then click the** Outline View button **in the Presentation Views group**

2. **Click the** Slide 8 icon ▢ **in the Outline pane, click the** Home tab **on the Ribbon, click the** New Slide button arrow **in the Slides group, then click** Slides from Outline
   Slide 8 appears in the Slide pane. The Insert Outline dialog box opens. Before you insert an outline into a presentation, you need to determine where you want the new slides to be placed. You want the text from the Word document inserted as new slides after Slide 8.

3. **Navigate to the location where you store your Data Files, click the Word document file** Support_PPT_6_Outline.docx, **then click** Insert
   Two new slides (9 and 10) are added to the presentation, and the new Slide 9 appears in the Slide pane. Notice, the Notes pane automatically opens by default when you display your presentation in Outline view, as shown in **FIGURE 6-1**. The two new slides retain formatting from the Word document and need to be set to default format settings.

4. **Scroll down the Outline pane until Slide 10 appears, press and hold** SHIFT, **click the** Slide 10 ▢, **release** SHIFT, **then click the** Reset button **in the Slides group**
   The new slides now follow the presentation design and font themes.

5. **In the Outline pane on Slide 9, double-click to the right of the word "agents," press** SPACEBAR, **type** and their expertise, **then drag the** Slide 9 ▢ **above the** Slide 8 ▢
   New text is added to Slide 9. As you drag the slide in the Outline pane, a horizontal line appears to show you the new placement as Slide 9 becomes Slide 8.

6. **Click the** Reading View button 🖼 **on the status bar, click the** Next button ⟩ **on the status bar, then click the** Normal button 🖺 **on the status bar**
   You viewed the slides using Reading view navigating between Slides 8 and 9. Slide 1 appears in the Slide pane.

QUICK TIP
You can also use Slide Sorter view to move slides around in the presentation.

7. **Click the** View tab **on the Ribbon, click the** Normal button **in the Presentation Views group, click the** Notes button **in the Show group, then click the** Home tab **on the Ribbon**
   The Notes button is a toggle to open and close the Notes pane as needed. You return to Slide 1 in Normal view and close the Notes pane.

8. **Click the** Slide 8 thumbnail **in the Slides tab, then click the** Save button 🖫 **on the Quick Access toolbar**
   Compare your screen to **FIGURE 6-2**.

FIGURE 6-1: Outline pane showing imported text

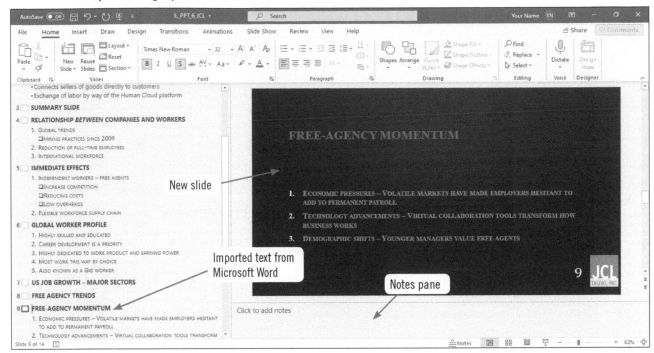

FIGURE 6-2: New slides from outline

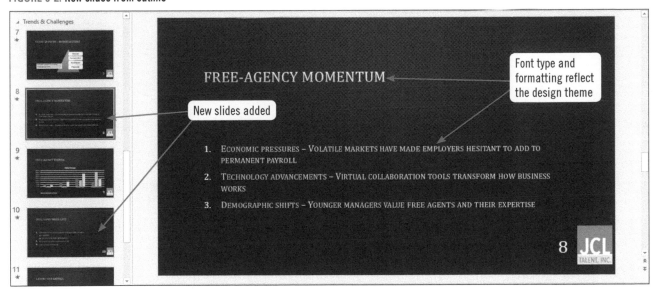

Recording a slide show

With the Record Slide Show feature you have the ability to record and save audio narrations, slide and animation timings, and laser pointer gestures for each slide during a slide show. This feature is great to use if you want to record audience comments so that people who were unable to attend the presentation live can view and listen to it later. To record a slide show, click the Slide Show tab, click the Record Slide Show button arrow in the Set Up group, then start recording from the beginning or the current slide. You then have to choose which elements you want to record during the slide show. If you choose to record audio narrations, you must have a microphone and speakers. A sound icon appears on every narrated slide.

Enhancing Charts and Tables

Change Chart Design and Style

Learning Outcomes
- Modify a chart layout
- Change the chart type

Being able to use Excel to create and modify charts in PowerPoint offers you many advantages, including the ability to use Excel Chart tools to customize chart design, layout, and formatting. After you create a chart, you can immediately alter the way it looks by changing individual chart elements or by applying a predefined chart layout or style. For example, you can select a chart layout that adds a chart title and moves the legend to the bottom of the chart. You can also easily change the color and effects of chart elements by applying one of the styles found in the Chart Styles gallery. **CASE** ▶ *You change the chart layout, style, and type of chart on Slide 9.*

STEPS

1. **Click the** Slide 9 thumbnail **in the Slides tab, click a blank area of the** chart, **then click the** Chart Design tab **on the Ribbon**

   The chart is selected and ready for you to make additional changes.

2. **Click the** Quick Layout button **in the Chart Layouts group, then click** Layout 3 **in the Layout gallery**

   ScreenTips identify each layout. Layout option 3 adds a legend to the bottom of the chart as shown in **FIGURE 6-3**.

QUICK TIP
To add an axis to a chart, click the Add Chart Element button in the Chart Layouts group, point to Axes, then click an option.

3. **Click the** Chart Elements button ▦ **on the slide next to the chart, click the** Axis Titles arrow, **click the** Primary Vertical check box, **click** ▦, **select** Axis Title **on the chart, then type** Percentage Change

   The new axis title helps identify the meaning of the values in the chart.

4. **Click the** Change Chart Type button **in the Type group**

   The Change Chart Type dialog box opens. The current chart is a Clustered Column chart, which is a chart with column data series markers.

5. **Click** Line **in the left pane, make sure that** Line **is selected at the top of the dialog box, then click** OK

   All of the data series markers are now lines.

6. **Click the** Chart Styles button ✑ **next to the chart, scroll down the Chart Style gallery, then click** Style 4

   The Style 4 option changes the weight of the data series markers, adds tick marks to the horizontal axis, and enlarges the chart title.

QUICK TIP
You can also click the Change Colors button in the Chart Styles group to change the chart colors.

7. **Click** Color **at the top of the Chart Style gallery, click** Colorful Palette 4 **in the Colorful section, then click** ✑

   The line colors change to reflect the new color scheme.

8. **Press and hold** SHIFT, **click the** bottom-left sizing handle, **drag down and to the left as shown in** FIGURE 6-4, **release the mouse, then release** SHIFT

   The chart is resized proportionally.

9. **Click a blank area of the slide, then save your presentation**

FIGURE 6-3: **New layout applied to the chart**

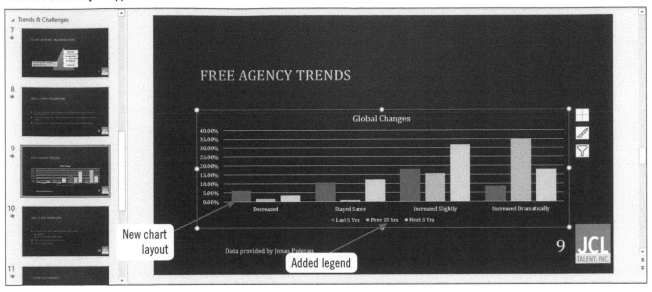

FIGURE 6-4: **Resizing the chart**

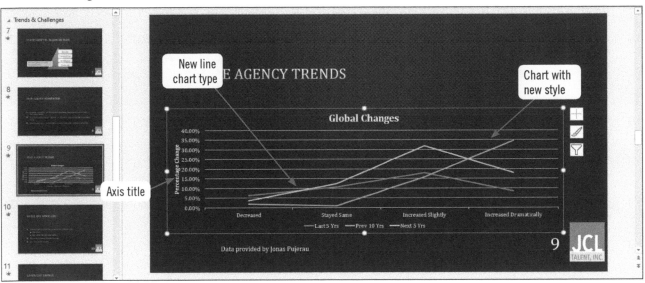

Using AutoFit Options to divide and fit body text

If the AutoFit Options button ⊞ appears while you are entering text in a body text object on a slide with either the Title and Content or the Content with Caption layout, you can click the button and choose from one of three options for dividing up the text in the object. The first option is to split text between two slides. If you choose this option, PowerPoint creates a second slide with the same title and then automatically divides the text between the two slides. The second option is to continue the text on a new slide. Here again, PowerPoint creates a second slide with the same title, but instead of splitting the text between the slides, you are given a blank body text object on the new slide to insert more text. The final option on the AutoFit Options button for splitting text in a body text object is to change the body text object from one column to two columns.

Customize a Chart

One of the many advantages of creating charts in PowerPoint is the ability you have to customize chart elements, such as labels, axes, gridlines, and the chart background. For example, you can change the plot area color so the data markers are distinctly set off, or you can add gridlines to a chart. Gridlines help make the data easier to read in the chart and extend from the horizontal axis or the vertical axis across the plot area. There are two types of gridlines: major gridlines and minor gridlines. **Major gridlines** identify major units on the axis and are usually identified by a tick mark. **Tick marks** are small lines of measurement that intersect an axis and identify the categories, values, or series in a chart. **Minor gridlines** identify minor units on the axis and can also be identified by a tick mark. **CASE** ▷ *You decide to improve the appearance of the chart on Slide 14 by customizing some elements of the chart.*

STEPS

1. **Click the** Slide 14 thumbnail **in the Slides tab, click a blank area above any column in the chart, click the** Chart Design tab **on the Ribbon, click the** Add Chart Element button **in the Chart Layouts group, then point to** Gridlines

   The Gridlines gallery opens. Notice that Primary Major Horizontal is already selected indicating the chart already has major gridlines on the horizontal axis.

2. **Move** ⌖ **over each gridline option to see how the gridlines change on the chart, then click** Primary Major Vertical

   Major vertical gridlines appear on the chart, as shown in **FIGURE 6-5**.

3. **Click the** Add Chart Element button, **point to** Data Table, **move** ⌖ **over each data table option to see how the chart changes, then click** No Legend Keys

   You like seeing the data displayed in the chart because it helps define the data markers.

4. **Click the** Chart Elements button ▦ , **then click the** Data Labels check box

   Data labels, the actual value for each data series marker, appear just above each data marker. You like the data labels, but you want to move them to the inside of the data markers.

5. **Click the** Data Labels arrow, **click** Center, **then click** ▦

   The data labels are placed to the inside center of each of the data series markers.

6. **Right-click** 25% **on the vertical axis, click** Format Axis, **click** Tick Marks **in the Format Axis pane, then scroll down**

   The Format Axis pane opens with options for changing the axes, tick marks, labels, and numbers.

7. **In the Tick Marks section, click the** Major type arrow, **click** Cross, **click the** Fill & Line icon ◇ **at the top of the pane, click** Line, **click the** Color button arrow ▨▾ , **click** Red **under Standard Colors, then close the Format Axis pane**

   The tick marks on the chart's vertical axis change to red and are easier to see.

8. **Click** ▦ , **click the** Trendline arrow, **click** More Options, **then click** OK **in the Add Trendline dialog box to add a Trendline based on the United States**

   The Format Trendline pane opens.

9. **Click** ◇ , **click the** Width up arrow **until** 3 pt **appears, click** ▨▾ , **click** Red, **close the Format Trendline pane, click a blank area of the slide, then save your presentation**

   Compare your screen to **FIGURE 6-6**.

FIGURE 6-5: Major vertical gridlines applied to the chart

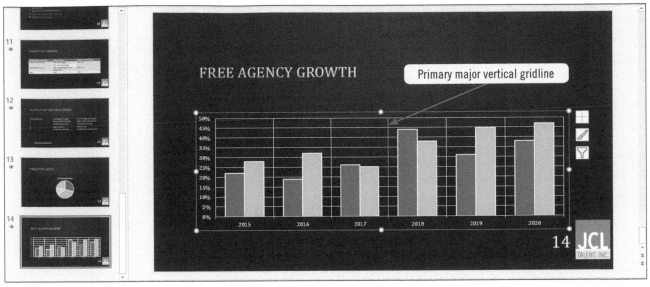

FIGURE 6-6: Chart with additional formatted elements

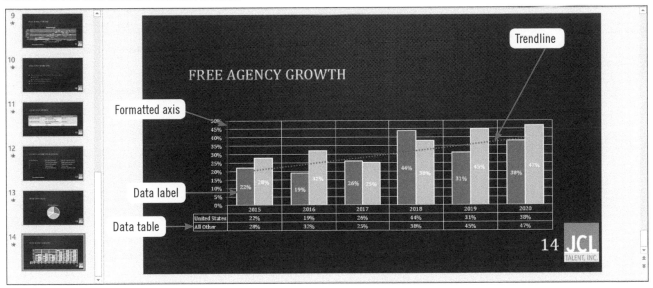

Using the Search pane

Sometimes when you are developing a presentation, you need help formulating your ideas or researching a particular subject. Using the Search pane, you can find information on a selected word or phrase, such as definitions, web articles, images, and other related information. To open and use the Search pane, click the Search button in the Insights group on the Review tab, type a word or phrase in the Search pane text box, then press ENTER. To see more information from a particular online source, click the More button in the Search pane, then select one of the options. The information that appears in the Search pane is generated by the Microsoft Bing search engine.

Enhancing Charts and Tables

Modify Chart Elements

Learning
Outcomes
• Change data series
  color
• Explode pie chart
• Add a legend to a
  chart

Quick Styles in PowerPoint provide you with a number of choices to modify all the elements in a chart at one time. Even with all the Quick Style choices, you still may want to format individual elements to make the chart easy to read and understand. **CASE** ▶ *You make modifications to the chart on Slide 13.*

STEPS

QUICK TIP
You can also click
the Chart Elements
arrow in the Current
Selection group on
the Format tab to
select any of the
chart elements.

1. **Click the** Slide 13 thumbnail **in the Slides tab, click the chart to select it, click the** dark gray pie data series marker **twice, right-click the** dark gray data marker, **click the** Fill button **on the Mini toolbar, then click** Orange, Accent 6

   The data series marker now has an orange fill color.

2. **Right-click the** orange data marker, **then click** Format Data Point **on the Shortcut menu**

   The Format Data Point pane opens. Using this pane you can format an individual data point.

3. **Click the** Point Explosion up arrow **until** 40% **appears, click the** Angle of first slice up arrow **until** 50° **appears, then close the Format Data Point pane**

   The orange pie wedge explodes away from the pie chart and the chart is rotated to the right 50 degrees, as shown in **FIGURE 6-7**.

4. **Click a blank area of the chart, click the** Format tab **on the Ribbon, click the** Shape Fill button **in the Shape Styles group, point to** Texture, **then click** Walnut (6th row)

   A texture effect is added to the chart background.

5. **Click the** Chart Elements button ▦, **click the** Chart Title check box, **then type** JCL Sales by Division

   A title is added to the top of the chart.

6. **Click the** Shape Outline button **in the Shape Styles group, click** Gold, Accent 4, **then click a blank area of the chart**

   The chart title now has a gold border.

7. **Click** ▦, **click the** Legend arrow, **click** Left, **then click** ▦

   A legend appears on the left side of the chart.

8. **Click the** Chart Design tab **on the Ribbon, click the** Edit Data button **in the Data group, click** cell B2, **type** 7.4, **press** ENTER, **then close the Excel worksheet**

   The National data value in the chart is changed.

9. **Click a blank area of the slide, then save the presentation**

   Compare your screen to **FIGURE 6-8**.

FIGURE 6-7: **Pie chart with exploded wedge**

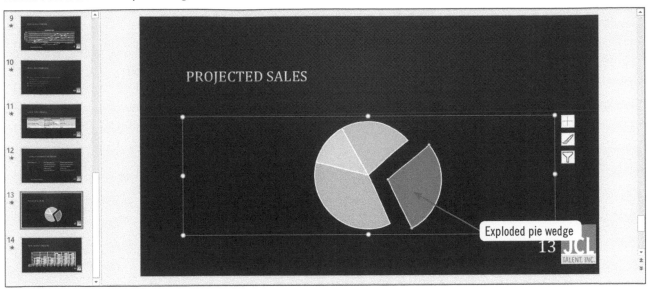

FIGURE 6-8: **Completed chart**

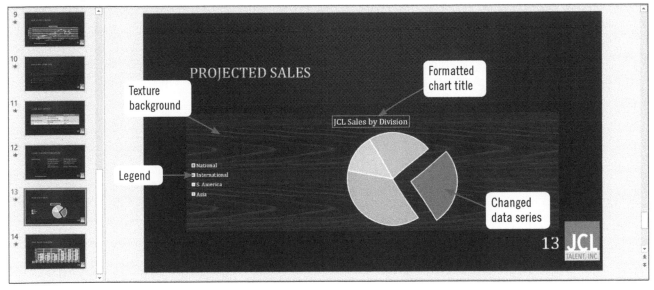

Changing PowerPoint options

You can customize your installation of PowerPoint by changing various settings and preferences. To change PowerPoint settings, click the File tab on the Ribbon, then click Options to open the PowerPoint Options dialog box. The sections in the left pane offer you ways to customize PowerPoint. For example, the General area includes options for viewing the Mini Toolbar, enabling Live Preview, and personalizing your copy of Office. You can also set Language options for editing and proofing as well as which language appears on buttons and ScreenTips.

Embed an Excel Chart

Learning Outcomes
• Insert an Excel chart
• Modify an Excel chart

When a chart is the best way to present information on a slide, you can either create one within PowerPoint or you can embed an existing Excel chart directly to the slide. When you use another program to create an object, the program, Excel in this case, is known as the **source program**. The object you create with the source program is saved to a file called the **source file**. When you embed a chart into a presentation, the presentation file in which the chart is embedded becomes the **destination file**. **CASE** *You want to include last year's sales numbers in your presentation, so you embed an Excel chart in a new slide.*

STEPS

QUICK TIP
You can also press CTRL+D to duplicate a slide in the Slides tab.

1. **Click the** Home tab **on the Ribbon, click the** New Slide arrow **in the Slides group, then click the** Title Only layout
   A new slide with the Title Only layout is added to the presentation as Slide 14.

2. **Click the** slide title placeholder, **type** International, **click the** Insert tab **on the Ribbon, then click the** Object button ⊡ **in the Text group**
   The Insert Object dialog box opens. Using this dialog box, you can create a new chart or locate an existing one to insert on a slide.

QUICK TIP
Another way to embed a chart is to open the chart in Excel, copy it, then paste it into your slide.

3. **Click the** Create from file option button, **click** Browse, **navigate to the location where you store your Data Files, click the file** Support_PPT_6_International.xlsx, **click** OK, **then click** OK **in the Insert Object dialog box**
   The chart from the Excel data file containing sales figures is embedded in the slide. You can open the chart and use the commands in Excel to make any changes to it.

4. **Drag the chart's** lower-left sizing handle **down and to the left to enlarge the chart, then using Smart Guides drag the** chart **to the middle of the blank area of the slide**
   The chart is now easier to read and is centered on the slide.

5. **Double-click the** chart **to open it in Excel**
   The chart appears inside an Excel worksheet on the slide of the open PowerPoint presentation. Both PowerPoint and Excel are open together, and Excel commands and tabs appear on the Ribbon under the PowerPoint title bar, as shown in **FIGURE 6-9**.

6. **Click the** Sheet 1 tab **at the bottom of the Excel worksheet to view the chart data, click cell** C6, **type** 45,660, **press** ENTER, **then click the** Sheet 2 tab
   The changed value is reflected for the Quarter 2 India data series in the chart.

QUICK TIP
If the chart you want to embed is in another presentation, open both presentations, then copy and paste the chart from one presentation to the other.

7. **Click the** chart **in Excel, click the** Chart Design tab **on the Excel Ribbon, click the** More button ⊡ **in the Chart Styles group, then click** Style 9 **(bottom row)**
   The chart style changes with new data marker effects.

8. **Right-click the** Vertical (Value) Axis, **click** Font **on the shortcut menu, click the** Font style arrow, **click** Bold, **click** OK, **click the** Horizontal (Category) Axis, **then press** F4
   Pressing F4 repeats the last formatting action. Both the value and category axes labels are bold and now easier to read.

9. **Right-click the** legend, **click** Format Legend **on the shortcut menu, click the** Top option button, **then click** OK
   The legend moves to the top of the chart.

10. **Click outside the chart to exit Excel, click a blank area of the slide, then save the presentation**
    Compare your screen to **FIGURE 6-10**.

FIGURE 6-9: Embedded Excel chart

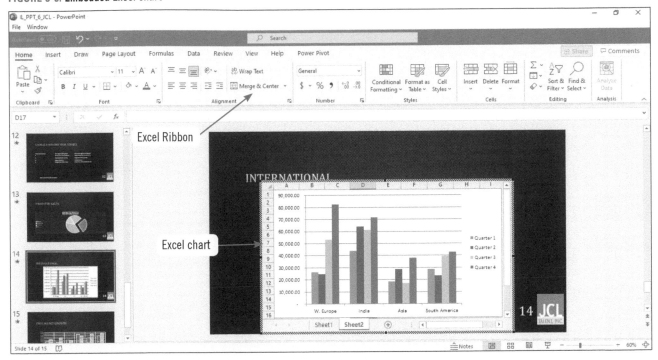

FIGURE 6-10: Formatted Excel chart

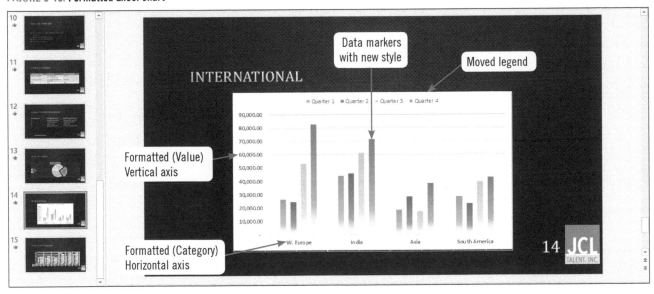

Embedding a worksheet

You can embed all or part of an Excel worksheet in a PowerPoint slide. To embed an entire worksheet, go to the slide where you want to place the worksheet. Click the Insert tab on the Ribbon, then click the Object button in the Text group. The Insert Object dialog box opens. Click the Create from file option button, click Browse, locate and double-click the worksheet filename, then click OK. The worksheet is embedded in the slide. Double-click it to edit it using Excel commands as needed to work with the worksheet. To insert only a portion of a worksheet, open the Excel workbook and copy the cells you want to include in your presentation.

PowerPoint

Link an Excel Worksheet

Learning Outcomes
• Link an Excel worksheet
• Format a linked worksheet

Another way to insert objects to your presentation is to establish a **link**, or connection, between the source file and the destination file. Unlike embedded objects, a linked object is stored in its source file, not on the slide or in the presentation file. So when you link an object to a PowerPoint slide, a representation (picture) of the object, not the object itself, appears on the slide. Any changes made to the source file of a linked object are automatically reflected in the linked representation in your PowerPoint presentation. Use linking when you want to be sure your presentation contains the latest information and when you want to include an object, such as an accounting spreadsheet, that may change over time. **CASE** *You link and format an Excel worksheet to the presentation.*

STEPS

QUICK TIP
If you plan to do the steps in this lesson again, make a copy of the Excel file Support_PPT_6_Account.xlsx to keep the original data intact.

1. **Right-click the** Slide 14 thumbnail **in the Slides tab, click** Duplicate Slide **on the shortcut menu, click the** chart **on the slide, then press** DELETE

   A new slide, Slide 15, is created and the duplicated chart is deleted.

2. **Click the** Insert tab **on the Ribbon, then click the** Object button 🔲 **in the Text group**

   The Insert Object dialog box opens.

3. **Click the** Create from file option button, **click** Browse, **navigate to the location where you store your Data Files, click the file** Support_PPT_6_Account.xlsx, **click** OK, **click the** Link check box, **then click** OK

   The Excel worksheet appears on the slide. The worksheet would be easier to read if it were larger and had a background fill color.

QUICK TIP
To edit or open a linked object in your presentation, the object's source program and source file must be available on your computer or network.

4. **Drag the** lower-left sizing handle **down and to the left, right-click the** worksheet, **then click** Format Object **on the shortcut menu**

   The Format Object pane opens.

5. **Click the** Fill & Line button 🖾, **click the** Gradient fill option button, **then close the Format Object pane**

   A gradient fill background color is applied to the worksheet as shown in **FIGURE 6-11**.

6. **Right-click the** Excel worksheet, **point to** Linked Worksheet Object, **then click** Edit

   The linked worksheet opens in an Excel window.

QUICK TIP
If the presentation is closed when you update a linked object, a security dialog box will open when you open your presentation again; click Update Links to update the linked object.

7. **Drag the edge of the** Excel window **to see all the data if necessary, click cell** B6, **type** 99,897.66, **click cell** D11, **type** 180,453.83, **then press** ENTER

   The Fiscal Yr. 2020 Quarter 1 value for South America and the Fiscal Yr. 2021 Quarter 3 value for W. Europe change. All totals that include these values in the Total cells are updated accordingly.

8. **Click the** Excel window Close button ⊠, **click** Save **to save your changes, click a blank area of the slide, then save your presentation**

   The Excel window closes. The Excel worksheet on Slide 15 is now updated with the new data. PowerPoint automatically makes all of the changes to the linked object. Compare your screen to **FIGURE 6-12**.

FIGURE 6-11: Linked Excel worksheet

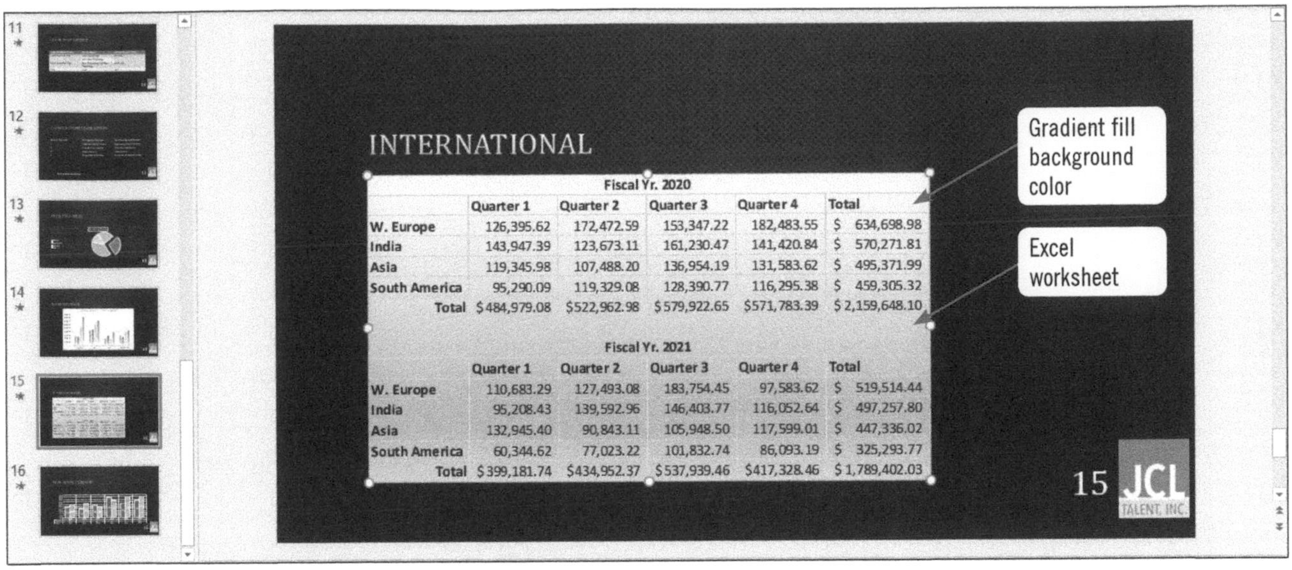

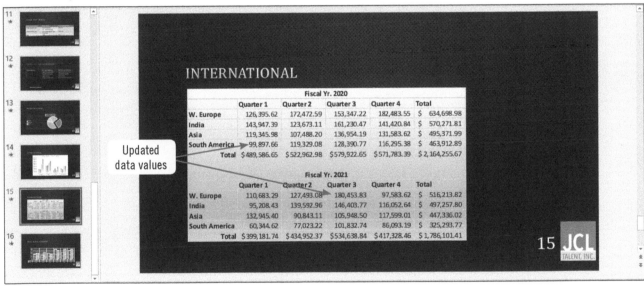

FIGURE 6-12: Updated linked worksheet

Editing links

Once you link an object to your presentation, you have the ability to edit its link. Using the Links dialog box, you can update a link, open or change a linked object's source file, break a link, and determine if a linked object is updated manually or automatically. The Links dialog box is the only place where you can change a linked object's source file, break a link, and change the link updating method. To open the Links dialog box, click the File tab on the Ribbon, click Info, then click Edit Links to Files button under Related Documents in the Info pane.

PowerPoint

Create a Custom Table

Learning Outcomes
- Add a table border
- Format a table border
- Resize a table

Tables provide a way to organize information for your audience. In PowerPoint, you have the ability to create vibrant tables. Tables you create in PowerPoint automatically display the style as determined by the theme assigned to the slide, including color combinations and shading, line styles and colors, and other effects. It is easy to customize the table border style, color, weight, and alignment of cells in a table.
CASE ➤ *You format a table on Slide 12 by adding color to the table cells and then you add a table border and format it.*

STEPS

1. **Click the** Slide 12 thumbnail **in the Slides tab, click the** table, **press and hold** SHIFT, **then drag the** bottom-right sizing handle **down to the right to enlarge the table**
   The table is resized proportionally.

QUICK TIP
To erase a cell border, click the Eraser button in the Draw Borders group, then click a table cell border.

2. **Click any** cell, **click the** Layout tab **on the Ribbon, click the** Select button **in the Table group, click** Select Table, **then click the** Table Design tab **on the Ribbon**
   The table object is selected.

3. **Click the** Borders button arrow **in the Table Styles group, then click** All Borders
   A border appears around the outside of the table and around all cells.

4. **Click the** Shading button **in the Table Styles group, then click** Orange, Accent 6, Darker 25%
   All the table cells have an orange background fill as shown in **FIGURE 6-13**.

QUICK TIP
You can also draw a custom table. Click the Draw Table button, then in a blank area of the slide, draw a box. Draw cell borders within the box.

5. **Click the** Pen Style button **in the Draw Borders group, click the** dot style (3rd style), **click the** Pen Weight button **in the Draw Borders group, click** 3 pt, **click the** Pen Color button **in the Draw Borders group, then click** Yellow **in the Standard Colors section**
   The pointer changes to 🖊, which indicates that you are in drawing mode.

6. **Click the** white vertical column line **in the first row that divides the Rank of Concerns and the Free Agency Employer columns, then click the** vertical column line **for each row in that column**
   A yellow dotted column line separates the first two columns.

7. **Click the** white horizontal row line **just below the Rank of Concerns row, then click the** horizontal row line **for each column in that row**
   A yellow dotted row line separates the first two rows.

8. **Click the** Draw Table button **in the Draw Borders group, click outside the table, then save your presentation**
   Compare your screen to **FIGURE 6-14**.

FIGURE 6-13: Formatted table

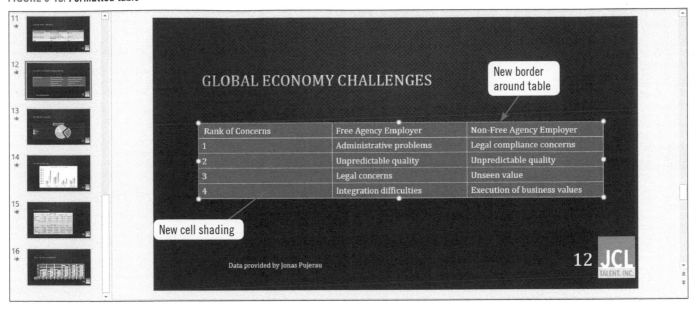

FIGURE 6-14: Table with formatted table borders

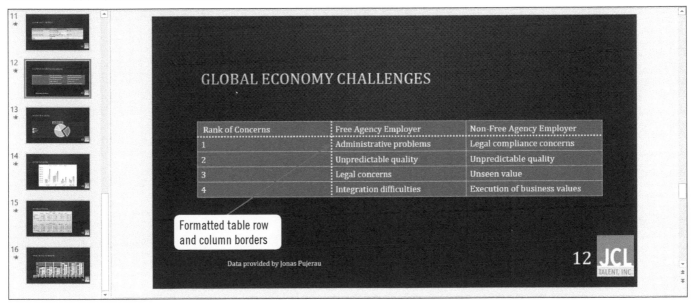

Resizing table rows and columns

Rows and columns in a table can be resized to approximate dimensions based on how the data is displayed in the table. To resize a row or column this way, select the row or column, then drag the row or column border to the desired position. If you want an exact row or column dimension, select the row or column, then adjust the row or column value in the Height or Width text boxes in the Cell Size group on the Layout tab.

Modify Data in a Table

Once you have data entered in a table, you can modify it to emphasize certain data or organize differently to help your audience understand the information. It is easy to customize the layout of a table or change how data is organized. You can delete and insert rows or columns, merge two or more cells together, or split one cell into more cells. **CASE** ➤ *You have worked on the table on Slide 11 and now it needs to be customized.*

STEPS

1. **Click the** Slide 11 thumbnail **in the Slides tab, then click the** Total cell **in the table**
   Slide 11 appears in the Slide pane with the insertion point in the Total cell.

2. **Click the** Layout tab **on the Ribbon, click the** Select button **in the Table group, click** Select Row, **then click the** Table Design tab **on the Ribbon**
   The last row is selected.

3. **Click the** Total Row check box **in the Table Style Options group, click the** Shading button **in the Table Styles group, click** Orange, Accent 5, **then click the** Total cell
   Clicking the Total Row check box applies special formatting to the bottom row. Compare your screen to **FIGURE 6-15**.

> **QUICK TIP**
> To change the text direction in a text box or a table, select the text, click the Text Direction button in the Alignment group, then click the appropriate option.

4. **Click the** Layout tab **on the Ribbon, click the** Align button **in the Arrange group, then click** Align Middle
   The table moves up to the center of the slide aligned relative to the slide edge.

5. **Click the** Select button **in the Table group, click** Select Table, **then click the** Center button ☰ **in the Alignment group**
   The data in the table is centered in the table cells.

6. **Click the** 194 - Technology cell, **then click the** Split Cells button **in the Merge group**
   The Split Cells dialog box opens. The default setting is 2 columns and 1 row.

> **QUICK TIP**
> To distribute the height of selected rows equally between them, click the Distribute Rows button in the Cell Size group.

7. **Click the** Number of columns down arrow **once, click the** Number of rows up arrow **once, then click** OK
   You split the cell to create a new row in that cell.

8. **Drag to select** 351 - Non-Technology, **right-click the** selected text, **click** Cut **on the shortcut menu, right-click the** new row, **click the** Keep Source Formatting Paste Options button 📝 **on the shortcut menu, then press** BACKSPACE
   The text 351 - Non-Technology is in a separate row. See **TABLE 6-1** for Paste button options.

9. **In the last column drag to select the** 1832 cell **and the bottom** All cell, **then click the** Merge Cells button **in the Merge group**
   The two cells are merged together into one as shown in **FIGURE 6-16**.

10. **Click outside the table, then save your presentation**

FIGURE 6-15: Table with formatted total row

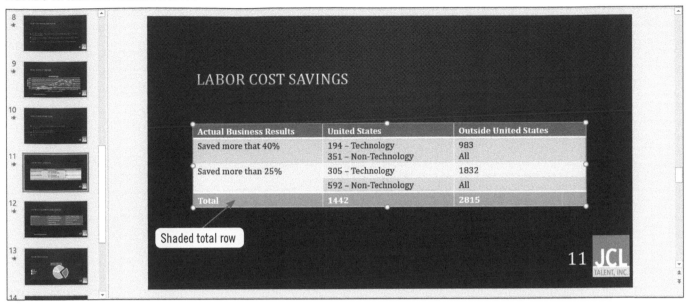

FIGURE 6-16: Modified table

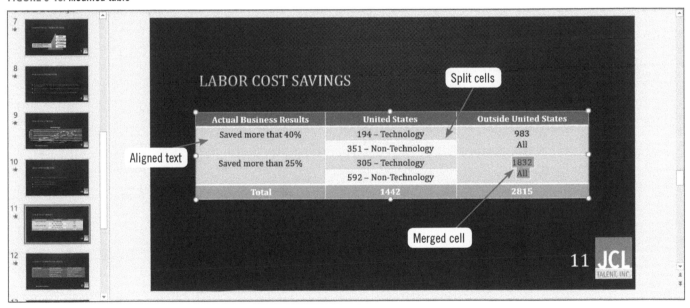

TABLE 6-1: Understanding common Paste button options

button	button name	result
	Use Destination Theme	Use the current theme of the presentation
	Keep Source Formatting	Use the formatting characteristics from the object's source file
	Picture	Insert the object as a picture
	Keep Text Only	Insert the object as text only with no formatting
	Embed	Insert the object as an embedded object

Add Effects to Table Data

Learning
Outcomes
• Apply effects to a
  table
• Change margin
  spacing

PowerPoint has a number of formatting effects that you can apply to the cells of a table. Effects, such as, reflections and shadows allow you to create dynamic tables that have a unique appearance. You also have the ability to modify the space between table cells by changing cell margins. Cell margin refers to the space between cell text and the cell border. **CASE** *Modify the table on Slide 12 by adding effects and changing cell margins. You also review when it's better to link an object and when it's better to embed. See* TABLE 6-2 *for suggestions on when to embed an object and when to link an object.*

STEPS

1. **Click the** Slide 12 thumbnail **in the Slides tab, then click anywhere in the** table
   Slide 12 appears in the Slide pane with the table selected.

2. **Click the** Layout tab **on the Ribbon, click the** Select button **in the Table group, click** Select Table, **then click the** Table Design tab **on the Ribbon**

3. **Click the** Effects button **in the Table Styles group, point to** Cell Bevel, **then click** Round
   The round bevel effect is applied to all of the cells and the yellow dotted border lines that were present are removed as shown in **FIGURE 6-17**.

4. **Click the** Layout tab **on the Ribbon, then click the** Cell Margins button **in the Alignment group**
   A list of cell margin options opens.

5. **Click** Wide, **click the** Table Design tab **on the Ribbon, click the** Effects button **in the Table Styles group, then point to** Shadow
   The Shadow effects menu opens.

6. **Click** Offset: Bottom **(top row)**
   Because of the slide background color, the shadow effect is not visible, so you decide to apply a different effect.

7. **Click the** Effects button, **point to** Reflection, **then click** Tight Reflection: Touching **(top row)**
   A reflection effects appears below the table.

8. **Click the** Shading button **in the Table Styles group, then click** Gold, Accent 4 **(top row)**
   The table is easier to read now as shown in **FIGURE 6-18**.

9. **sam↑ Click outside the table, save your presentation, submit your presentation to your instructor, then exit PowerPoint**

QUICK TIP

If you want to customize cell margins, click Custom Margins at the bottom of the Cell Margins menu to open the Cell Text Layout dialog box. Specify custom text layout and internal margin options in this dialog box.

QUICK TIP

You can also fill a cell background with a picture or symbol. Select the cell, click the Shading button in the Table Styles group, then locate and insert a picture. Choose a picture from the Insert Pictures dialog box, then click Insert.

FIGURE 6-17: Table with bevel effect applied to cells

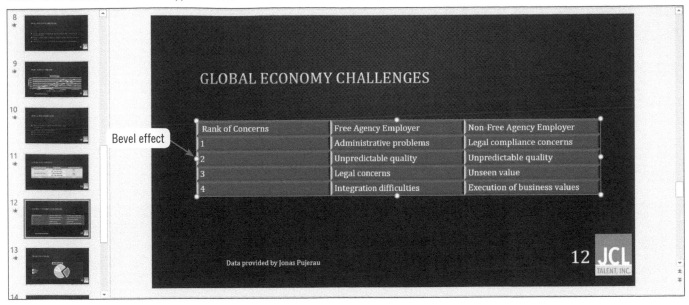

FIGURE 6-18: Table with distributed cells

TABLE 6-2: Embedding vs. linking

situation	action
When you are the only user of an object and you want the object to be a part of your presentation	Embed
When you want to access the object in its source program, even if the original file is not available	Embed
When you want to update the object manually while working in PowerPoint	Embed
When you always want the latest information in your object	Link
When the object's source file is shared on a network for other users to access and change	Link
When you want to keep your presentation file size small	Link

Practice

Skills Review

1. Insert text from Microsoft Word.

   a. Open IL_PPT_6-2.pptx from the location where you store your Data Files, save it as **IL_PPT_6_Alpine**, then open Outline view. You will work to create the completed presentation as shown in **FIGURE 6-19**.

FIGURE 6-19

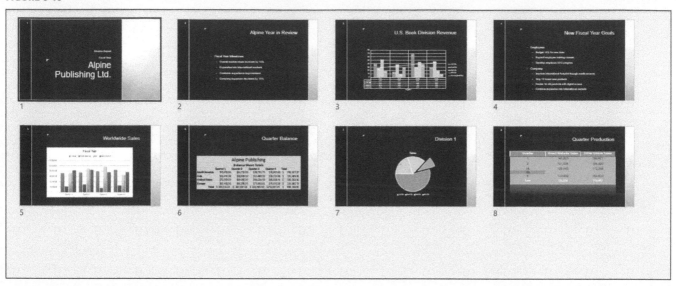

   b. Click the Slide 2 icon in the Outline pane, then use the Slides from Outline command to insert the file Support_PPT_6_Alpine.docx from the location where you store your Data Files.

   c. In the Outline pane on Slide 4 click after the word "access," then press ENTER to add a 4th bullet under the Company heading.

   d. Type **Continue expansion into international markets**, press and hold SHIFT, click the Slide 3 icon in the Outline pane, then release SHIFT.

   e. On the Home tab, click the Reset button in the Slides group, click the Layout button in the Slides group, then click Title and Content.

   f. In the Outline pane, drag Slide 3 above Slide 2, then click the Slide 4 icon in the Outline pane.

   g. Open Reading view, click the Next button until you return to Outline view, then click the Normal button in the status bar.

2. Change chart design and style.

   a. Go to Slide 3, select the chart, then click the Chart Design tab.

   b. Change the chart layout to Layout 10, then resize the chart proportionally smaller so the legend fits on the black background.

   c. Change the chart type to Clustered Column, then add an axis title on the horizontal axis.

   d. Type **Regions**, then change the chart color to Colorful Palette 1.

   e. Click a blank area of the chart, then save your changes.

Skills Review (continued)

3. Customize a chart.

   a. Select the chart on Slide 3, then click the Chart Design tab.

   b. Click the Add Chart Element button in the Chart Layouts group, then add Primary Major Vertical gridlines to the chart.

   c. Click the Add Chart Element button in the Chart Layouts group, then add a data table with legend keys to the chart.

   d. Click the Chart Elements button next to the chart, then add data labels to the inside end of the data series markers.

   e. Add a linear trendline based on the 2nd quarter, then close the Chart Elements menu.

   f. Select the vertical axis, click the Format tab, click the Shape Outline button in the Shape Styles group, change the axis color to yellow, then change the axis weight to 2 1/4 pt.

   g. Click a blank area of the slide, then save your work.

4. Modify chart elements.

   a. Go to Slide 6, select the chart, click the 4th Qtr pie wedge (*Hint*: use ScreenTips to identify each wedge), right-click the pie wedge, then click Format Data Point.

   b. Change the angle of the first slice to 75 degrees, change the point explosion of the pie wedge to 35%, then close the Format Data Point pane.

   c. Click the Shape Fill button in the Shape Styles group, then change the pie wedge color to green.

   d. Click the Shape Outline button in the Shape Styles group, then add a 3 pt yellow border to the pie wedge.

   e. Add a legend to the bottom of the chart, add a chart title to the top of the chart, then, if necessary, type **Sales** in the chart title object.

   f. Click a blank area of the slide, then save your changes.

5. Embed an Excel chart.

   a. Go to Slide 5, click the Insert tab, then click the Object button in the Text group.

   b. Click the Create from file option button, click Browse, then locate and embed the file Support_PPT_6_Chart.xlsx from the location where you store your Data Files.

   c. Drag the lower-right sizing handle to increase the size of the chart so it fills most of the blank space between the title and the bottom of the slide and then center on the slide.

   d. Double-click the chart, click the Sheet1 tab in the worksheet that opens, change the value in cell D8 to **74820.33**, change the value in cell B6 to **21,473.53**, then click the Sheet2 tab. (*Note*: The hashtags indicate that the column isn't wide enough to display the full values in the cells, it won't affect your chart.)

   e. Right-click the legend, click Format Legend in the shortcut menu, click Top, then click OK.

   f. Click a blank area of the slide, then save your changes.

6. Link an Excel worksheet.

   a. Insert a new slide after Slide 5 with the Title Only layout.

   b. Type **Quarter Balance**, click the Insert tab, then click the Object button in the Text group.

   c. Click the Create from file option button, click Browse, locate the file Support_PPT_6_Balance.xlsx from the location where you store your Data Files, then link it to the slide. (*Hint*: Make a copy of the Excel file Support_PPT_6_Balance.xlsx to keep the original data intact.)

   d. Resize the worksheet object to fit in the blank area of the slide by dragging its sizing handles, then center-align it in the blank area of the slide.

   e. Right-click the worksheet, click Format Object, click the Solid fill option button, click the Color arrow, then click Gold, Accent 2.

   f. Close the Format Object pane, then double-click the worksheet.

   g. Drag to select cells B4 to E7, click the Number Format list arrow in the Number group, then click Currency.

   h. Click cell B6, type **75003.07**, click cell E5, type **31742.93**, then press ENTER.

   i. Close the Excel window, then click Save to save your changes to the Excel worksheet. The changes appear in the linked worksheet on the slide.

Skills Review (continued)

7. Create a custom table.

   a. Go to Slide 8, click in the table, then click the Table Design tab.

   b. Right-click the table, click Select Table in the shortcut menu, click the Borders button arrow in the Table Styles group, then add outside borders to the table.

   c. Click the Shading button in the Table Styles group, then change the color of the cells to Blue, Accent 4.

   d. Click the Pen Weight arrow in the Draw Borders group, click 3 pt, click the Pen Color button, click Red under Standard Colors, click the Pen Style arrow, then click the 4th option in the list.

   e. Click the bottom border of each cell in the first row, then click the Draw Table button in the Draw Borders group.

   f. Press and hold SHIFT, then drag the bottom-left sizing handle down to increase the size of the table so it touches the white vertical line.

   g. Click a blank area of the slide, then save your changes.

8. Modify data in a table.

   a. Click in the table, click the Table Design tab, then add a total row to the table.

   b. Right-click the table, click Select Table in the shortcut menu, click the Layout tab, then align the table cells to the center.

   c. Click the Distribute Columns button in the Cell Size group, click the Align button in the Arrange group, then align the table to the middle of the slide.

   d. Click the 3A cell, split the cell into 1 column and 2 rows, then type **3B** in the new cell.

   e. Click a blank area of the slide, then save your changes.

9. Add effects to table data.

   a. Select the first row in the table, click the Table Design tab, then apply the Round bevel effect.

   b. Click the 3B cell, then apply an Orange, Accent 1 shading to the cell.

   c. Apply the Inside Center shadow and the Tight Reflection: Touching effects to the table.

   d. Right-click the table, click Select Table in the shortcut menu, then change the cell margins to None.

   e. Save your work, submit your presentation to your instructor, close the presentation, and exit PowerPoint.

Independent Challenge 1

Riverwalk Medical Clinic (RMC), is a large medical facility in Cambridge Massachusetts. You have been asked by your supervisor to create a presentation on the Riverwalk Clinic EMS system. You have been working on the presentation and now you insert text from Microsoft Word and format charts to enhance the presentation.

a. Start PowerPoint, open the presentation IL_PPT_6-3.pptx from the location where you store your Data Files, then save it as **IL_PPT_6_RMC**. You will work to create the completed presentation as shown in FIGURE 6-20.

b. Insert the outline Support_PPT_6_EMS.docx after Slide 1, then open Outline view.

c. In the Outline pane insert a new Slide 4 after Slide 3 using the Title and Content layout, then type **Purpose** in the title text object.

d. In the text object, type **Standardization**, then type the following second level bullet text:
- **Training programs**
- **Levels of certification**
- **Patient care**

e. Select Slide 2 and Slide 3 in the Outline pane, reset the two slides, then change their layout to Title and Content.

f. Move Slide 4 above Slide 2, then close Outline view.

g. Switch to Reading view, then navigate the slides to the end of the presentation.

h. Go to Slide 7, change the chart layout to Layout 1, then change the chart colors to Colorful Palette 3.

i. Change the chart type to Line, add an axis title to the horizontal axis, then type **Response** in the axis title text box.

j. Change the size of the chart so it is proportionally smaller, then add data labels above the data series markers.

k. Add a data table with legend keys to the chart, then format the vertical axis outline with a 3 point red color.

l. Add primary major vertical gridlines, go to Slide 6, then change the color of the largest pie wedge to Red, Accent 5.

m. Explode the largest pie wedge to 25%, apply a 50 degree angle on the slice, then apply a legend on the right side of the chart.

n. Apply a 4 point yellow border around the largest pie wedge, add a title to the top of the chart, then if necessary type **Systems** in chart title text box.

o. Save the presentation, submit your presentation to your instructor, close the presentation, then exit PowerPoint.

FIGURE 6-20

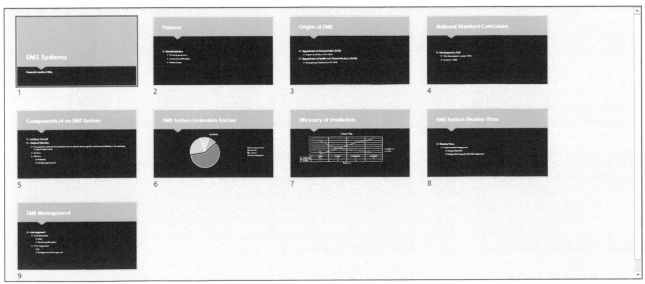

Independent Challenge 2

Generac Products is a large company that develops and produces medical equipment and technical machines for operating and emergency rooms throughout the United States. You are one of the client representatives in the company, and one of your assignments is to prepare a presentation for the division management meetings on the profitability and efficiency of each division in the company. (*Hint:* Before you complete this step make a copy of the Data File Support_PPT_6_G2.xlsx.)

a. Open the file IL_PPT_6-4.pptx from the location where you store your Data Files, then save it as **IL_PPT_6_Generac**. You will work to create the completed presentation as shown in FIGURE 6-21.

b. Go to Slide 5, select the table, then shade the cells with Green, Accent 3.

c. Format the border between the first and second row with a 3 point dark red dotted line.

d. Resize the table proportionally so it fills the width of the slide, then center it in the blank area of the slide.

e. Split the cell System manager into two rows and one column, then type **Allegis UI** into the new cell.

f. Select the table, distribute the rows, then align the data in the cells to the center.

g. Select the top row, apply the Slant bevel, apply the Inside: Bottom shadow to the table, then apply the Tight Reflection: 4 point offset to the table.

h. Apply a Wide cell margin to all the cells, then go to Slide 3.

i. Embed the chart in the Excel file Support_PPT_6_G1.xlsx from the location where you store your Data Files.

j. Drag the corner sizing handles of the chart so it fills the blank area of the slide, double-click the chart, click the Sheet 1 tab, click cell C5, then type -2.

k. Click the Sheet 2 tab, click the Chart Design tab, click the Add Chart Element button in the Chart Layouts group, point to Legend, click Top, then click a blank area of the slide.

l. Go to Slide 4, then link the worksheet in the Excel file Support_PPT_6_G2.xlsx from the location where you store your Data Files.

m. Open the linked worksheet in Excel, select cells B4 through F10, click the Accounting Number Format button in the Number group, click cell B8, type **40,000.00**, save the changes to the worksheet, then close Excel.

n. Right-click the linked worksheet, click Format Object, click the Solid fill option button, if necessary, click the Color button, click White, Text 1, then close the Format Object pane.

o. Resize the worksheet to fill the slide, then view your presentation in Slide Show view.

p. Submit your presentation to your instructor, close the presentation, then exit PowerPoint.

FIGURE 6-21

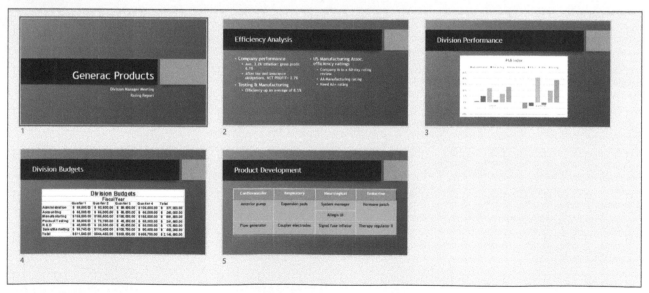

Visual Workshop

Create slides that look like the examples in **FIGURE 6-22** and **FIGURE 6-23**. Start a new presentation, then embed the Excel chart Support_PPT_6_Trac.xlsx from the location where you store your Data Files. Resize the chart larger, then in Excel move the legend to the top of the chart. Format the first row in the table with a Round bevel effect, then center all the data in the center of the cells. Apply a wide margin to all the cells, proportionally resize the table larger, then align the table to the center of the slide. Save the presentation as **IL_PPT_6_TracTec**. Add the slide number as a footer to the slides, then submit your presentation to your instructor.

FIGURE 6-22

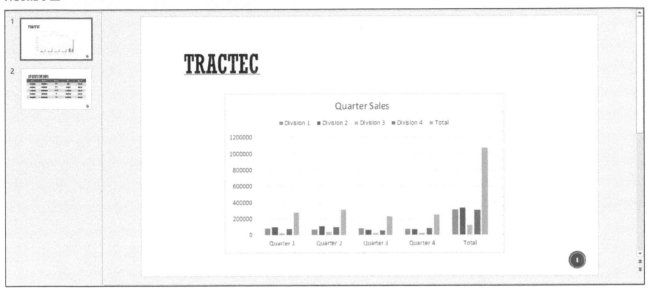

FIGURE 6-23

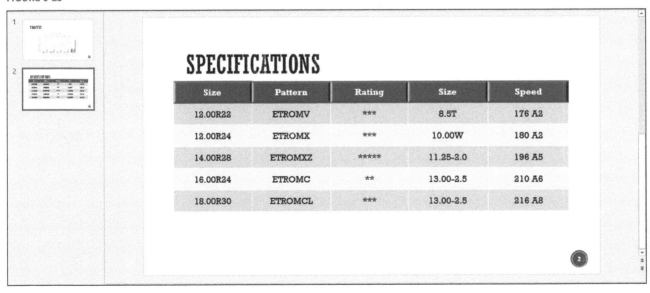

Inserting Graphics, Media, and Objects

CASE In this module, you work on a shortened version of the presentation you have been working on that describes global workforce trends. You use the advanced features in PowerPoint to customize a SmartArt graphic, a digital video, an audio clip, and a picture. You then insert action buttons and hyperlinks for better navigation. And finally, you insert and animate a 3-D model to enhance the presentation.

Module Objectives

After completing this module, you will be able to:

- Design a SmartArt graphic
- Enhance a SmartArt graphic
- Customize digital video
- Insert and trim audio

- Edit and adjust a picture
- Add action buttons
- Insert hyperlinks
- Insert and animate 3-D models

Files You Will Need

IL_PPT_7-1.pptx
Support_PPT_7_Desk.mp4
Support_PPT_7_Audio.mp3
Support_PPT_7_Woman.jpg
Support_PPT_7_Tables.docx
Support_PPT_7_Charts.pptx
IL_PPT_7-2.pptx
IL_PPT_7-3.pptx
Support_PPT_7_Office_Group.jpg
Support_PPT_7_Video.mp4

Support_PPT_7_Company.jpg
Support_PPT_7_Alpine.pptx
IL_PPT_7-4.pptx
Support_PPT_7_Doctor.mov
Support_PPT_7_ER.jpg
Support_PPT_7_RMC.pptx
IL_PPT_7-5.pptx
IL_PPT_7-6.pptx
Support_PPT_7_R2G.jpg

Design a SmartArt Graphic

SmartArt graphics improve your ability to create vibrant content on slides. SmartArt allows you to easily combine your content with an illustrative diagram, improving the overall quality of your presentation. Better presentations lead to improved understanding and retention by your audience. In a matter of minutes, and with little training, you can create a SmartArt graphic using slide content that would otherwise have been placed in a simple bulleted list. **CASE** ▷ *You continue working on the presentation by changing the graphic layout, adding a shape and text to the SmartArt graphic, and then changing its color and style.*

STEPS

1. **sam ↓ Start PowerPoint, open the presentation IL_PPT_7-1.pptx from the location where you store your Data Files, save the presentation as IL_PPT_7_JCL, click the Slide 2 thumbnail in the Slides tab, then click the bottom shape in the SmartArt graphic**

   The SmartArt graphic is selected. Each shape in the SmartArt graphic is separate and distinct from the other shapes and can be individually edited, formatted, or moved within the boundaries of the SmartArt graphic. The bottom shape is selected.

2. **Click the SmartArt Design tab on the Ribbon, click the Text Pane control button ◁ to open the Text pane, click the Add Bullet button in the Create Graphic group, then type Digital labor force in the Text pane**

   A new bullet appears indented beneath the bullet above it in the Text pane and in the graphic.

3. **Click the Promote button in the Create Graphic group, click the Move Up button in the Create Graphic group, then click the third shape in the graphic**

   The new bullet indents to the left, appears in its own shape, and moves up in the list. Compare your screen with FIGURE 7-1.

4. **Click the Add Shape arrow in the Create Graphic group, click Add Shape After, then click the Move Down button once in the Create Graphic group**

   A new shape in the same style appears with a new bullet in the Text pane and then is moved down in the Text pane.

5. **Type 75% increase in last 5 years, click the Demote button in the Create Graphic group, then click the top shape in the SmartArt graphic**

6. **Click Intense Effect in the SmartArt Styles group, then click the Right to Left button in the Create Graphic group**

   The style of the SmartArt graphic changes and the graphic layout switches from left to right. The new bullet point does not move, so you return the graphic to its original layout.

7. **Click the Right to Left button in the Create Graphic group, click the Change Colors button in the SmartArt Styles group, then click Colorful - Accent Colors in the Colorful section**

   Each shape now has a different color that follows the Theme colors of the presentation.

8. **Click the Text Pane button in the Create Graphic group to close the Text pane, then click a blank area of the slide**

   Compare your screen to FIGURE 7-2.

FIGURE 7-1: **SmartArt graphic with added text**

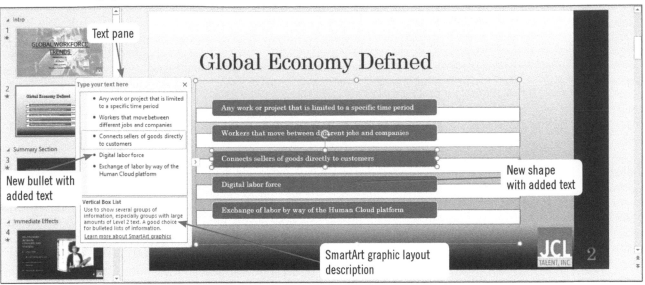

FIGURE 7-2: **Formatted SmartArt graphic**

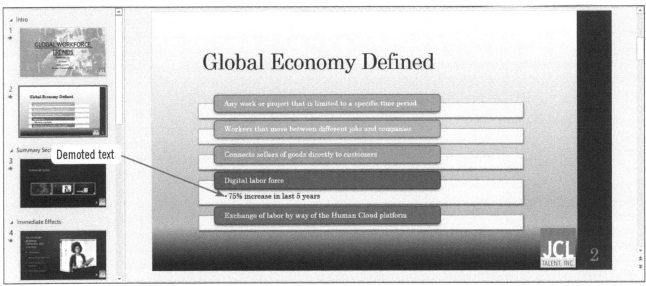

Creating mathematical equations

You can insert or create mathematical equations using the Equation button in the Symbols group on the Insert tab. Click the Equation button list arrow to access nine common equations, which include the area of a circle, the Pythagorean Theorem (my personal favorite), and the Quadratic Formula (my editor's favorite). To create your own equations, click the Equation button to open the Equation tab. On this tab you can use the Ink Equation button to insert an equation using your own handwriting, or you can create an equation using eight different types of mathematical symbols including basic math, geometry, operators, and scripts. You also have the ability to create mathematical structures such as integrals and functions.

Enhance a SmartArt Graphic

Even though you can use styles and themes to quickly format a SmartArt graphic, you still may need to refine individual aspects of the graphic. You can use the commands on the Format tab to change shape styles, fills, outlines, and effects. You can also convert text within the SmartArt graphic to WordArt and format the text using any of the WordArt formatting commands. Individual shapes in the SmartArt graphic can be resized or even changed into a different shape. **CASE** *You continue working on the SmartArt graphic on Slide 8 by adjusting shapes, adding pictures to the shapes, and resizing the graphic.*

STEPS

1. **Click the** Slide 8 thumbnail **in the Slides tab, click the** SmartArt graphic, **click the** Format tab **on the Ribbon, then click the** picture placeholder shape **(not the picture icon) next to the Economic pressures shape**

   The circle shape behind the picture icon is selected.

2. **Click the** Change Shape button **in the Shapes group, then click** Rectangle: Top Corners Rounded **in the Rectangles section**

   The form of the picture placeholder shape changes.

3. **Click the** middle placeholder shape, **press and hold** CTRL, **click the** bottom picture placeholder shape, **release** CTRL, **press** F4, **then click the** Technology advancements shape

   The picture placeholder shapes now have the top rounded corner rectangle shape.

4. **Click the** Shape Fill button **in the Shape Styles group, click** Gold, Accent 4, **then click the** picture icon 🖾 **in the picture placeholder shape next to the Economic pressures shape**

   The Insert Pictures dialog box opens.

5. **Click** From a File, **navigate to the location where you store your Data Files, click** Support_PPT_7_Woman.jpg, **then click** Insert

   The picture is placed in the picture placeholder shape. Notice the picture fills the contour of the shape, as shown in **FIGURE 7-3**.

6. **Following the instructions in Step 5, insert the file** Support_PPT_7_Woman.jpg **into the remaining two picture placeholders**

   All three shapes in the SmartArt graphic have pictures in them.

7. **Click the** picture **next to the Economic pressures shape, click the** Larger button **in the Shapes group, click the** picture **next to the Technology advancements shape, press and hold** CTRL, **click the remaining** picture, **release** CTRL, **then press** F4

   The three pictures are a little larger now.

8. **Click a blank area inside the SmartArt graphic, click the** Shape Effects button **in the Shape Styles group, point to** 3-D Rotation, **then click** Perspective: Right **in the Perspective section**

   A 3-D effect is applied to the SmartArt graphic that turns it to the right.

9. **Click the** Size button, **click the** Shape Height up arrow **in the Size group until** 4 **appears, click a blank area of the slide, then save your work**

   The SmartArt graphic increases in size, as shown in **FIGURE 7-4**.

FIGURE 7-3: New shapes in SmartArt graphic

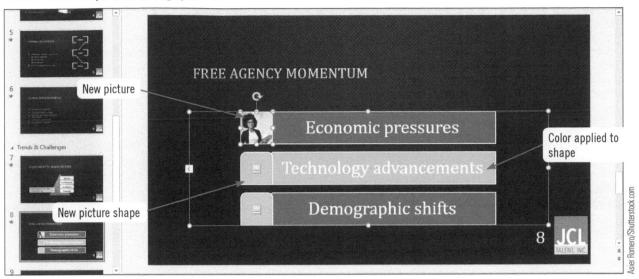

FIGURE 7-4: Completed SmartArt graphic

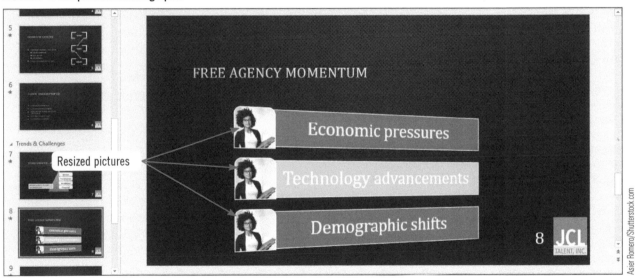

Saving a presentation in PDF, XPS, or other fixed file formats

In certain situations, such as when sharing sensitive or legal materials with others, you may find it necessary to save your presentation file in a fixed layout format. A **fixed layout format** is a specific file format that "locks" the file from future changes and allows others only the ability to view or print the presentation. To save a presentation in one of these fixed formats, click the File tab on the Ribbon, click Export, make sure Create PDF/XPS Document is selected, then click the Create PDF/XPS button. The Publish as PDF or XPS dialog box opens. Select the appropriate file type in the Save as type list box, choose other options (optimization), then publish your presentation in a fixed layout format. To view a fixed layout format presentation, you need appropriate viewer software that you can download from the Internet. Other common file formats supported in PowerPoint include PowerPoint Template (.potx), PowerPoint Show (.ppsx), OpenDocument Presentation (.odp), and PowerPoint Picture Presentation (.pptx). On the File tab, click Save As, then click the Change File Type arrow to save a file in another file format and to view descriptions of these and other supported file formats.

PowerPoint

Customize Digital Video

Learning
Outcomes
• Insert a video
• Apply a poster
  frame
• Compress a video

In your presentation, you may want to use special effects to illustrate a point or capture the attention of your audience. You can do this by inserting digital or animated video. **Digital video** is live action captured in digital format by a video camera. You can embed or link a digital video file from your computer or link a digital video file from a webpage on the Internet. **Animated video** contains multiple images that stream together or move to give the illusion of motion. If you need to edit the length of a video or add effects or background color to a video, you can use PowerPoint video-editing tools to accomplish those and other basic editing tasks. **CASE** *You continue to develop your presentation by inserting and editing a video clip on Slide 6.*

STEPS

1. **Click the** Slide 6 thumbnail **in the Slides tab, click the** Insert tab **on the Ribbon, click the** Video button **in the Media group, then click** This Device

   The Insert Video dialog box opens.

2. **Navigate to the location where you store your Data Files, click** Support_PPT_7_Desk.mp4, **then click** Insert

   The Support_PPT_7_Desk.mp4 video clip is inserted on the slide and fills the slide. You resize the video so it fits better on the slide.

3. **Click the** Width text box **in the Size group, type** 6, **press** ENTER, **then drag the** video clip **to the middle of the blank area on the right side of the slide**

   The video clip is proportionally smaller and fits better on the slide.

4. **Move** ⃗ **over the** video control timeline **located below the video, click the** video control timeline **at about** 00:06.60, **click the** Poster Frame button **in the Adjust group, then click** Current Frame

   The video frame at about 06 seconds is now set as the preview video image, as shown in **FIGURE 7-5**.

5. **Click the** Play/Pause button ▶ **in the video control bar**

   The short video plays through once but does not rewind to the beginning.

6. **Click the** Playback tab **on the Ribbon, click the** Rewind after Playing check box **in the Video Options group, then click the** Play button **in the Preview group**

   The video plays through once, and this time the video rewinds back to the beginning and displays the preview image.

7. **Click the** Start list button **in the Video Options group, click** When Clicked On, **then click the** Play Full Screen check box **in the Video Options group**

   Now the video will play full screen only when clicked during a slide show.

8. **Click the** Slide Show button 🖳 **on the status bar, move** ⃗ **over the video, the pointer changes to** 🖑, **then click the** video

   The video clip fills the screen and plays and then Slide 6 appears in Slide Show view again.

9. **Press** ESC, **click the** File tab **on the Ribbon, click** Info, **click the** Compress Media button, **then click** Standard (480p)

   The Compress Media dialog box opens and the video is compressed.

10. **Click** Close **in the dialog box, click the** Back button 🔙, **click a blank area of the slide, then save your work**

    Compare your screen to **FIGURE 7-6**.

FIGURE 7-5: Video clip inserted on the slide

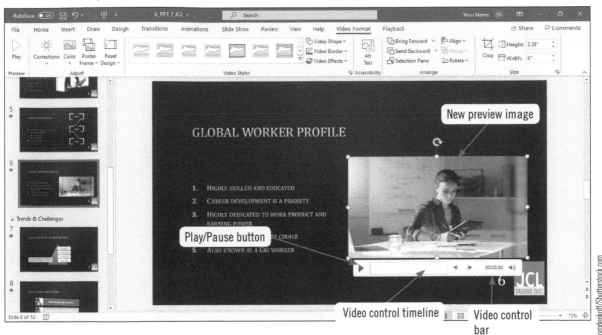

FIGURE 7-6: Edited video on slide

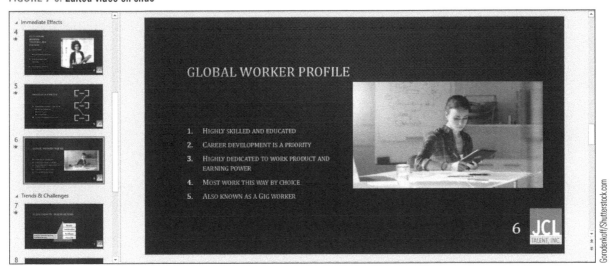

Trimming a video

After you watch a video clip, you may determine certain portions of the video are not relevant to your slide show. From PowerPoint, a video clip can be trimmed only from the beginning or the end of the clip; you can't use PowerPoint to trim out the middle of a clip. To trim a video clip, select the video, click the Playback tab, then click the Trim Video button in the Editing group. The Trim Video dialog box opens. To trim the beginning of the video clip, drag the start point (green marker) to the right until you reach a new starting point. To trim the end of a video clip, drag the end point (red marker) to the left until you reach a new ending point. If you want to precisely choose a new beginning or ending point for the video clip, you can click the up or down arrows on the Start Time and End Time text boxes.

Insert and Trim Audio

Learning
Outcomes
• Insert, edit, and
 play a sound file

PowerPoint allows you to insert sound files in your presentation to help narrate a slide or add audio effects. You can add sounds to your presentation from files on a removable storage device, the Internet, or a network drive. The primary use of sound in a presentation is to provide emphasis to a slide or an element on the slide. For example, if you are creating a presentation about a tour up the Nile River, you might consider inserting a rushing water sound on a slide with a photograph showing people on the Nile. **CASE** *You insert a recorded sound file on Slide 1 that will play during a slide show.*

STEPS

QUICK TIP
If you have two or more audio clips on the same slide, you can group them by clicking the Group button in the Arrange group on the Audio Format tab.

1. **Click the** Slide 1 thumbnail **in the Slides tab, click the** Insert tab **on the Ribbon, click the** Audio button **in the Media group, then click** Audio on My PC
   The Insert Audio dialog box opens. Common sound formats you can insert into a presentation include Windows audio files (waveform) (.wav), MP3 and MP4 audio files (.mp3 / .mp4), and Windows Media Audio Files (.wma).

2. **Navigate to the location where you store your Data Files, click** Support_PPT_7_Audio.mp3, **click the** Insert arrow, **then click** Link to File
   A sound icon with an audio control bar appears in the center of the slide, as shown in **FIGURE 7-7**.

3. **Drag the** sound icon ◁⟩) **to the lower-left corner of the slide, click the** Play button ▶ **in the audio control bar, listen to the music for about a minute, then click the** Pause button ❚❚
   You decide to trim the audio clip.

QUICK TIP
You can use bookmarks to manually start or end an audio or jump to a precise point in the audio.

4. **Click the** Trim Audio button **in the Editing group on the Playback tab**
   The Trim Audio dialog box opens, as shown in **FIGURE 7-8**. Notice on the audio timeline there is a start point (green marker) and an end point (red marker), which identify the beginning and end of the audio. The blue marker identifies where you stopped listening. The audio is just over three minutes long.

5. **Drag the** start point ▯ **to the right to about** 00:09.135, **then drag the** end point ▯ **to the left to about** 02:07.221
   The audio will now start and end at the new selected points, as shown in **FIGURE 7-9**.

QUICK TIP
Click the Rewind after Playing check box in the Audio options group to rewind an audio clip after playing.

6. **Click** OK, **click the** Play Across Slides check box **in the Audio options group, click the** Loop Until Stopped check box **in the Audio options group, then click** ▶ **on the audio control bar**
   The audio now plays between the new start and end points and then loops back to the beginning when the audio clip reaches the end. By default, the audio plays when you click the sound icon during a slide show.

7. **Click the** Pause button **in the Preview group, then click the** Play in Background button **in the Audio Styles group**
   Notice that by clicking the Play in Background button the Hide During Show check box is selected and the Start option is set to Automatically in the Audio Options group. The audio will now be hidden from view and run automatically as soon as the slide appears in Slide Show view.

8. **Click the** Volume button **in the Audio options group, click** Medium, **click the** Slide Show button 🖵 **on the status bar, then listen to the audio**
   The sound icon does not appear during the slide show.

9. **Click through each slide, watch all animations and the movie clip, press** ESC **on the last slide, then save your changes**

FIGURE 7-7: **Sound clip inserted on the slide**

Rawpixel.com/Shutterstock.com

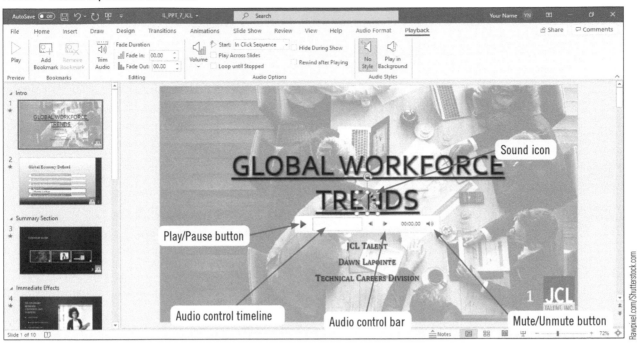

FIGURE 7-8: **Trim Audio dialog box**

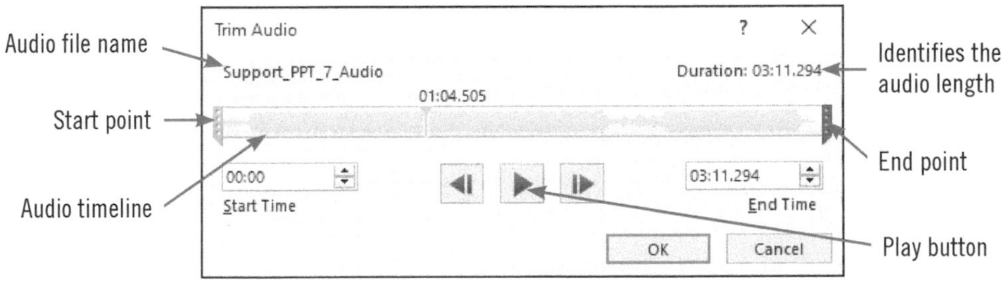

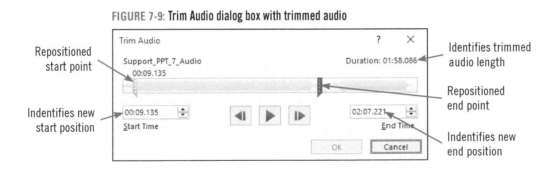

FIGURE 7-9: **Trim Audio dialog box with trimmed audio**

PowerPoint

Edit and Adjust a Picture

Learning
Outcomes
• Replace a picture
• Remove picture
  background
• Convert picture to
  SmartArt graphic

Inserting pictures and other media to your slides can dynamically enhance the message of your presentation. When working with pictures in PowerPoint, you have a number of available design options you can use to format pictures in creative ways, including artistic effects, color saturation, color tone, recoloring, sharpening, brightness, contrast, and background removal. These advanced picture-formatting features can dramatically change how a picture appears, and they can be useful when you are trying to match the picture to other content in the presentation. **CASE** ➤ *On Slide 10 you experiment with PowerPoint picture tools.*

STEPS

QUICK TIP

To insert an online picture without a content placeholder, click the Pictures button in the Images group on the Insert tab, click Online Pictures, then locate a picture.

1. **Click the** Slide 10 thumbnail **in the Slides tab, click the** picture, **click the** Picture Format tab **on the Ribbon, click the** Height text box **in the Size group, type** 3.5, **then press** ENTER

   The picture proportionally increases slightly in size.

2. **Drag the** picture **to the blank area of the slide, then click the** Change Picture button **in the Adjust group**

   The Change Picture list box opens. Using this list you can search for a replacement picture from your computer or the Internet.

3. **Click** From a File, **navigate to the location where you store your Data Files in the Insert Picture dialog box, click** Support_PPT_7_Woman.jpg, **click** Insert, **review the Design Ideas pane, then close the Design Ideas pane**

   A new picture takes the place of the original picture. Eliminating the background of a picture can highlight the subject or remove distracting aspects of the picture.

4. **Click the** Remove Background button **in the Adjust group**

   The Background Removal tab opens on the Ribbon. The suggested background is highlighted in pink, as shown in **FIGURE 7-10**.

5. **Click the** Mark Areas to Keep button **in the Refine group, the pointer changes to** ⌀, **drag a line to match** FIGURE 7-11, **drag a** small line **at the top of the woman's hair, then click the** Keep Changes button **in the Close group**

   Most of the background portion of the picture is removed from the picture.

6. **Click the** Reset Picture button **in the Adjust group, view the** picture, **then click the** Undo button 🔄 **on the Quick Access toolbar**

   After looking at the picture in its original condition, you decide to keep the picture as is.

QUICK TIP

To make one color in a picture transparent, select the picture, click the Color button in the Adjust group, click Set Transparent Color, then click the color on the picture you want to make transparent.

7. **Click the** Color button **in the Adjust group, click** Saturation: 66% **in the Color Saturation section, click the** Corrections button **in the Adjust group, then click** Brightness: +20% Contrast: 0% (Normal) **in the Brightness/Contrast section (3rd row)**

   The picture color, saturation, brightness, and contrast change.

8. **Click the** Rotate button **in the Arrange group, click** Flip Horizontal, **click** Compress Pictures **in the Adjust group, then click** OK **in the Compress Pictures dialog box**

   The picture is flipped horizontally and compressed.

9. **Click a blank area of the slide, save your work, then compare your screen to** FIGURE 7-12

FIGURE 7-10: Picture with background area to be removed

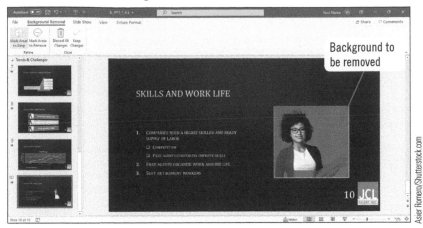

Background to be removed

FIGURE 7-11: Background removal line

Background area to be removed

Drag a line to here

FIGURE 7-12: Picture with removed background

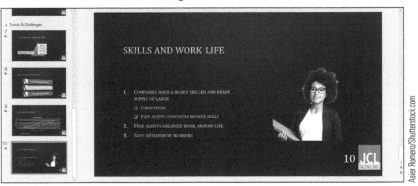

Compressing pictures

To compress all pictures in a presentation, select a picture, click the Compress Pictures button in the Adjust group, remove the Apply only to this picture check mark, then click OK. It's important to know that when you compress a picture you change the amount of detail in the picture, so it might look different than it did before the compression. By default, all inserted pictures in PowerPoint are automatically compressed based on default settings in the PowerPoint Options dialog box. To locate the compression settings, click the File tab, click Options, click Advanced in the left pane, then go to the Image Size and Quality section.

Add Action Buttons

Learning
Outcomes
• Create action
  buttons
• Edit action
  buttons

An **action button** is an interactive button that you create from the Shapes gallery to perform a specific task. For example, you can create an action button to play a video or a sound, or to link to another slide in your presentation. Action buttons can also link to a webpage on the Internet, a different presentation, or any file created in another program. Action buttons are commonly used in self-running presentations and presentations published on the web. **CASE** ▶ *You add action buttons to the slides of your presentation, which will allow you to move from slide to slide in Slide Show view.*

STEPS

1. **Click the** Slide 1 thumbnail **in the Slides tab, click the** Shapes button **in the Drawing group, click** Action Button: Go Forward or Next ▷ **in the Action Buttons section, press and hold** SHIFT, **drag to create a button as shown in** FIGURE 7-13, **then release** SHIFT

   A small action button appears on the slide, and the Action Settings dialog box opens. Pressing and holding SHIFT while you create a shape maintains the shape's proportions as you change its size.

2. **Make sure** Next Slide **is selected in the Hyperlink to list, then click** OK

   The dialog box closes. The action button now has an action, in this case, linking to the next slide.

3. **Click the** Shape Format tab **on the Ribbon, click the** More button ▾ **in the Shape Styles group, then click** Gradient Fill - Orange, Accent 6, No Outline **in the last row of the Presets section**

   The new theme fill makes the action button easier to see on the slide.

4. **Drag the** action button **to the upper-left corner of the slide, click the** Home tab, **then click the** Copy button **in the Clipboard group**

5. **Click the** Slide 2 thumbnail **in the Slides tab, then click the** Paste button

   An exact copy of the action button, including the associated action, is placed on Slide 2.

6. **Paste a copy of the** action button **on Slides 4 through 9, click the** Slide 10 thumbnail **in the Slides tab, click the** Shapes button **in the Drawing group, then click** Action Button: Go Home ⌂ **in the Action Buttons section**

7. **Press and hold** SHIFT, **create a similar-sized action button as you did for Slide 1, release** SHIFT, **make sure** First Slide **is selected in the Hyperlink to list, click** OK, **then drag the** action button **to the upper-left corner of the slide**

   Compare your screen to FIGURE 7-14.

8. **Click the** Slide 2 thumbnail **in the Slides tab, right-click the** action button, **click** Edit Link **in the shortcut menu, click the** Hyperlink to list arrow, **then click** Slide

   The Hyperlink to Slide dialog box opens.

9. **Click** 4. Relationship Between Companies, **click** OK, **click** OK again, **click the** Slide 1 thumbnail **in the Slides tab, then click the** Slide Show button ▭ **on the status bar**

10. **Click the** action buttons **on each slide, click the** Home action button **on Slide 10, press** ESC **to end the slide show, then save your changes**

    The pointer changes to 🖑 when you click each action button.

FIGURE 7-13: Inserted action button

FIGURE 7-14: Home action button on last slide

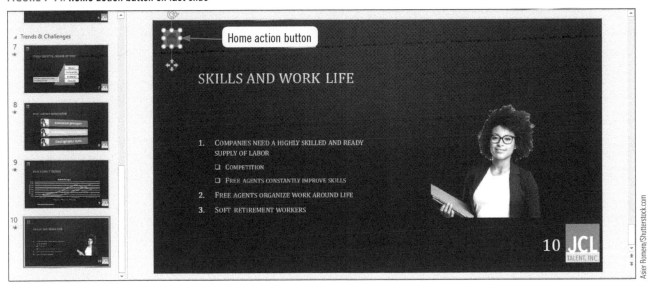

Changing the transparency of a picture

Pictures in PowerPoint are commonly used as slide backgrounds, individual objects on a slide, or inserted in another object, such as a SmartArt graphic. To change the transparency of a picture used as a slide background, insert the picture as a slide background using the Format Background button on the Design tab, then adjust the Transparency slider in the Format Background pane. To change the transparency of a picture on a slide, right-click the picture. Click Format picture on the shortcut menu, click Fill & Line, click the Picture or texture fill option button, then move the Transparency slider in the Format Picture pane.

PowerPoint

Insert Hyperlinks

Learning Outcomes
• Create hyperlinks
• View and use hyperlinks

While creating a presentation, there might be a circumstance in which you want to view a document that either won't be easily viewed on a slide or is too detailed for your presentation. In these cases, you can insert a **hyperlink**, a specially formatted word, phrase, graphic, or drawn object that you click during a slide show to "jump to," or display, another slide or PowerPoint presentation in your current presentation; a document from another program, like Word; or a webpage. A hyperlinked object is similar to a linked object because you can modify the object in its source program from within PowerPoint. **CASE** ▶ *You add two hyperlinks to your presentation.*

STEPS

1. **Click the** Slide 7 thumbnail **in the Slides tab, click the** grey triangle **to select the SmartArt graphic, click the** Insert tab **on the Ribbon, click the** Link button **in the Links group to open the Insert Hyperlink dialog box, then, if necessary, click** Existing File or Web Page **in the Link to: pane**

   The Existing File or Web Page button is selected in the Link to: pane, and Current Folder is selected in the Look in pane. The location where you store your Data Files should be the open folder.

   QUICK TIP
   Links can also be established between slides of the same presentation, a new presentation, an email address, or any webpage.

2. **Click the file** Support_PPT_7_Tables.docx, **click** OK, **then click a blank area of the slide**

   Now you have made the grey triangle a hyperlink to the file Support_PPT_7_Tables.docx.

3. **Click the** Slide Show button 🖵 **on the status bar, point to the** grey triangle, **notice the pointer change to** 🖑, **then click the** grey triangle

   Microsoft Word opens, and the Word document containing tables of information appears, as shown in **FIGURE 7-15**.

4. **Read the two-page document, then close the** Word window

   The PowerPoint slide reappears in Slide Show view.

5. **Press** ESC, **click the** Slide 10 thumbnail **in the Slides tab, right-click the** picture, **click** Link, **click** Support_PPT_7_Tables.docx, **then click** OK

   The picture is now linked to the Word document. You realize this is the wrong linked document.

   QUICK TIP
   To open, copy, or remove a hyperlink, right-click the hyperlink, then click the appropriate command on the shortcut menu.

6. **Right-click the** picture, **click** Edit Link **in the shortcut menu, click** Support_PPT_7_Charts.docx **as shown in** FIGURE 7-16, **then click** OK

   The PowerPoint presentation Support_PPT_7_Charts.pptx is now linked to the picture on Slide 10.

7. **Click the** Slide 1 thumbnail **in the Slides tab, click** 🖵 **to start the slide show, then click the** action buttons **to view the slides in the presentation**

   Be sure to watch the movie on Slide 6 and to trigger the animation on Slide 7 to move the SmartArt graphic.

8. **Click the** linked objects **on Slide 7 and Slide 10, press the** Home action button **on Slide 10, press** ESC **to end the slide show, then save your changes**

   The hyperlinks and action buttons all work correctly.

9. **sam ▲ Submit your presentation to your instructor, then close the presentation but do not close PowerPoint**

FIGURE 7-15: **Linked Word document**

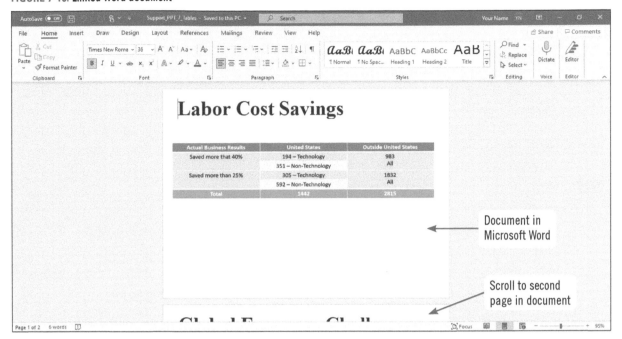

Document in Microsoft Word

Scroll to second page in document

FIGURE 7-16: **Open Edit Hyperlink dialog box**

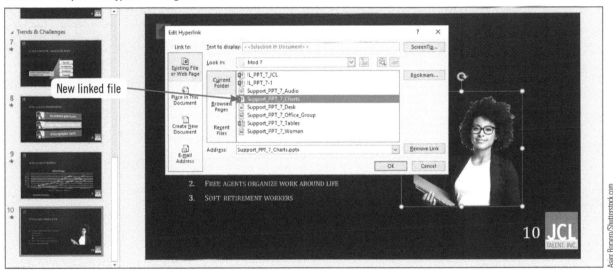

New linked file

Asier Romero/Shutterstock.com

Inserting a screenshot

Using the Screenshot button in the Images group on the Insert tab, you can insert a picture, or screenshot, of an open program window or a specific part of the window. A screenshot is simply a picture of the window displayed on your screen. For example, you could use the screenshot feature to insert a picture of information you found on a webpage or found in other documents or programs that might not be easily transferable to PowerPoint. Screenshots are static and are not able to be updated if the source information changes. Only open, nonminimized windows are available to be captured as a screenshot. When you click the Screenshot button, all open program windows appear in the Available Windows gallery. To take a screenshot of part of a window, click the Screenshot button, then click Screen Clipping.

Inserting Graphics, Media, and Objects

Insert and Animate 3-D Models

Learning Outcomes
- Insert and modify a 3-D model
- Animate a 3-D model

Three-dimensional models are high-quality objects that you can modify by rotating or tilting to view different angles of the object to suit your needs. Once the 3-D model is inserted, you can manually adjust it or choose one of the standard views in the 3D Model Views group. Some 3-D models are animated and provide a dynamic way to display the model in your presentation. Animated 3-D models have different cinematic scenes that cause the 3-D model to perform different actions, such as walking or flying.

CASE ➤ *You open a presentation and experiment with 3-D models to use in future presentations.*

STEPS

1. **sam'** ⬇ **Open the presentation** IL_PPT_7-2.pptx **from the location where you store your Data Files, then save the presentation as** IL_PPT_7_3DModel

2. **Click the** Insert tab **on the Ribbon, click the** 3D Models button **in the Illustrations group, then click** Animated for Education **in the Online 3D Models dialog box**

   The animated models in the Animated for Education group appear. All of these 3-D models are animated.

3. **Click the** astronaut, **then click** Insert

   The 3-D animated model of an astronaut appears in the middle of the slide. The astronaut appears to float on the slide, which is this 3-D model's animation movement. A 3D Rotate handle appears in the middle of the 3-D model.

4. **Drag the** 3D Rotate handle **up, down, and around, watch how the 3-D model reacts, click the** More button ⬇ **in the 3D Model Views group, move the pointer over each of the options to see the changes, then click** Above Front Left **(middle row, last column)**

   Dragging the 3D Rotate handle manipulates the astronaut in many different angles. The astronaut appears turned to the right, as shown in **FIGURE 7-17**.

5. **Click the** Scenes button **in the Play 3D group, then click** Scene 2

   The animation changes and the astronaut appears to turn from side to side.

6. **Click the** Scenes button **in the Play 3D group, click** Scene 3, **click the** Scenes button, **click** Scene 4, **then click the** Pause button **in the Play 3D group**

   The other two animation scenes play and then the 3-D animation is paused. This 3-D model dramatically increases the presentation file size, so you change the 3-D model.

7. **Press DELETE, click the** Insert tab **on the Ribbon, click the** 3D Models button **in the Illustrations group, click** 3D Icons, **click the** Gears 3D model, **then click** Insert

   The astronaut 3-D model is deleted and the gears 3-D model now appears, as shown in **FIGURE 7-18**.

8. **Drag the** 3-D model Rotate handle **so the model is in a new position, click the** Animations tab **on the Ribbon, click** Turntable, **click the** Slide Show button ⬜ **on the status bar, then click the** 3D Model

   The 3-D model animates by turning around.

9. **sam'** ⬆ **Press ESC, submit your presentation to your instructor, close the presentation, then close PowerPoint**

FIGURE 7-17: Slide with astronaut 3-D model

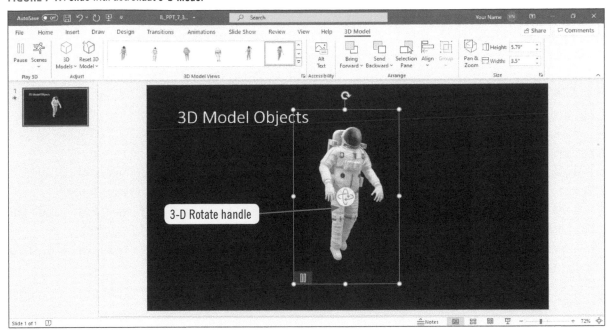

FIGURE 7-18: Slide with gears 3-D model

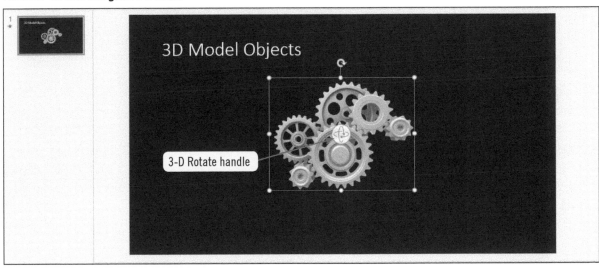

Zooming in on a 3-D model

With 3-D models you have the option of zooming in or out. You can also pan the 3-D model around to see a specific area. With the 3-D model selected, click the Pan & Zoom button in the Size group on the 3D Model tab. A magnifying glass appears on the right side of the 3-D model. To zoom in or out click the magnifying glass, then drag up or down depending on the direction you want to zoom. To pan the 3-D model, simply drag the 3-D model inside its selection box. When you are finished, click the Pan & Zoom button again.

Practice

Skills Review

1. **Design a SmartArt graphic.**
   a. Start PowerPoint, open the presentation **IL_PPT_7-3.pptx** from the location where you store your Data Files, then save it as **IL_PPT_7_Alpine**.
   b. Go to Slide 4, click the left shape in the SmartArt graphic, click the SmartArt Design tab, then open the Text pane.
   c. Click the Add Bullet button in the Create Graphic group, then type **Expand sales force by 5%**.
   d. Click the Promote button in the Create Graphic group, click the Add Shape list arrow in the Create Graphic group, then click Add Shape After.
   e. Type **Trim budget by 10%**, press ENTER, click the Demote button in the Create Graphic group, then type **Combine development projects**.
   f. Close the Text pane, click the Change Colors button in the SmartArt Styles group, then click Colorful - Accent Colors in the Colorful section.
   g. Click the left shape, click the Move Down button in the Create Graphic group, then click the right shape.
   h. Click the Move Up button in the Create Graphic group, then save your changes.

2. **Enhance a SmartArt graphic.**
   a. Click the Format tab, click the left picture shape in the SmartArt graphic, click the Larger button in the Shapes group, then increase the size of the other picture shapes.
   b. Click a blank area of the SmartArt graphic, click the Width text box, type **9.5**, then press ENTER.
   c. Click the Insert picture icon in the left picture shape, click From a File, then locate and insert the file Support_PPT_7_Office_Group.jpg from the location where you store your Data Files.
   d. Follow the above instructions and insert the file Support_PPT_7_Office_Group.jpg to the other picture shapes.
   e. Click the left picture, click the Shape Effects button in the Shape Styles group, point to Bevel, then click Round.
   f. Select the four other pictures, press F4, then select the light green colored shape behind the pictures.
   g. Click the Shape Fill button in the Shape Styles group, click Aqua, Accent 3, then save your changes.

3. **Customize digital video.**
   a. Go to Slide 2, click the Insert tab on the Ribbon, click the Video button in the Media group, then click This Device.
   b. Locate the file Support_PPT_7_Video.mp4 from the location where you store your Data Files, click Insert, then click the Video Format tab.
   c. Click the number in the Height text box in the Size group, type **3.5**, press ENTER, then move the video clip to the center of the blank area of the slide.
   d. Move the pointer over the video control timeline, click at approximately 00:09.02 in the timeline, click the Poster Frame button in the Adjust group, then click Current Frame.
   e. On the Playback tab, click the Rewind after Playing check box, then click the Play Full Screen check box in the Video options group.
   f. Click the File tab, click Info, click the Compress Media button, click Standard, then click Close in the Compress Media dialog box.
   g. Click the Back button, preview the video clip in Slide Show view, then save your presentation.

4. **Insert and trim audio.**
   a. Go to Slide 1, click the Insert tab, click the Audio button in the Media group, then click Audio on My PC.
   b. Locate the sound file Support_PPT_7_Audio.mp3 from the location where you store your Data Files, click the Insert arrow, then click Link to File.
   c. In the Audio Options group click the Play Across Slides check box, click the Loop until Stopped check box, then drag the sound icon to the lower-left corner of the slide.

Skills Review (continued)

    d. Use the Trim Audio dialog box to change the start point of the audio clip to 02:04.800 and the end point to 03:05.900.

    e. Click the Play in Background button in the Audio Styles group, click the Volume button in the Audio Options group, click Medium, then click the Slide Show button on the status bar.

    f. Click through the slides in Slide Show view, review the movie on Slide 2, press ESC, then save your presentation.

5. Edit and adjust a picture.

    a. Go to Slide 5, click the Picture, change the picture with Support_PPT_7_Company.jpg, review the designs in the Design Ideas pane, then close the Design Ideas pane.

    b. Change the color saturation of the picture to Saturation: 0%, then correct the picture to Brightness: -20% Contrast: -20%.

    c. Click the Remove Background button in the Adjust group, click the Mark Areas to Keep button in the Refine group, then draw small lines on all the people, the table, and the items on the table in the picture.

    d. Reset the picture, click the Rotate Objects button in the Arrange group, then click Flip Horizontal.

    e. Compress all the pictures in the presentation, click the Width text box in the Size group, type 6, then press ENTER.

    f. Save your changes.

6. Add action buttons.

    a. Go to Slide 1, click the Shapes button in the Drawing group, then click Action Button: Go Forward or Next.

    b. Draw a small button, click OK in the Action Settings dialog box, then move the button to the left edge of the slide.

    c. Click the Shape Format tab on the Ribbon, click the More button in the Shape Styles group, then click Colored Fill - Orange, Accent 5 in the second row.

    d. Copy and paste the action button on all the other slides.

    e. Right-click the action button on Slide 5, click Edit Link on the shortcut menu, click the Hyperlink to: arrow, click First Slide, then click OK.

    f. Go to Slide 1, run the slide show, test the action buttons, exit the slide show, then save your work.

7. Insert hyperlinks.

    a. Go to Slide 3, then click the green shape to select it.

    b. Click the Insert tab on the Ribbon, click the Link button, locate the file Support_PPT_7_Alpine.pptx from the location where you store your Data Files, then click OK.

    c. Go to Slide 4, right-click the left picture in the SmartArt graphic, then click Link in the shortcut menu.

    d. In the Insert Hyperlink dialog box, click Place in This Document in the Link to: section, click 5. New Fiscal Year Goals in the Select a place in this document: section, then click OK.

    e. Go to Slide 1, open Slide Show view, click the action buttons to Slide 3, then click the hyperlink shape.

    f. Click through the slides of the linked presentation, click the action button to Slide 4, then click the hyperlink in the SmartArt graphic.

    g. Press ESC, go to Slide 4, right-click the SmartArt picture with the hyperlink, click Edit Link, click 2. Alpine Year in Review in the Select a place in this document section, then click OK.

    h. Go to Slide 1, open Slide Show view, click the action buttons to move between slides, watch the video on Slide 2, click the hyperlinks on Slides 3 and 4, press ESC when you are finished, then save your changes.

8. Insert and animate 3-D models.

    a. Go to Slide 1, click the Insert tab, then click the 3D Models button in the Illustrations group.

Skills Review (continued)

b. Click 3D Icons, locate the 3-D model shown in **FIGURE 7-19**, then click Insert.

c. Drag the 3-D model to the lower-right corner of the slide, then drag the 3-D Rotate handle to change the angle of the model.

d. Click the Width text box in the Size group, type **3**, press ENTER, then reposition the model, if necessary.

e. Click the 3D Model Views More button, click Above Front Right, then click the Animations tab.

f. Click Jump & Turn in the Animation group, click the Effect Options button in the Animation group, then click Clockwise in the Direction section.

g. Click the Slide Show button on the status bar, view the animation on Slide 1, use the action buttons to go through the slide show, watch the video, view all hyperlinks, then press ESC when you are finished. The completed presentation is shown in **FIGURE 7-20**.

h. Save your work, submit your presentation to your instructor, then close the presentation.

FIGURE 7-19

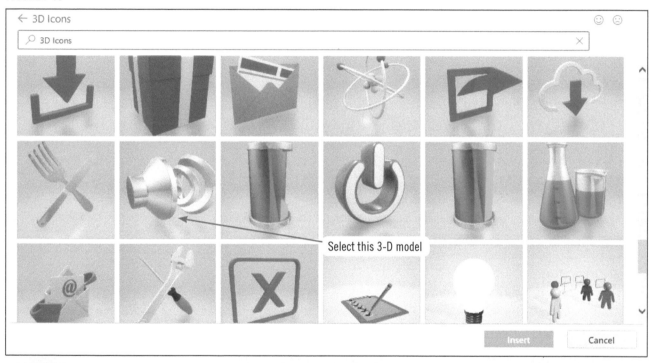

FIGURE 7-20

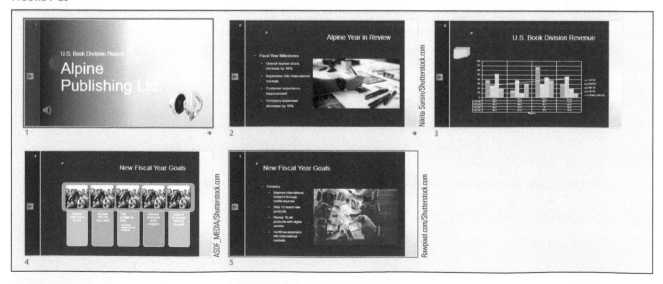

Independent Challenge 1

Riverwalk Medical Clinic (RMC), is a large medical facility in Cambridge, Massachusetts. Your supervisor has asked you to create a presentation on the Riverwalk Clinic EMS system. You have been working on the presentation and now you add video, audio, a hyperlink, and a 3-D model to the presentation.

a. Open the file IL_PPT_7-4.pptx, save it as **IL_PPT_7_RMC**, then go to Slide 6.

b. Locate and insert the video file Support_PPT_7_Doctor.mov from the location where you store your Data Files.

c. Resize the video to a width of 6.25", then drag the video to the middle of the blank area of the slide.

d. Apply a poster frame at about 00:10.00 in the video, then click the Playback tab.

e. Click the Play Full Screen check box, then click the Rewind after Playing check box.

f. Click the File tab, click Info, compress the video using the Standard (480p) format, then review the video in Slide Show view.

g. Go to Slide 1, locate and link the audio Support_PPT_7_Audio.mp3 from the location where you store your Data Files, then drag the audio icon to the lower-right corner of the slide.

h. Click the Playback tab, click the Play Across Slides check box, then click the Play in Background button.

i. Trim the audio clip so the start time is 00:06 and the end time is 02:17.200, then change the volume to Low.

j. Go to Slide 3, then change the existing picture to a new picture. Locate and insert the picture Support_PPT_7_ER.jpg from the location where you store your Data Files.

k. Change the picture color saturation to 200%, then change the brightness and contrast of the picture to Brightness: 0% (Normal) Contrast: -40%.

l. Resize the picture to a width of 7", using the Remove Background feature remove the parking lot from the picture, then keep your changes.

m. Reset the picture, then compress all pictures in the presentation.

n. Make sure the picture is still selected, click the Link button on the Insert tab, locate the file Support_PPT_7_ER.jpg from the location where you store your Data Files, then click OK.

o. Open Slide Show view, click the picture to view the linked picture, close the picture window, then press ESC when you return to Slide 3.

p. Right-click the picture, click Edit Link, locate the file Support_PPT_7_RMC.pptx from the location where you store your Data Files, then click OK.

q. Go to Slide 1, open Slide Show view, click through the presentation, click the linked picture on Slide 3, watch the video on Slide 6, then press ESC when you are finished. Your completed presentation should look similar to FIGURE 7-21.

r. Check the presentation spelling, submit your presentation to your instructor, then close the presentation and close PowerPoint.

FIGURE 7-21

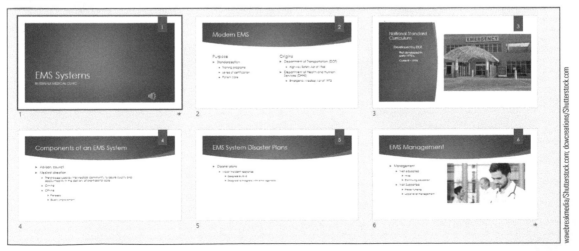

PowerPoint

Independent Challenge 2

You work for JR Capital Group, a global financial services firm. You have been given the task of enhancing a presentation by modifying SmartArt graphics, adding action buttons, and adding a 3-D model.

a. Open the file IL_PPT_7-5.pptx from the location where you store your Data Files, then save it as **IL_PPT_7_JR**.

b. On Slide 2, open the SmartArt graphic Text pane, add a bullet to the first shape, type **U.S. Employees - 920**, then press ENTER.

c. Click the Promote button, type **30 years in business**, click the Move Up button, then click the Add Shape button to add a shape.

d. Type **Global reach**, then click the Move Down button, click the number 14 in the Text pane, then click the Move Up button.

e. Click the Change Colors button, click Colorful - Accent Colors, then click a blank area of the slide.

f. Go to Slide 4, click the middle shape in the SmartArt graphic, click the Format tab, click the Shape Fill button, then click Lavender, Accent 4.

g. Click the Larger button, click the Size button, click the number in the Height text box, then type **1.5**.

h. Click the picture icon in the top shape, then locate and insert the file Support_PPT_7_Company.jpg from the location where you store your Data Files.

i. Insert the same picture in the other two picture placeholders, then click a blank area of the SmartArt graphic.

j. Click the Shape Effects button, point to Preset, then click Preset 4.

k. Go to Slide 1, insert the shape Action Button: Go Forward or Next, make sure Next Slide appears in the Hyperlink to text box, then drag the shape to the upper middle of the slide.

l. Change the shape style of the action button to Subtle Effect - Red, Accent 3, then copy and paste the action button to the other three slides.

m. Right-click the action button on Slide 4, click Edit Link, click the Hyperlink to arrow, click First Slide, then click OK.

n. Open Slide Show view, click the action buttons to make sure they work correctly, then press ESC. The action button Slide 4 should return you to Slide 1.

o. Go to Slide 1, click the Insert tab, open the Online 3D Models dialog box, open the 3D Shapes section, then insert the dark red shape shown in **FIGURE 7-22**.

p. Change the width of the 3-D model to 2", then drag the model to the blank area to the right of the title text.

FIGURE 7-22

Independent Challenge 2 (continued)

q. Use the Rotate handle to change the angle of the model, then apply the Below Front 3D model view.

r. Apply the Turntable animation to the 3-D model, apply the effect option Continuous, click the Start list arrow in the Timing group, then click With Previous.

s. Open Slide Show view, watch the 3-D model animation, click the action buttons to view each slide, then press ESC when you are finished. Your completed presentation should look similar to **FIGURE 7-23**.

t. Submit your presentation to your instructor, close the presentation, then close PowerPoint.

FIGURE 7-23

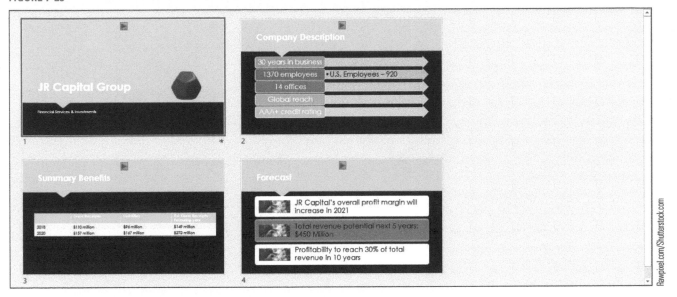

Rawpixel.com/Shutterstock.com

PowerPoint

Visual Workshop

Open the file IL_PPT_7-6.pptx from the location where you store your Data Files, then save it as **IL_PPT_7_R2G**. Locate the file Support_PPT_7_R2G.jpg from the location where you store your Data Files, insert the picture, then close the Design Ideas pane. Change the slide background to solid Gold, Accent 4. Change the width of the picture to 7.2", then remove the background from the picture. On the Background Removal tab, click the Mark Areas to Keep button, then click the areas of the picture to keep it, as shown in **FIGURE 7-24**. Click the Keep Changes button in the Close group to save the changes to the picture and create a finished slide that looks like the example in **FIGURE 7-25**. Save the presentation, submit the presentation to your instructor, then close PowerPoint.

FIGURE 7-24

FIGURE 7-25

Delivering Presentations

CASE ▶ Before you complete your presentation, you work with PowerPoint views and customize Handout and Notes masters. You will then create a custom slide show, change slide show options, prepare the presentation for distribution, and then make it possible for others to view on the Internet. You end your day by creating a photo album of a recent trip to the state capital in Austin, Texas.

Module Objectives

After completing this module, you will be able to:

- Work with presentation views
- Customize Handout and Notes masters
- Set up a slide show
- Create a custom show
- Prepare a presentation for distribution
- Deliver a presentation online
- Create a photo album

Files You Will Need

IL_PPT_8-1.pptx
Support_PPT_8_Austin1.jpg
Support_PPT_8_Austin2.jpg
Support_PPT_8_Austin3.jpg
Support_PPT_8_Austin4.jpg
IL_PPT_8-2.pptx
Support_PPT_8_Pic1.jpg
Support_PPT_8_Pic2.jpg

Support_PPT_8_Pic3.jpg
Support_PPT_8_Pic4.jpg
IL_PPT_8-3.pptx
Support_PPT_8_ICPic1.jpg
Support_PPT_8_ICPic2.jpg
Support_PPT_8_ICPic3.jpg
Support_PPT_8_ICPic4.jpg

Work with Presentation Views

Learning Outcomes
- Use PowerPoint views
- Use Presenter view
- Use Notes Page view
- Create a PowerPoint Show

PowerPoint has five primary views: Slide view, Slide Sorter view, Outline view, Slide Show view, and Notes Page view. Each of these views is designed for a specific purpose and provides you with a variety of tools to easily and quickly develop and present a presentation. There is also Presenter view, which you can access only while in Slide Show view and is designed to help a presenter give a presentation using two monitors. Presenter view along with Notes Page view and the features in these views are important to understand before you attempt to give a presentation to an audience. **CASE** *In this lesson, you examine Notes Page view and Presenter view and then you insert a symbol and change the slide orientation.*

STEPS

1. **sam✦ Start PowerPoint, open the presentation** IL_PPT_8-1.pptx **from the location where you store your Data Files, then save the presentation as** IL_PPT_8_JCL

QUICK TIP
To change the slide orientation, click the Design tab, then click the Slide Size button in the Customize group. Click Custom Slide Size, then click the landscape or portrait option buttons for slides.

2. **Click the** View tab **on the Ribbon, then click the** Notes Page button **in the Presentation Views group**
   Notes Page view appears, showing a reduced image of the current slide above a large text placeholder. You can enter text in this placeholder, which as the presenter you can see during a slide show.

3. **Click in the** text placeholder, **type** Be sure to introduce guest speaker, **click the** Normal button 🔲 **on the status bar, then click the** Notes button **on the status bar**
   The text you typed appears in the Notes pane, as shown in **FIGURE 8-1**.

4. **Click the** Insert tab **on the Ribbon, click after the word** Talent **in the subtitle text object, click the** Symbol button **in the Symbols group, then scroll to the seventh row from the top of the dialog box to view the Registered symbol**
   The Symbol dialog box opens with the Normal font selected. You want to select the registered symbol, which is the letter "R" inside a circle.

5. **Click the** Registered Sign symbol, **click** Insert, **then click** Close
   The Registered symbol appears after the word "Talent" on Slide 1.

6. **Click the** Slide Show view button **on the status bar, click the** More slide show options button 🔘 **on the Slide Show menu, then click** Show Presenter View
   Presenter view opens.

7. **Click the** See all slides button 🔳, **click the** Slide 5 thumbnail, **click** 🔳, **then click the** Slide 8 thumbnail

8. **Click the** Zoom into the slide button 🔍, **click the chart, compare your screen to** FIGURE 8-2, **click** 🔍, **then press** ESC
   You can zoom in on any part of the slide in Presenter view.

9. **Save the presentation, click the** File tab **on the Ribbon, click** Save As, **click the** PowerPoint Presentation arrow, **click** PowerPoint Show (*.ppsx), **then click the** Save button
   Your presentation is saved as a PowerPoint Show, which is a special file format that automatically starts your presentation in Slide Show view when opened.

10. **Click the** File tab, **click** Close **to close the PowerPoint Show presentation, then open the presentation** IL_PPT_8_JCL.pptx **from the location where you store your Data Files**

FIGURE 8-1: Text entered in the Notes pane

FIGURE 8-2: Zoomed-in slide in Presenter view

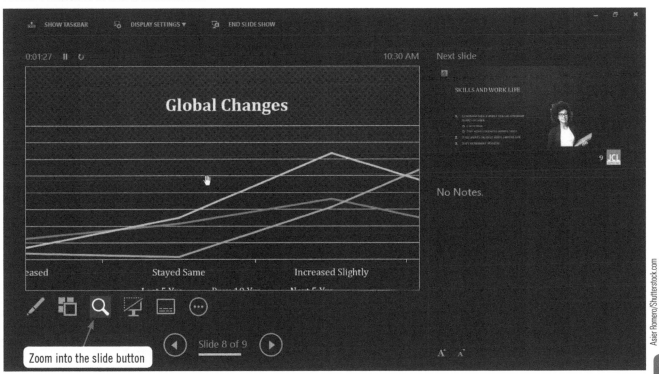

Recording a narration on a slide

If you have a microphone, you can record a voice narration and then play it during a slide show. To record a narration, click the Insert tab on the Ribbon, click the Audio button in the Media group, then click Record Audio. The Record Sound dialog box opens. To start recording, click the Record button in the dialog box, then click the Stop button when you are finished. A sound icon appears on the slide. Narration recordings and other sounds are embedded in the presentation and will increase the PowerPoint file size. You can preview a narration in Normal view by pointing to the sound icon on the slide, then clicking the Play/Pause button in the audio control bar.

Customize Handout and Notes Masters

Learning Outcomes
• Modify the handout master
• Change page orientation

It is often helpful to provide your audience with supplemental materials of the presentation. Creating handouts for your audience provides them a way to follow along and take notes during your presentation. As the presenter, creating notes pages that you can refer to while giving the presentation can be useful, especially when your presentation is complex or detailed. Before you create handouts or notes pages, you might want to customize them to fit your specific needs. **CASE** > *You plan to create supplemental materials to hand out when you give the presentation. You customize the Handout master by changing the slides per page and the background style. Then you modify the Notes master by changing the page setup and the notes page orientation.*

STEPS

1. **Click the** Slide 1 thumbnail **in the Slides tab, click the** View tab **on the Ribbon, then click the** Handout Master button **in the Master Views group**

   The Handout Master view opens. The master has six large empty placeholders that represent where the slides will appear on the printed handouts. The four smaller placeholders in each corner of the page are the header, footer, date, and page number placeholders. The date placeholder displays today's date.

   QUICK TIP
   To save one or more slides as a picture, click the File tab on the Ribbon, click Save As, click the arrow next to the Save button, click a picture format (such as .jpg or .tif), click the Save button, then choose which slides to export.

2. **Click the** Background Styles button **in the Background group, then click** Style 10

   When you print handouts on a color printer, they will have a gradient gray background.

3. **Click the** Slides Per Page button **in the Page Setup group, then click** 3 Slides **on the menu**

   Three slide placeholders appear on the handout, as shown in **FIGURE 8-3**.

4. **Click the** Header placeholder, **drag the** Zoom Slider **on the status bar to** 100%, **type** JCL Talent, **press** PAGE DOWN, **click the** Footer placeholder, **then type your name**

   Now your handouts are ready to print when you need them.

5. **Click the** Fit slide to current window button ⊕ **on the status bar, then click the** Close Master View button **in the Close group**

   Your presentation is in Normal view, so you don't see the changes you made to the Handout master.

   QUICK TIP
   To create custom theme fonts, click the View tab, click the Slide Master button, click the Fonts button, then click Customize Fonts.

6. **Click the** View tab **on the Ribbon, then click the** Notes Master button **in the Master Views group**

   Notes Master view opens. It has four corner placeholders—one each for the header, footer, date, and page number—a large notes text box placeholder, and a large slide master image placeholder.

7. **Click the** Notes Page Orientation button **in the Page Setup group, click** Landscape, **click the** Footer placeholder, **type** JCL Talent, **then click a blank area of the slide master**

   The page orientation changes to landscape. Notice that all the text placeholders are now resized to fill the width of the page. Compare your screen to **FIGURE 8-4**.

8. **Click the** Close Master View button **in the Close group, click the** File tab **on the Ribbon, click** Print, **click** Full Page Slides, **click** 9 Slides Horizontal, **click** Print, **then save your work**

   The presentation prints nine slides per page. The presentation has nine slides, so one page was all that was needed to print this presentation.

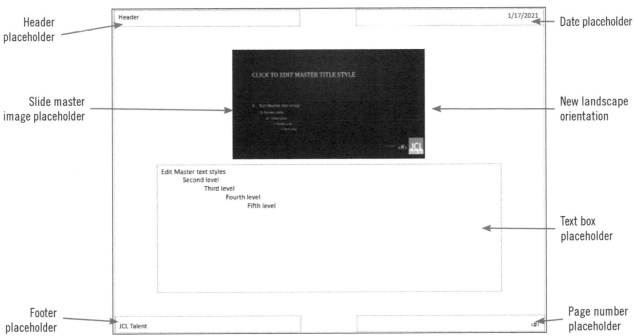

FIGURE 8-3: Handout Master view

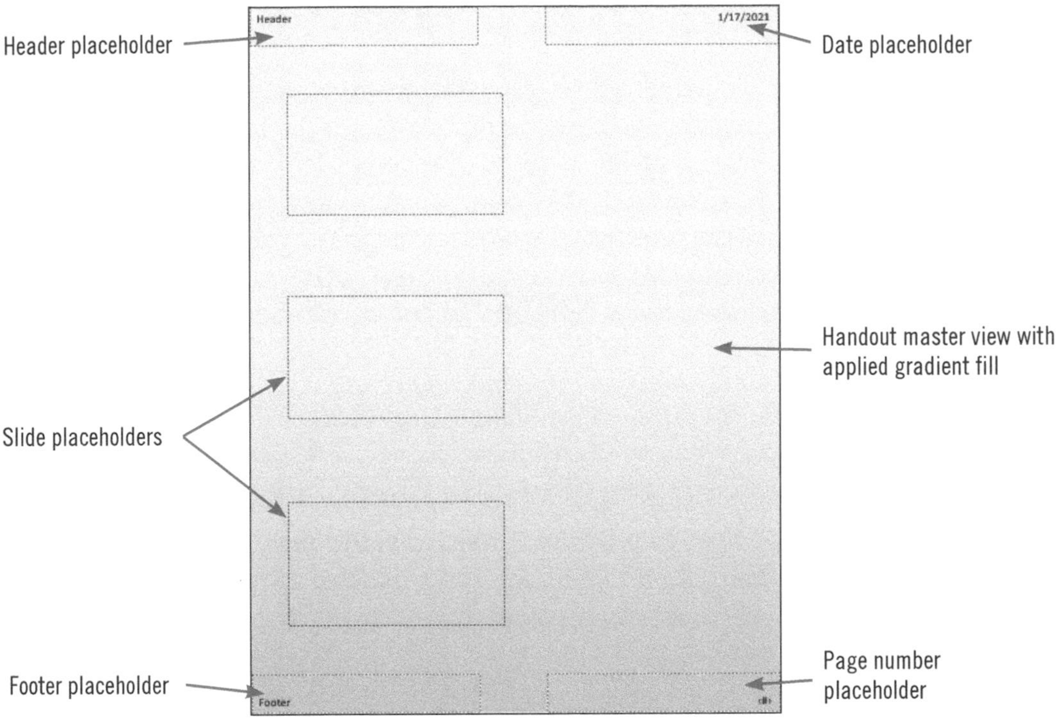

Header placeholder ← Header — 1/17/2021 → Date placeholder

Handout master view with applied gradient fill

Slide placeholders

Footer placeholder ← Footer — Page number placeholder

FIGURE 8-4: Notes Master view in landscape orientation

Header placeholder ← Header — 1/17/2021 → Date placeholder

Slide master image placeholder — CLICK TO EDIT MASTER TITLE STYLE

New landscape orientation

Edit Master text styles
Second level
Third level
Fourth level
Fifth level

Text box placeholder

Footer placeholder ← JCL Talent — Page number placeholder

Creating handouts in Microsoft Word

Sometimes it's helpful to use a word processing program like Microsoft Word to create detailed handouts or notes pages. You might also want to create a Word document based on the outline of your presentation. To send your presentation to Word, click the File tab on the Ribbon, click Export, click Create Handouts, then click the Create Handouts button. The Send to Microsoft Word dialog box opens and provides you with five document layout options. Two layouts include notes entered in the Notes pane. Select a layout, then click OK. Word opens and a new document opens with your inserted presentation, using the layout you selected. To send just the text of your presentation to Word, click the Outline only page layout. To link the slides to your Word document, which will reduce the file size of the handout, click the Paste link option button.

Set Up a Slide Show

Learning Outcomes
• Automate a slide show
• Hide a slide

With PowerPoint, you can create a self-running slide show that plays without user intervention. For example, you can set up a presentation so that viewers can watch a slide show on a stand-alone computer, in a booth or **kiosk**, at a convention, trade show, or some other public place. You can also create a self-running presentation on a DVD or flash drive. You have a number of options when designing a self-running presentation; for example, you can include hyperlinks or action buttons to assist your audience as they move through the presentation. You can also add a synchronized voice that narrates the presentation, and you can set either manual or automatic slide timings. **CASE** ▷ *You prepare the presentation so that it can be self-running.*

STEPS

1. **Click the** Slide Show tab **on the Ribbon, then click the** Set Up Slide Show button **in the Set Up group**

   The Set Up Show dialog box has options you use to specify how the show will run.

2. **Make sure the** All option button **is selected in the Show slides section, then verify that the** Using timings, if present option button **is selected in the Advance slides section**

   All the slides in the presentation are included in the slide show, and PowerPoint will advance the slides at time intervals you set.

3. **Click the** Slide show monitor arrow, **click** Primary Monitor, **click the** Resolution arrow, **then click the resolution closest to** 1360 x 768

   The primary monitor resolution is set to 1360 x 768.

4. **Click the** Browsed at a kiosk (full screen) option button **in the Show type section of the Set Up Show dialog box**

   This option allows you to have a self-running presentation that can be viewed without a presenter. See **FIGURE 8-5**.

5. **Click** OK, **click the** Transitions tab **on the Ribbon, click the** On Mouse Click check box **in the Timing group to remove the checkmark, click the** After up arrow **until** 00:05.00 **appears, then click the** Apply To All button **in the Timing group**

   Each slide in the presentation will now be displayed for 5 seconds before advancing.

6. **Click the** Slide Show button 🖳 **on the status bar, view the show, let it start over from the beginning, press** ESC, **then click the** Slide Show tab **on the Ribbon**

   PowerPoint advances the slides automatically at 5-second intervals. After the last slide, the slide show starts over because the kiosk slide show option loops the presentation until someone presses ESC.

7. **Click the** Set Up Slide Show button **in the Set Up group, click the** Presented by a speaker (full screen) option button, **then click** OK

   The slide show options are back to their default settings.

8. **Click the** Slide 1 thumbnail **in the Slides tab, click the** Hide Slide button **in the Set Up group, click the** From Beginning button **in the Start Slide Show group, watch Slide 2 appear, then press** ESC

   The slide show begins with Slide 2. Notice the Slide 1 thumbnail in the Slides tab is dimmed and has a backslash through its number indicating it is hidden, as shown in **FIGURE 8-6**.

9. **Right-click the** Slide 1 thumbnail **in the Slides tab, click** Hide Slide **in the shortcut menu, then save your changes**

   Slide 1 is no longer hidden.

FIGURE 8-5: Set Up Show dialog box

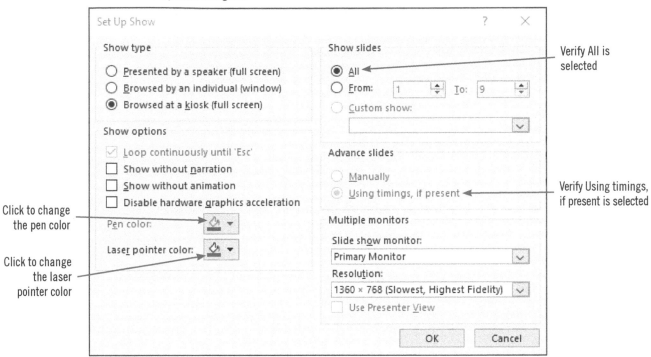

Verify All is selected

Click to change the pen color

Click to change the laser pointer color

Verify Using timings, if present is selected

FIGURE 8-6: Slide 1 is a hidden slide

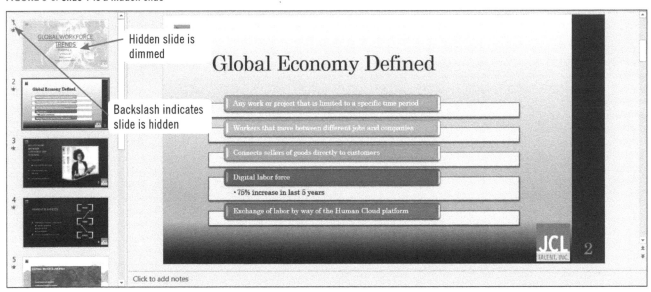

Hidden slide is dimmed

Backslash indicates slide is hidden

Global Economy Defined

Installing and managing Office Add-ins

Office add-ins are applications you can download to PowerPoint and your other Office programs for free (or for a small fee) from the Microsoft Office Store on the Internet. Typical add-ins available to download to PowerPoint include navigation and mapping add-ins, dictionary and word usage add-ins, and news and social media add-ins. To install an add-in, click the Get Add-ins button in the Add-ins group on the Insert tab, then search through the add-in categories and add it to PowerPoint. To manage or uninstall an add-in, click the My Add-ins arrow, click Manage Other Add-ins, click Go at the bottom of the PowerPoint Options dialog box, then add or uninstall add-ins.

Create a Custom Show

Learning Outcomes
- Create and modify a custom slide show
- Use the laser pointer

A custom show gives you the ability to adapt a presentation for use in different circumstances or with different audiences. For example, you might have a 25-slide presentation that you show to new customers, but only 12 of those slides are necessary for a presentation for existing customers. PowerPoint provides two types of custom shows: basic and hyperlinked. A basic custom show is a separate presentation or a presentation that includes slides from the original presentation. A hyperlinked custom show is a separate (secondary) presentation that is linked to a primary custom show or presentation. You can also use the laser pointer to help you focus the audience's attention on specific areas of slides. **CASE** ▷ *You have been asked to create a short version of the presentation for a staff meeting, so you create a custom slide show containing slides appropriate for that audience. You also learn to use the laser pointer during a slide show.*

STEPS

QUICK TIP
To print a custom show, click the File tab, click Print, click Print All Slides under Settings, then click the name of the custom show under Custom Shows.

1. **Click the** Slide Show tab, **click the** Custom Slide Show button **in the Start Slide Show group, click** Custom Shows **to open the Custom Shows dialog box, then click** New

   The Define Custom Show dialog box opens. The slides that are in your current presentation are listed in the Slides in presentation list box.

2. **Click the** Slide 1 check box, **click the** Slides 4–9 check boxes, **then click** Add

   The seven slides you selected move to the Slides in custom show list box, indicating that they will be included in the custom show. See **FIGURE 8-7**.

3. **Click** 7. Skills and Work Life **in the Slides in custom show list, then click the** Up button **twice**

   The slide moves from seventh place to fifth place in the list. You can arrange the slides in any order in your custom show by clicking the slide order Up or Down buttons.

QUICK TIP
Clicking the Remove button does not delete the slide from the presentation; it only deletes the slide from the custom show.

4. **Click** 7. Free Agency Trends **in the Slides in custom show list, click the** Remove button, **drag to select the existing text in the Slide show name text box, type** Meeting, **then click** OK

   The Custom Shows dialog box lists your custom presentation. The custom show is not saved as a separate presentation file even though you assigned it a new name. To view a custom slide show, you must first open the presentation you used to create the custom show in Slide Show view. You can edit, remove, and open a custom show from the Custom Shows dialog box.

5. **Click** Website **in the Custom Shows list, click** Remove, **click** Show, **view the** Meeting slide show, **then press** ESC **to end the slide show**

   The slides in the custom show appear in the order you set in the Define Custom Show dialog box. At the end of the slide show, you return to the presentation in Normal view.

6. **Click the** From Beginning button **in the Start Slide Show group, right-click the screen, point to** Custom Show, **then click** Meeting

   The Meeting custom show appears in Slide Show view.

QUICK TIP
To change the color of the laser pointer, click the Slide Show tab, click the Set Up Slide Show button, then click the Laser pointer color button.

7. **When Slide 4 appears, press and hold** CTRL, **press and hold the** left mouse button, **move the laser pointer around the slide as shown in** FIGURE 8-8, **release** CTRL, **then release the** left mouse button

   Automatic slide timings are set so your slide show can advance to the next slide even though you use the laser pointer. You can use the laser pointer in any presentation on any slide during a slide show.

8. **Press** ESC **at any point to end the slide show, then save your changes**

FIGURE 8-7: Define Custom Show dialog box

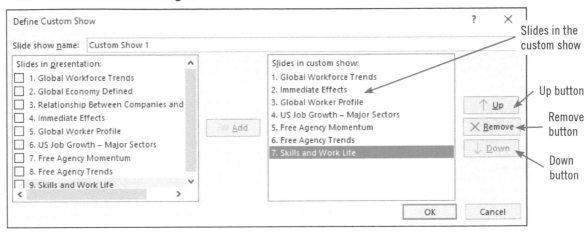

FIGURE 8-8: First slide of custom slide show with laser pointer

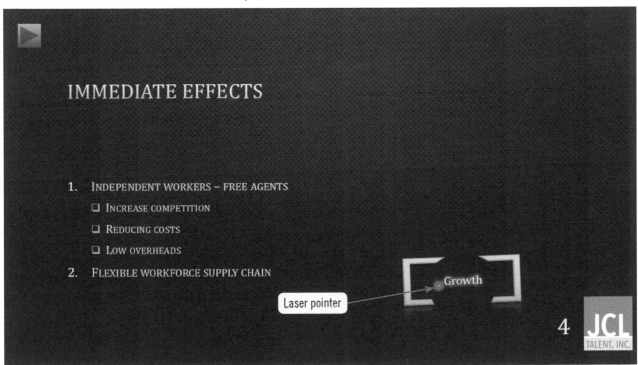

Linking to a custom slide show

You can use action buttons to switch from the "parent" show to the custom show. Click the Shapes button in the Drawing group on the Home tab, then click an action button. Draw an action button on the slide. Click the Hyperlink to arrow, click Custom Show, click the custom show you want to link, then click OK.

Now when you run a slide show you can click the action button you created to run the custom show. You can also create an interactive table of contents using custom shows. Create your table of contents entries on a slide, then hyperlink each entry to the section it refers to using a custom show for each section.

Delivering Presentations

Prepare a Presentation for Distribution

Learning Outcomes
- Protect a presentation with a password
- Check presentation compatibility
- Check for accessibility

Reviewing and preparing your presentation before you share it with others is an essential step, especially with so many security and privacy issues on the Internet. One way to help secure your PowerPoint presentation is to set a security password, so only authorized people can view or modify its content. If you plan to open a presentation in an earlier version of PowerPoint, it is a good idea to determine if the presentation is compatible. Some features in PowerPoint, such as sections and SmartArt graphics, are not compatible in earlier versions of PowerPoint. **CASE** ▶ *You want to learn about PowerPoint security and compatibility features so that you can use them on presentations and other documents.*

STEPS

1. **Click the** Slide 1 thumbnail **in the Slides tab, click the** File tab **on the Ribbon, click** Info, **click the** Protect Presentation button, **then click** Encrypt with Password **on the menu**
   The Encrypt Document dialog box opens.

2. **Type** 123abc
   As you type, solid black symbols appear in the text box, as shown in **FIGURE 8-9**, which hides the password and makes it unreadable. This protects the confidentiality of your password if anyone happens to be looking at your screen while you type.

3. **Click** OK **to open the Confirm Password dialog box, type** 123abc, **then click** OK
   A password is now required to open this presentation. Once the presentation is closed, this password must be entered in the Password dialog box to open it. The presentation is now password protected.

4. **Click** Close, **click** Save **to save changes, click the** File tab, **then click** IL_PPT_8_JCL.pptx **in the Presentations list**
   The Password dialog box opens.

5. **Type** 123abc, **then click** OK **to open the presentation**
   The presentation opens. Be aware that if you don't remember your password, you will not be able to open or view the presentation.

6. **Click the** File tab **on the Ribbon, click** Info, **click the** Protect Presentation button, **click** Encrypt with Password, **select the** password, **press** DELETE, **click** OK, **then click** Save
   The password is removed and is no longer needed to open the presentation.

7. **Click the** File tab **on the Ribbon, click** Info, **click the** Check for Issues button, **then click** Check Compatibility
   The Compatibility Checker analyzes the presentation, and the Microsoft PowerPoint Compatibility Checker dialog box opens, as shown in **FIGURE 8-10**. Each item in the dialog box represents a feature that is not supported in earlier versions of PowerPoint.

8. **Click the** down scroll arrow, **read all the items in the dialog box, click** OK, **click the** File tab, **click** Info, **click the** Check for Issues button, **then click** Check Accessibility
   The Check Accessibility feature analyzes the presentation for content that people with certain disabilities might find hard to read, as shown in **FIGURE 8-11**.

9. **Read the items in the Accessibility pane, close the Accessibility pane, then save your work**

FIGURE 8-9: Encrypt Document dialog box

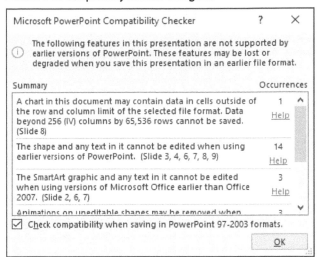

Hidden password →

Encrypt Document

Encrypt the contents of this file

Password:
●●●●●●

Caution: If you lose or forget the password, it cannot be recovered. It is advisable to keep a list of passwords and their corresponding document names in a safe place.
(Remember that passwords are case-sensitive.)

OK   Cancel

FIGURE 8-10: Compatibility Checker dialog box

Microsoft PowerPoint Compatibility Checker   ?   ×

ⓘ The following features in this presentation are not supported by earlier versions of PowerPoint. These features may be lost or degraded when you save this presentation in an earlier file format.

Summary   Occurrences

A chart in this document may contain data in cells outside of the row and column limit of the selected file format. Data beyond 256 (IV) columns by 65,536 rows cannot be saved. (Slide 8)   1   Help

The shape and any text in it cannot be edited when using earlier versions of PowerPoint. (Slide 3, 4, 6, 7, 8, 9)   14   Help

The SmartArt graphic and any text in it cannot be edited when using versions of Microsoft Office earlier than Office 2007. (Slide 2, 6, 7)   3   Help

Animations on uneditable shapes may be removed when   3

☑ Check compatibility when saving in PowerPoint 97-2003 formats.

OK

FIGURE 8-11: Accessibility pane open

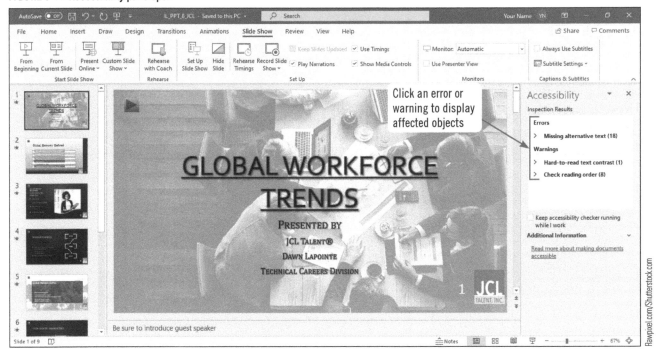

Digitally signing a presentation

What is a digital signature, and why would you want to use one in PowerPoint? A digital signature is similar to a handwritten signature in that it authenticates your document; however, a digital signature, unlike a handwritten signature, is created using computer cryptography and is not visible within the presentation itself. There are three primary reasons you would add a digital signature to a presentation: one, to authenticate the signer of the document; two, to ensure the content of the presentation has not been changed since it was signed; and three, to assure the reader of the origin of the signed document. To add a digital signature, click the File tab on the Ribbon, click Info, click the Protect Presentation button, click Add a Digital Signature, then follow the instructions in the dialog boxes.

PowerPoint

Deliver a Presentation Online

Being able to assemble everyone in the same room for a presentation can be difficult, which is why PowerPoint provides a way to share your presentation with remote viewers. Using PowerPoint, you can host an online presentation in real time over the Internet to viewers using the free Microsoft Office Presentation Service. Viewers of an online presentation need to have a computer connected to the Internet, a web browser, and a link to an Internet address, called a **URL**, which is automatically supplied by PowerPoint. The URL link for your online broadcast can be emailed to viewers directly from PowerPoint. **CASE** ▶ *In preparation for hosting an online presentation to others in your company, you test the online broadcasting features in PowerPoint. (NOTE: To complete this lesson as a host, you need to be logged into PowerPoint with a Microsoft account and have Internet access. As a viewer, you need Internet access and the URL link entered into a web browser.)*

STEPS

1. **Click the** Slide 1 thumbnail **in the Slides tab, click the** Slide Show tab **on the Ribbon, then click the** Present Online button **in the Start Slide Show group**

   Read the information on the screen. If you don't have a Microsoft account, you need to acquire one from the Microsoft website before you proceed.

TROUBLE
If you get a service error message, try to connect again. See your instructor or technical support person for additional help.

2. **Click** CONNECT

   The Present Online dialog box opens, and PowerPoint connects to the Office Presentation Service online. Once connected, PowerPoint prepares your presentation to be viewed online, which may take a short time. The Present Online dialog box eventually displays a URL link, as shown in **FIGURE 8-12**.

3. **If approved by your instructor, click the** Send in Email link **to open a new Outlook message window, type an** email address **in the To text box, then click** Send

   The Microsoft Outlook window opens with the URL link in the message box and is then sent to the person you want to view the online presentation. Anyone to whom you provide the URL link can enter the link into their web browser and watch the broadcast.

4. **Click the** START PRESENTATION button

   The first slide of the presentation opens in Slide Show view. Make sure viewers can see the presentation in their web browser.

QUICK TIP
Until you end the broadcast or close the presentation, you are continuously broadcasting the presentation.

5. **Press** SPACEBAR, **wait for your viewers to see the slide, press** SPACEBAR, **wait for your viewers to see the slide, end the slide show, then click the** Present Online tab **on the Ribbon**

   Each slide in the presentation is viewed by you and your online viewers. The Present Online tab opens, as shown in **FIGURE 8-13**. Use this tab to start the slide show from different slides, share meeting notes using OneNote, invite others to view the broadcast, and end the broadcast.

6. **When you are finished broadcasting click the** End Online Presentation button **in the Present Online group**

   A message box opens asking if you want to end the online presentation.

7. **Click** End Online Presentation, **close the presentation, click the** File tab **on the Ribbon, then click** Blank Presentation

   The online presentation stops, the presentation closes, and a new blank presentation opens.

FIGURE 8-12: Present Online dialog box

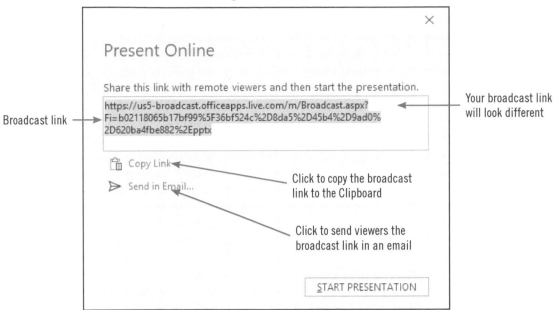

FIGURE 8-13: Online presentation broadcast

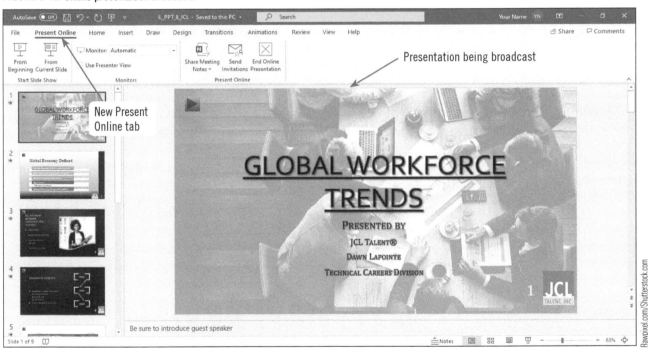

Coauthoring a presentation

By using collaboration software, such as SharePoint Online or saving a presentation to a OneDrive location, you have the ability to work with others on a presentation over the Internet at the same time. To set up a presentation to be coauthored with you as the original author, click the File tab, click Share, click Share with People, click Save To Cloud, then click your OneDrive location. Choose a shared location or server to store a primary copy of your presentation, then click the Save button. Open the presentation and begin working, and if someone else is working on the presentation, you will see their thumbnail picture in the upper-right corner of the Ribbon. All changes made to the presentation are recorded, including who is working on the presentation and where in the presentation they are working. When you save the presentation, PowerPoint notifies you about changes made by the coauthors. To use this feature, all authors must have PowerPoint 2010 or later installed on their computers.

PowerPoint

Create a Photo Album

Learning
Outcomes
• Create a photo
album
• Customize a photo
album

A PowerPoint photo album is a presentation designed specifically to display photographs. You can add pictures to a photo album from any storage device, such as a hard drive, flash drive, digital camera, scanner, or web camera. As with any presentation, you can customize the layout of a photo album presentation by adding title text to slides, applying frames around the pictures, and applying a theme. You can also format the pictures of the photo album by adding a caption, converting the pictures to black and white, rotating them, applying artistic effects, and changing their brightness and contrast. **CASE** ▷ *On a break from work, you decide to create a personal photo album showing some of the pictures you took on a trip to the state capitol building in Austin, Texas.*

STEPS

1. **Click the** Insert tab **on the Ribbon, click the** Photo Album arrow **in the Images group, then click** New Photo Album

   The Photo Album dialog box opens.

QUICK TIP

In the Photo Album dialog box, click a picture check box, then click New Text Box to create a text box after the picture.

2. **Click** File/Disk, **select the file** Support_PPT_8_Austin1.jpg **from the location where you store your Data Files, then click** Insert

   The picture appears in the Preview box and is listed in the Pictures in album list, as shown in **FIGURE 8-14**.

3. **Click** Create, **save the presentation as** IL_PPT_8_AustinAlbum **to the location where you store your Data Files, then change the presentation title from "Photo Album" to** Austin Photos

   A new presentation opens. PowerPoint creates a title slide along with a slide for the picture you inserted. The computer username appears in the subtitle text box by default.

TROUBLE

If the Design Ideas pane didn't open, it was not enabled in the PowerPoint options dialog box.

4. **Review the options in the** Design Ideas pane, **close the** Design Ideas pane, **click the** Slide 2 thumbnail **in the Slides tab, click the** Photo Album arrow **in the Images group on the Insert tab, then click** Edit Photo Album

   The Edit Photo Album dialog box opens. You can use this dialog box to add and format pictures and modify the slide layout in the photo album presentation.

5. **Click** File/Disk, **click** Support_PPT_8_Austin2.jpg, **press and hold** SHIFT, **click** Support_PPT_8_Austin4.jpg, **release** SHIFT, **click** Insert, **click the** Support_PPT_8_Austin3 check box **in the Pictures in album list, then click the** Rotate Right button ⬛

   Three more pictures are added to the presentation, and picture Support_PPT_8_Austin3.jpg is rotated to the right 90 degrees.

QUICK TIP

Click the ALL pictures black and white check box to change all the pictures in the photo album to black and white.

6. **Click the** Support_PPT_8_Austin2 check box, **click to deselect the** Support_PPT_8_Austin3 check box, **click the** Down arrow twice, **click the** Picture layout arrow, **click** 2 pictures, **then click the** Captions below ALL pictures check box

7. **Click the** Frame shape arrow, **click** Simple Frame, White, **click** Update, **then click the** Slide 2 thumbnail **in the Slides tab**

   Two pictures with a caption below each picture (currently the picture file name) appear on each slide, and each picture is formatted with a white frame.

8. **Click the** Slide Sorter view button ⬛, **then drag the** Zoom Slider ▯ **on the status bar until your screen looks similar to** FIGURE 8-15

9. **sam↑** **Save your changes, submit your presentation to your instructor, close the presentation, then close PowerPoint**

FIGURE 8-14: Photo Album dialog box

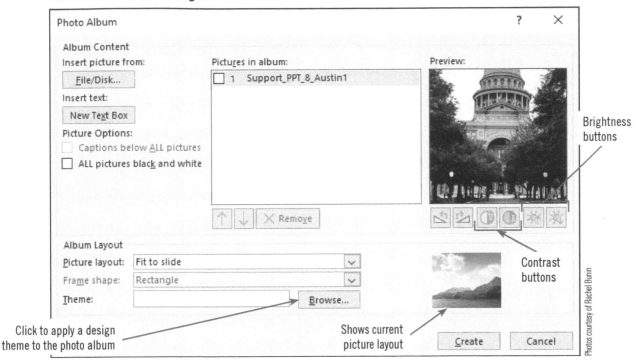

Brightness buttons

Contrast buttons

Click to apply a design theme to the photo album

Shows current picture layout

Photos courtesy of Rachel Bunin

FIGURE 8-15: Completed photo album

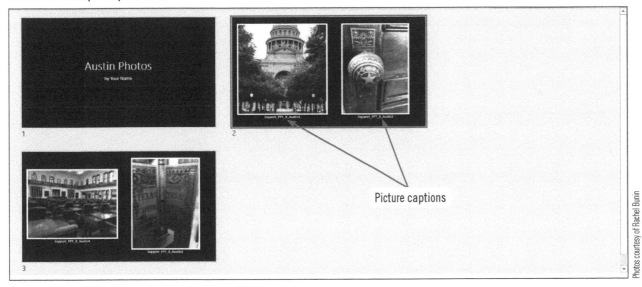

Picture captions

Photos courtesy of Rachel Bunin

Working with macros

A macro is a recording of an action or a set of actions that you use to automate tasks. The contents of a macro consist of a series of command codes that you create in the Visual Basic for Applications programming language using Microsoft Visual Basic. You can use macros to automate almost any action that you perform repeatedly when creating presentations, which saves you time. Any presentation with the .pptm file extension is saved with a macro. To use a macro in PowerPoint, click the View tab, click the Macros button in the Macros group, name the macro, then click Create to open the Microsoft Visual Basic for Applications window and create your macro.

Practice

Skills Review

1. Work with presentation views.

  a. Start PowerPoint, open the file IL_PPT_8-2.pptx from the location where you store your Data Files, then save it as **IL_PPT_8_Water**.

  b. Go to Slide 4, switch to Notes Page view, click in the text placeholder, then type **Refer to development projects**.

  c. Switch to Normal view, click the Notes button on the status bar, click after the word "projects", then type **in Uganda**.

  d. Go to Slide 1, click after the word "project" in the title text, click the Insert tab, then click the Symbol button in the Symbols group.

  e. Locate and insert the Copyright Sign, then switch to Slide Show view.

  f. Open Presenter view, display all the slides in the presentation, click the Slide 7 thumbnail, zoom in on Slide 7, then press ESC when you are finished.

  g. Save the presentation, then save the presentation as a PowerPoint Show.

  h. Close the PowerPoint Show presentation, open the file IL_PPT_8_Water.pptx from the location where you store your Data Files, then go to Slide 1.

2. Customize Handout and Notes masters.

  a. Switch to Handout Master view, then change the slides per page to 3 slides.

  b. Change the handout orientation to Landscape, then type **Uganda** in the header text placeholder.

  c. Switch to Notes Master view, change the background style to Style 10, type **Uganda** in the header text placeholder, close Notes Master view, then save your work.

  d. Print handouts 3 per page.

3. Set up a slide show.

  a. Click the Slide Show tab, click the Set Up Slide Show button, verify automatic slide timings is selected, set up a slide show so that it will be browsed at a kiosk, make sure the monitor resolution is set to Automatic, close the Set Up Show dialog box, then click the Transitions tab.

  b. Remove the checkmark from the On Mouse Click check box, set a slide timing of 3 seconds to all the slides, run the slide show all the way through to Slide 1, then end the slide show.

  c. Change the slide show options to be presented by a speaker, then change the slide timings to manual in the Set Up Show dialog box.

  d. Manually run through the slide show from Slide 1. Move forward and backward through the presentation, then press ESC when you are finished.

  e. When you have finished viewing the slide show, reset the slide timings to automatic, then save your work.

4. Create a custom show.

  a. Open the Custom Shows dialog box, remove Custom Show 1, then create a custom show called **Development** that includes Slides 1, 4, 5, and 6.

  b. View the show from within the Custom Shows dialog box, then press ESC to end the slide show.

  c. Go to Slide 1, then save your work.

5. Prepare a presentation for distribution.

  a. Click the File tab, click Info, click Protect Presentation, then click Encrypt with Password.

  b. Type **123abc**, then type the same password in the Confirm Password dialog box.

  c. Close the presentation, save your changes, open the presentation, then type **123abc** in the Password dialog box.

Skills Review (continued)

d. Open the Encrypt Document dialog box again, then delete the password.

e. Click the File tab, click Info, click Check for Issues, click Check Compatibility, read the results, then close the dialog box.

f. Click the File tab, click Info, click Check for Issues, click Check Accessibility, then read the information.

g. If the Keep accessibility checker running while I work check box is selected, click the check box to remove the checkmark, close the Accessibility pane, then save your work.

6. **Deliver a presentation online.**

a. Click the Slide Show tab, click Present Online button, then click Connect.

b. Send invitations to people you want to view the broadcast using the Send in Email link in the Present Online dialog box.

c. Start the online presentation, then move through each slide in the presentation.

d. When you are finished broadcasting, end the online presentation, save your work, close the presentation, then submit the presentation to your instructor. The completed presentation is shown in FIGURE 8-16.

FIGURE 8-16

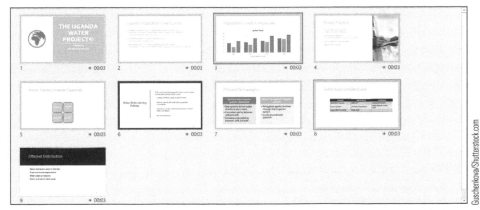

7. **Create a photo album.**

a. Create a new photo album presentation, navigate to the location where you store your Data Files, then insert the files Support_PPT_8_Pic1.jpg, Support_PPT_8_Pic2.jpg, Support_PPT_8_Pic3.jpg, and Support_PPT_8_Pic4.jpg.

b. Rotate picture Support_PPT_8_Pic1.jpg to the right, move the picture so that it is third in the list, create the photo album, then save it as **IL_PPT_8_Album** to the location where you store your Data Files.

c. Change the title on the title slide to **Best Things in Life**, then type your name in the subtitle text box.

d. Open the Edit Photo Album dialog box, change the picture layout to 1 picture, then change the frame shape to Soft Edge Rectangle.

e. Save your changes, submit your presentation to your instructor, close the presentation, then close PowerPoint. The completed photo album is shown in FIGURE 8-17.

FIGURE 8-17

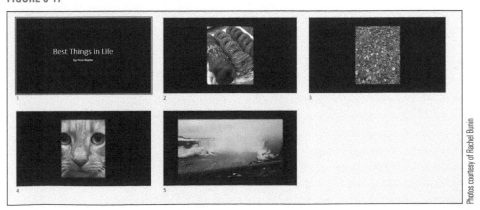

PowerPoint

Independent Challenge 1

Riverwalk Medical Clinic (RMC) is a large medical facility in Cambridge, Massachusetts. You have been working on an EMS system presentation for the clinic, and you have just a couple things left to do before you are finished. In this challenge, you customize handouts and notes pages, create a custom show, and prepare the presentation for distribution.

a. Start PowerPoint, open the presentation IL_PPT_8-3.pptx from the location where you store your Data Files, then save it as **IL_PPT_8_RMC**.

b. Switch to Notes Page view, type **Start online feed** in the text placeholder, switch to Normal view, then switch to Slide Show view.

c. Open Presenter view, display all slides, go to Slide 3, use the zoom feature, then press ESC when you are finished.

d. Go to Slide 3, click after the word "curriculum", open the Symbol dialog box, then insert the Section Sign symbol located on the same row as the copyright symbol.

e. Use the Compatibility Checker on the presentation and review the results.

f. Use the Accessibility Checker on the presentation, then review the results.

g. Open Handout Master view, change the slides per page to 4, then apply background Style 5.

h. Click the footer text, type **RMC**, click in the header text box, type **EMS System**, then close the master view.

i. Switch to Notes Master, change the background to Style 9, then close the master view.

j. Create a custom slide show that displays slides 1, 5, and 6 from the presentation, then save it as **EMS**.

k. Run the custom slide show, press ESC when you are finished, save the presentation, then save the presentation as a PowerPoint Show. The completed presentation is shown in **FIGURE 8-18**.

l. Submit your presentation to your instructor, close the presentation, then close PowerPoint.

FIGURE 8-18

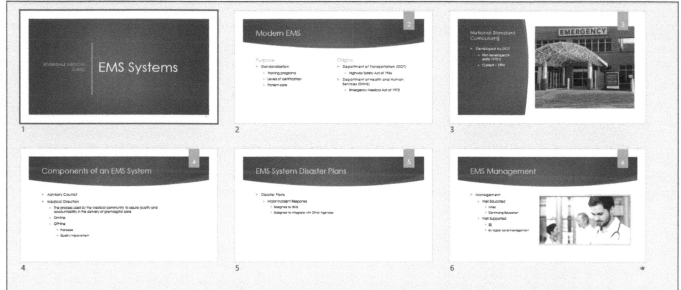

Independent Challenge 2

You have just been given an assignment in your Cultural Geography class to create a photo album that shows aspects of your living environment. Include photos of buildings, landscapes, means of travel, anything you think is relevant to your life. You are encouraged to use your own pictures for this assignment or you can use the pictures provided.

a. Start PowerPoint, create a photo album presentation, insert your pictures, then save the presentation as **IL_PPT_8_Geography** to the location where you store your Data Files. If you don't have your own pictures, then locate the following pictures where you store your Data Files: Support_PPT_8_ICPic1.jpg, Support_PPT_8_ICPic2.jpg, Support_PPT_8_ICPic3.jpg, and Support_PPT_8_ICPic4.jpg.

b. Enter the title Urban Life in the title text placeholder, add your name to the subtitle text placeholder, then apply a design.

c. Use the Edit Photo Album dialog box to format the pictures as needed. An example of a photo album is shown in **FIGURE 8-19**.

d. Check the spelling of the presentation, save your changes, then broadcast this presentation to two friends using the Present Online feature.

e. Print handouts 2 slides per page, then save the presentation as a PowerPoint Show.

f. Submit your presentation and your handouts to your instructor. Close the presentation, then close PowerPoint.

FIGURE 8-19

Photos courtesy of Rachel Bunin

PowerPoint

Visual Workshop

Use an instructor-approved topic for your presentation and the following task list to help you complete this Visual Workshop:

- Create a new presentation, save the presentation as **IL_PPT_8_FinalProject** to the location where you store your Data Files, then enter and format slide text.
- Create and format new slides, create slide sections, then create Zoom links.
- Apply a design theme, then modify the design theme by changing its variation.
- Format a slide background, then use the Design Ideas pane to customize a slide.
- Insert and format at least one picture, video, and audio.
- Use the Remove Background feature to remove part or all of a picture background.
- Insert, format, and merge shapes, then insert and format a SmartArt graphic.
- Insert and format a table and a chart, then apply animations, transitions, and timings to objects and slides.
- Insert, modify, and animate a 3-D model.
- Modify slide, handout, and notes masters, then create a custom show.
- Insert action buttons or hyperlinks, then send to a class member for revision changes and comments.
- Merge the reviewed presentation with your original presentation; make necessary changes and keep comments. Check the presentation for accessibility, making any suggested changes that might make the presentation more accessible.
- Deliver the presentation online to members of your class.

Add your name as a footer on the slide, save the presentation, submit the presentation to your instructor, close the presentation, then close PowerPoint. FIGURE 8-20 shows an example of a presentation you can create.

FIGURE 8-20

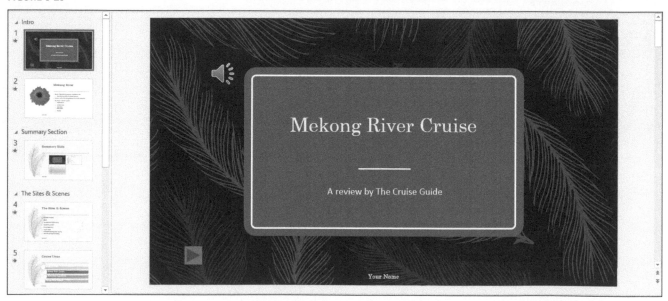

Index

9 780357 675137